Faithful Warriors

Faithful Warriors
A Combat Marine Remembers the Pacific War

By Lt. Col. Dean Ladd, USMCR (Ret.),
and Steven Weingartner

NAVAL INSTITUTE PRESS
Annapolis, Maryland

Naval Institute Press
291 Wood Road
Annapolis, MD 21402

First Naval Institute Press paperback edition published in 2013.
ISBN 978-1-59114-435-9

The Library of Congress has cataloged the hardcover edition as follows:
Ladd, Dean.
    Faithful warriors: a combat marine remembers the Pacific War / Dean Ladd, and Steven Weingartner.
        p. cm.
    Includes index.
    ISBN 978-1-59114-452-6 (alk. paper)
    1. Ladd, Dean—Travel—Pacific Area. 2. World War, 1939-1945—Campaigns—Pacific Area. 3. World War, 1939-1945—Personal narratives, American. 4. Marines—United States—Biography. 5. United States. Marine Corps—Biography. I. Weingartner, Steven. II. Title.
    D767.9.L25 2009
    940.54'1273092—dc22

                                                                                                2008055484

♾ This paper meets the requirements of ANSI/NISO z39.48-1992 (Permanence of Paper).
Printed in the United States of America.

18 17 16 15 14 13   6 5 4 3 2 1
First printing

To the memory of my wife, Vera, and to my mother, Gertrude

To the young men who gave their all for their country in far-flung World War II Pacific battle sites

> *They went with songs to the battle, they were young*
> *Straight of limb, true of eye, steady and aglow.*
> *They were staunch to the end against odds uncounted,*
> *They fell with their faces to the foe.*
>
> *They shall not grow old, as we that are left grow old.*
> *Age will not weary them nor the years condemn,*
> *At the going down of the sun and in the morning,*
> *We will remember them.*

—From "For the Fallen" (1914), by LAURENCE BINYON

Contents

Foreword

THE 1ST AND 2D MARINE DIVISIONS came into being on the same day: February 1, 1941. The 1st Division was activated at its base in North Carolina, which was then called New River and today is Camp LeJeune. The 2d Division formed and was activated at Camp Elliott, not too distant from downtown San Diego. Soon thereafter, however, the 2d Division began to split apart as major elements were dispatched independently to meet threats that cropped up in the Atlantic and Pacific oceans.

In May 1941, a Regimental Landing Team (RLT) built around the 6th Marines was deployed by ship through the Panama Canal for the intended purpose of reinforcing the 1st Marine Division on the East Coast. By the time it arrived at Charleston, South Carolina, its mission had been changed. Instead, RLT-6 became the nucleus of the 1st Provisional Marine Brigade with orders to assist British land forces in the defense of Iceland. And there it remained until relieved by a U.S. Army division in the spring of 1942. At about the same time, the 2d Engineer Battalion was sent to Hawaii to assist in the building of a logistic base at Camp Catlin in the vicinity of Pearl Harbor. Then, within a month following the attack at Pearl Harbor, a second RLT, this one built around the 8th Marines, became the nucleus of the 2d Marine Brigade, which likewise sailed independently for American Samoa. Its mission: to garrison and defend the island of Tutuila and prevent the Japanese from cutting critical U.S. supply lines to Australia and New Zealand.

While the 6th and 8th Marines guarded the far-flung ramparts of the United States, the 2d Marines remained at Camp Elliott engaged in training the host of new recruits flowing from the boot camps at Parris Island and San

Diego and conducting amphibious exercises off La Jolla. Even this interlude turned out to be brief. During the first week of July, following the strategic naval victory at Midway, the 2d Regiment embarked on amphibious ships as RLT-2 and sailed from San Diego. On 7 August, as the 1st Marine Division came ashore to establish a foothold on the north coast of Guadalcanal, the 2d Marines, along with the 1st Raider and 1st Parachute battalions, stormed ashore to seize Tulagi and Gavutu islands across the channel in the Florida group. During the latter part of October, the bulk of the 2d Marine Division was incrementally boated across the "Slot" to Guadalcanal to bolster the 1st Marine Division's very thin defensive perimeter surrounding Henderson Field. RLT-8 sailed from Samoa at the same time, and in early November it too was committed to the battle for Guadalcanal as an attachment to the 1st Marine Division.

After very heavy fighting during November, the steady arrival of fresh U.S. Army formations finally allowed the exhausted 1st Marine Division to be relieved in place and sent to Australia for rest and rehabilitation. (It would take a full year before the division could be ready for recommitment to battle.) Then, on New Year's Day 1943, the 6th Marine Regiment started coming ashore at Guadalcanal. For the first time during the war, the 2d Marine Division ceased to be a name on paper and became a fighting fact. A forward division command post established just east of the Matanikau River directed the division's four regiments and combat support battalions throughout the final four weeks of offensive operations under the operational control of the Maj. Gen. Alexander Patch, USA. By early February, the Japanese had succeeded in evacuating what was left of their half-starved army on the island, and Guadalcanal was declared secured.

The six-month nightmare of slugging it out with the Japanese army under the most adverse conditions of climate and malarial jungle terrain was over. By now, all elements of the division had been baptized by fire and had earned their combat spurs. They had also learned that the Japanese were indeed tough fighters, but not invincible. By 1 March, the entire division had reassembled in Wellington, New Zealand, eager to enjoy a well-earned rest and to receive replacements for those who had been killed or wounded in action. Within ten months the 2d Marine Division was back to full strength and once again fit and ready for combat. While the next assault into the Central Pacific was scheduled to be of shorter duration than the last one, it would prove to be a far more deadly type of fight.

★   ★   ★

The foregoing is merely a backdrop to Col. Dean Ladd and Steve Weingartner's gripping account of close combat in the Pacific theater. In November 1940, Dean Ladd was in his second year at Washington State College when his reserve unit was suddenly mobilized and redesignated Company B, 1st Battalion, 8th Marines. He thus became a "plank owner" of the 2d Marine Division when it was activated at Camp Elliott more than sixty-seven years ago. Except for several months of hospitalization while recuperating from a severe gunshot wound, the author served continuously for more than three and a half years with 1/8 through all of its World War II overseas deployments and four of its five major combat assault operations. He served first as a fast-trotting noncommissioned officer on American Samoa, then as a commissioned officer and platoon commander at Guadalcanal, as a rifle platoon commander at Tarawa, and as a platoon commander and company commander at Saipan and Tinian during the Mariana Islands campaign. He therefore saw action in all of the 2d Marine Division's World War II campaigns except Okinawa.

In the preface, Colonel Ladd explains his motivation and purpose in publishing a second book under the same title as his 1993 work. Instead of dwelling on the "big picture," as he puts it, with this volume he wanted to impart "a more personal and immediate account of the war in the Pacific," one that would "illuminate the valor and the sacrifices of the Marines who took part in the fighting." I believe the readers of this second version of *Faithful Warriors* will agree that Dean Ladd and his coauthor, Steven Weingartner, have achieved that aim superbly. Writing in an easy, crisp style, the authors paint a potent and vivid picture of some of the most fiercely contested amphibious assaults and most savage fighting to take place in the Pacific. The view is always as seen from the eyes of those who had the unenviable task of having to close those last few yards with the enemy. Clearly, the central theme and intent of *Faithful Warriors* is to underscore the close-up, human side of battle with all its anxieties, fears, misapprehensions, uncertainties, violence, and at times cruelties, along with many testaments of extraordinary valor and examples of both good and poor combat leadership. Above all, however, this is a story about human solidarity—about how a fraternity of men was forged in battle and bonded forever in blood.

In the prologue, the author recounts the hell that he and the men of his battalion endured on the morning of D+1 as they were forced to wade the last six hundred yards across the lagoon off Betio Island. After reading this horrific and starkly realistic narrative, one can easily understand why the battle for Tarawa became one of the defining moments in the history of the 2d Marine

Division—and arguably, perhaps, even the entire Leatherneck Corps. Equally compelling are the firsthand accounts that come from Dean and his friends and shipmates who found themselves desperately fighting hand to hand to hold their lines against the human waves of Japanese banzai charges that climaxed the battles for Saipan and Tinian.

Taken altogether, *Faithful Warriors* presents some of the most powerful descriptions of combat that I have ever read. I am confidant that this book will be widely read and treasured by both former and future members of the "Follow Me" Division, as well as deeply appreciated and frequently cited by future military historians writing on the Pacific theater during the Second World War.

MAJ. GEN. O. K. STEELE, USMC (RET.)
CG, 2d Marine Division, 1987–89

Preface

THIS BOOK HAS BEEN MANY YEARS IN THE MAKING—decades, actually. It is not the first book to appear under the title *Faithful Warriors*. In late 1993 I self-published a book with the same title and distributed it through an improvised network of friends, associates, and Marine Corps contacts. Although the book was well received, I soon realized that changes in emphasis and focus were needed. A principal goal in writing the book had been to convey something of the nature of Pacific War combat and, in doing so, to illuminate the valor and the sacrifices of the Marines who took part in the fighting. But I found, in retrospect, that the presentation and organization of the book's three primary elements—my recollections of the war interwoven with historical accounts and descriptions of my postwar travels to the Pacific and Japan—ran counter to that purpose. I had provided a "big picture" view of the war—too big, it turned out, for the story that I wished to tell.

I decided that a rewrite was in order, and to that end I teamed up with award-winning author and military historian Steve Weingartner. Much new material was added, derived in large measure from numerous interviews that Steve conducted with me and with other Marines, most of them men with whom I served. The result is a more personal and immediate account of the war in the Pacific, one chiefly concerned with the actions and events taking place within what Marine veteran and historian Joseph Alexander described as the "mythical fifty-yard circle" around every foxhole. It is our fervent hope that these efforts will provide insight and understanding of the conflict that will reach far beyond those circles of individual experience.

Many people helped us in the writing of this book, and we are deeply grateful to all for their invaluable contributions. In particular, we want to thank the "cadre" of 2d Division veterans whom we interviewed and whose remembrances add immeasurably to the overall narrative. Listed in alphabetical order, they are Bill Crumpacker, Ken Desirelli, Harry Gooch, Don Holzer, Paul Kennedy, Don Maines, Mike Masters, John Murdock, Harold Park, Hawk Rader, Rodney Sandburg, Clarence Shanks, Dick Stein, George Stein, Larry Wade, Warren Wallace, George Wasicek, and Don Weide. Semper fi, guys— well done!

Additionally, I wish to express my gratitude to the many individuals I met in the course of my travels and research who provided me with a wealth of information on the Pacific War and related matters.

A very special word of thanks goes to Joseph Alexander for his unflagging encouragement and support, and not least for his insightful comments and advice; and to Tom Cutler, our editor at the Naval Institute Press, for his support and, most of all, for his patience.

DEAN LADD
November 2007

Prologue

ON A BRIGHT AND VIOLENT MORNING in the Central Pacific, a dying Marine with part of his face shot off saved my life. He was perched atop the partially raised ramp of an LCVP: a big, solidly built man with a gaping, gory hole where his eye should have been, blood streaming from the wound. Moments earlier he had been standing in the water beside me at the bottom of the ramp, waiting with other wounded men for his turn to board, another casualty in the battle for Betio Island.

I was dying. I had been shot through the lower abdomen, hit as my unit waded toward shore to assault the island. Two men from my platoon hauled me back to the LCVP and struggled to lift me into the boat. The Marine with the ravaged face, who had just boarded, saw that they were having trouble with me. He reached down, grabbed me with one hand, and pulled me up and over the top of the ramp. Amazing.

And so I didn't die. That, too, was amazing. But not really all that significant in the grand scheme of things. That incident is just a small scene in a very big picture. Time to pull back in time and space for a wider field of vision, a deeper perspective—to start at the beginning, on the first day of the battle.

★   ★   ★

Aboard the troopship *Sheridan*. The time is 0200; the date, 20 November 1943. It's D-day for Operation Galvanic, the invasion of the Tarawa Atoll in the Gilbert Islands. Soon Marines in the first waves of the 2d Marine Division's five-thousand-man landing force will assault Betio, the main island in the atoll. Their immediate objectives are three narrow slivers of sand and coral codenamed "Red Beach 1," "Red Beach 2," and "Red Beach 3."

I'm a first lieutenant commanding a rifle platoon in B Company, 1st Battalion, 8th Regiment. The 1/8 won't be going ashore just now: it's being held in reserve. *Sheridan,* our home away from home, will remain offshore, beyond the outer reef encircling the atoll. We will be committed to battle as circumstances warrant—that is, if things go badly.

Things will soon go very badly.

A boatswain's pipe trills reveille over the ship's public address system. Then, from the loudspeakers, the voice of authority: "Now hear this," followed by announcements: go here, go there, do this, do that. The usual. I'm already half-awake, have been for hours, sleeping fitfully. Sleep doesn't come easy the night before an operation; a combination of excitement, worry, and anticipation keep chasing it off.

I share a compartment on the main deck with two or three other junior officers. When reveille sounds we rush out on deck for a look at the island. We press against the cable that serves as the ship's guardrail, talking in hushed, excited voices: "Where is it? Can you see it?"

We can, barely. Betio is about ten miles away, a speck on the eastern horizon (we're approaching Betio from the west), and it's burning from carrier aircraft strikes launched over the past few days. After a few minutes we go to the officers' mess to eat what is known as the "dead man's breakfast." It's a hearty meal, lots of protein—steak and powdered eggs: energy food. I'm not hungry; few of us are, but we eat our fill and then some, stoking up, taking in fuel for the exertions to come. Enjoy it if you can, while you can. After this it'll be nothing but K-rations until Betio is secured.

We don't say much while we're eating; we're too jittery for conversation. I feel as if I'm back at Washington State College on the morning of final exams. I've got a big test today, and I'm not ready to take it. I try to review my duties and responsibilities, but it seems I can't remember a damn thing. I've been a Marine for going on four years, I'm a combat veteran of the Guadalcanal campaign, and every lesson I've learned in training and battle, every soldierly skill I've developed, has disappeared from memory. On top of that, I'm bleary from lack of sleep and I'm nervous, nervous, nervous. Enjoy breakfast? Yeah, sure.

We finish chow and go back on deck to watch the show. Around this time we receive a pep talk, piped over the PA system, from *Sheridan's* captain, Cdr. John Mockrish. He informs us that the Japanese are "a strong and wily foe" and that "no quarter will be asked nor given."

The assault teams debark at 0320, before sunup. The bombardment starts at 0507, around daybreak, after Japanese shore batteries fire on our fleet. Our ships cut loose, BOOM! BOOM! BOOM! BOOM!, the big guns of the battlewagons and cruisers roaring salvo after salvo to greet the new day. The warships stand far off on one quarter, but we can see their guns flashing. We can even see the shells, red-hot and glowing like meteors, streaking across the sky in shallow trajectories toward the island. On Betio we see explosions, flames leaping up. We're impressed. "Wow, look at that," we say. "Look at the smoke, look at the fire. Wow."

Very quickly Betio is obscured by clouds of billowing black smoke shot through with flames and the fireballs of explosions. Beautiful, beautiful. The Navy has all but stomped Betio into the ocean. At 0610 carrier aircraft attack the island, adding to the destruction. The naval bombardment continues for several hours. When it ends, Betio is hardly more than a burning smear on the water. And the Japanese? Surely most of them are dead, wounded, or stunned senseless. *This operation is going to be a walkover,* we tell ourselves, *nothing more than a test of our new equipment and an opportunity to refine our technique for amphibious operations.*

The best of our new equipment is the LVT, which stands for Landing Vehicle, Tracked. These amphibian tractors ("amtracs" for short) are an innovation, designed for seaborne invasions. They float like boats, crawl like tanks. They'll carry the assault waves through a channel in the barrier reef leading into the atoll's lagoon, then trundle over Betio's fringing reef and roll right up on the beaches. That's assuming they don't get shot full of holes after crossing the fringing reef and sink or blow up. This is a distinct possibility. The darn things are awfully vulnerable to enemy fire, even small-arms fire. Many have steel plates installed on the crew cabs that provide some protection for the drivers and gunners, but nothing protects the passengers. With or without armor, and however inadequate that armor might be, there aren't enough amtracs to go around, and the follow-up waves will have to use LCVPs.

Popularly known as a Higgins boat, after its inventor, Andrew Jackson Higgins, the LCVP (Landing Craft, Vehicle, Personnel) is a rectangular box with a steel ramp in front that can be raised and lowered like a drawbridge. When the ramp drops, you charge from the boat. This is not the best way to enter a battle if the enemy is firmly entrenched and waiting for you on the beach you are charging. Ideally, though, the enemy will not be waiting. The preliminary bombardment and the first-attack waves in their amtracs will have driven them from their beach defenses. That's the plan, anyway.

We watch the amtracs head for the island. They enter the lagoon, and we lose sight of them. The minutes pass, and we know the assault has begun. The time is around 0900. Nothing to do now but wait. The warships have ceased firing. We smoke cigarettes, chat, check our weapons and gear, fidget. We can't hear any sounds of the battle: it's too far away. Maybe there isn't a battle. Maybe the amtracs are trundling ashore without incident, depositing the Marines on the beaches, and no one is even getting his feet wet.

It's a pleasant scenario. It's also a complete fantasy.

Betio isn't much of an island. About two and a half miles long and five hundred yards wide at its broadest point, and no more than ten feet above sea level, it barely qualifies as dry land. On a normal day you could walk from one end to the other in a half hour, across it in five minutes. But this day is anything but normal. On this day, and in the two days that follow, Betio is a place of havoc and slaughter.

The problem is that there are nearly five thousand enemy troops and support personnel on the island. That's a heck of a lot of men to pack into four hundred acres. As if that weren't bad enough, some twenty-six hundred of them are *rikusentai*, members of Japan's Special Naval Landing Forces— Japanese Marines, in other words. Like the U.S. Marines, they're crack troops. It's said that they're recruited for size and that many of them are six feet tall or more. Not that their size matters all that much. Big or small, tall or short, they'll fight ferociously because they're Japanese, and that's what the Japanese do. It's what they've been trained to do, what they've been brought up to do as loyal subjects of their emperor. The only way to beat those people is to kill them, kill them all. Which is what *we* do.

The Navy promised us a preliminary bombardment that would blow the Japanese and their defenses to kingdom come, leaving the Marines to carry out what would amount to little more than a mopping-up operation. During a preinvasion staff briefing at Efate, in the New Hebrides, an admiral announced that it was not the Navy's intention merely to neutralize Betio. "Gentlemen," he told the assemblage, "we will obliterate it." This statement was passed on to the rank and file, and we believed it. At the same briefing, a battleship captain declared, "We are going to bombard at six thousand yards. We've got so much armor we're not afraid of anything the Japs can throw back at us." After the war, it was revealed that the commander of the 2d Marine Division, Maj. Gen. Julian C. Smith, was incensed by the captain's brave words. "Gentlemen," he retorted, "remember one thing: when the Marines land and meet the enemy at bayonet point, the only armor a Marine will have is his khaki shirt."

Actually, we don't call them shirts; they're "dungarees" or "fatigues." And most are green, not khaki. Although we have all been issued mottled-camouflage helmet covers that feature dark splotches on a khaki background, only a few men have received the matching camouflage dungarees. But the general had made an excellent point. Too bad the Navy didn't heed it. Too bad the Marines had to prove it.

It's tough going right from the start. The Japanese are heavily armed, firmly and deeply entrenched, and as always, they resist fiercely, inflicting heavy casualties on our assault teams. The radio reports start coming in. They're spotty and intermittent, but we get the picture. Encountering heavy resistance . . . heavy machine-gun fire.boats destroyed . . . units scattered . . . many casualties. The voices on the loudspeakers enumerate these calamities in measured tones. They sound calm, almost detached. If you didn't know better, you'd think the situation wasn't too terrible. But we know better.

We look at each other, all thinking some version of, *Oh, boy, this is bad. This is really bad.* At first we scarcely believe what we're hearing. What happened to the Navy's promise to obliterate Betio? Sounds as though we're the ones being obliterated.

This is not the case. The assault teams are getting ashore. But they're getting chewed up in the process. Same goes for the follow-up waves, the ones riding in LCVPs. The original plan called for the landing craft to clear the reef and get to within a few yards of the beaches before dropping their ramps. But the tides, which were supposed to cover the reef to an adequate depth, have proved uncooperative: the water is too shallow, just inches deep in some spots, and always less than the needed three-foot draft. Consequently, the landing craft are running aground on the reef and discharging their passengers six hundred yards from the shore. The men have to wade all that distance, fully exposed, into withering fire. Many are killed; many are wounded. With casualties so high, we know it'll be our turn soon. Which is why we're not surprised when we're told to load our boats.

Sheridan's complement of LCVPs, which had been suspended from davits on both sides, have already been lowered into the water. Now they come chugging up to the side of the ship, one after the other, to collect their passengers. The boat for my platoon arrives. We shoulder our packs, tighten our helmet straps, sling our weapons, then go over the side and climb down the cargo net into the boat. There's a trick to doing this. You put your feet on the horizontal ropes, which are like rungs on a ladder, and grip the vertical ropes with your hands so the guy above you doesn't step on your fingers. Getting stepped on can be extremely painful, even fatal if the pain is enough to make you let go and fall and hit the LCVP. You can also fall between the LCVP and *Sheridan*. If the sea is rough, the waves will roll the boat against the ship's hull and you'll be crushed. Fortunately, the sea is calm today and we load without incident; nobody gets stepped on, at least not seriously, and nobody falls.

We climb into the idling boat, which rocks ever so slightly, backward and forward and side to side, gently nudging the ship. The unmuffled engine makes a throaty growling sound, and the water behind the boat is churning and the air is thick with diesel exhaust fumes. The fumes have a coarse, oily smell, but that doesn't keep some guys from lighting up and taking deep drags of cigarette smoke. Smoke 'em if you got 'em, while you got 'em—while there's time.

Our helmsman is a Navy coxswain who operates the boat from a lectern-like control console mounted atop the engine platform at the stern. He wears a gray helmet and a bulging life jacket, and you know he has one of the most hazardous jobs in this business of amphibious warfare, because his station is fully exposed to all the bullets that will be soon flying his way. It takes a real cool customer to be a coxswain. Right now, he's holding the boat against *Sheridan's* hull, steering wheel turned slightly toward the troopship to hold the boat steady, and he's watching us impassively as we climb aboard.

After the boat is loaded, the coxswain works the throttle; the engine growls a little louder and stronger, and the boat moves away from the troopship. We rendezvous with a formation of circling boats that loaded ahead of ours. When the entire battalion is loaded, our commander's boat peels off and heads for Betio with our boats following in single file. Passing through the channel in the barrier reef, the flotilla enters the lagoon and we start circling again. We don't know yet where the brass is sending us, but we expect to go where the fighting is hottest, and we expect to go soon.

We circle and circle in the lagoon. We're standing in the boat and either leaning against the sides or holding onto them for balance. In general we have a soft ride, because the water is mostly still except for the turbulence caused by all the boats. The turbulence buffets the LCVP, and this movement, combined with the stench of the engine exhaust and the nervous tension that we all feel, makes many of us sick. Some men stick their heads over the sides to retch, while others puke onto the wooden deck. The men standing next to them just step aside like it's no big deal to get sick—because it really isn't a big deal. When the sick men finish retching, they straighten up as if nothing had happened; no one thinks the worse of them for it. After awhile, and depending on how long we're out there in the boat, the deck might be slippery with puke, but that's no big deal either. You can't smell the vomit—or anything else, for that matter—because the exhaust fumes overpower every other smell.

The minutes go by, lengthening into hours. The hours go by, but we're going nowhere, we're just going around and around. It's hot, in the high eighties or low nineties, the sky is clear, and the equatorial sun is beating down. Lovely weather for a vacation. But this is no vacation and I'm betting that most of us would gladly trade this balmy tropical clime for the autumn cold stateside. We'd make that trade in a New York second. The tropics can be pleasant, but you get tired of them very quickly when everywhere you go people are shooting at you.

Nobody's shooting at us just yet, because our boat is too far from the action, several thousand yards off Betio's shore. The sounds of battle are muted this far out. We can hear artillery and explosions, but not small-arms fire. We're all peering over the sides, looking at Betio, looking at the fires and the smoke and the explosions. It's an awesome sight, a mass of smoke and flames. "Holy Moses, look at that," we say. Not for the last time we ask ourselves how any of the defenders could survive in a place so torn up. It's an irrelevant question, really. Many Japanese *have* survived, and they're killing a lot of Marines. We know that a lot of our men were killed going in, and we know that the men who did make it ashore are fighting for their lives.

We expect we'll have a tough go of it too. We're apprehensive—who wouldn't be?—and we're wondering how we'll behave in combat. I know the new guys are especially concerned with how they'll behave. The great fear, the *greatest* fear, is that you won't be able to handle it, that you'll turn yellow, that you'll let your buddies down. We fear this much more than we fear getting killed or wounded. One reason for that is no one really thinks he'll be killed or wounded. You never think it's going to happen to you—never. You acknowledge that it *could* happen to you, that it *might* happen to you; the rational part of your brain makes you understand this. But in such circumstances as we now find ourselves, emotion trumps rationality every time. We know we're too young to die, and somehow, in a kind of strange and protective twist of logic and feeling, we figure that because we're too young to die we certainly won't die.

You've got to do a lot of hard thinking to reach this conclusion, however, and because we're all thinking so hard we're not talking much. Just as well: the engine is so loud that you can't talk to or hear anyone except the guys standing next to you.

We wait for the word to begin our assault, but it doesn't come. We continue circling beneath the hot sun, breathing exhaust fumes, staring at the island. We

want to know what, for Pete's sake, is happening. We wonder where they're
going to send us. We wonder, *Gosh, how much longer can it go on like this?*

A lot longer, as it turns out.

Nightfall. One moment the sun is above the horizon and the sky is bright,
then the sun drops below the horizon and it's dark. That's how night comes in
the tropics: no twilight. It's bright one moment and dark the next. Betio isn't
dark, however. Betio is on fire and the sky above it is glowing red. We're too
tired to care. Now we're sitting or lying on the deck. Not much room for that,
we're on top of each other, crammed together like sardines in a can. Many
guys are sleeping or trying to sleep. This isn't easy, in part because of the engine
noise and exhaust but mostly because of the uncertainty and the waiting. We
realize that we have to be mentally ready for action, because we might be sent
in at any moment. But we don't get sent. Instead, we wait. As a result, we're all
keyed up and bored out of our minds at the same time. This is a very stressful
condition, hardly conducive to sleeping. You're as tense as a coiled spring and
you want to let go of that tension because it's so tiring to keep your body and
mind coiled so tightly. But you can't let go because the reason for the tension—
Betio—is still there, so you just get more tired, which makes you more tense,
which makes you more tired, and so on.

This all makes for a long and fatiguing night. But we can hack it. We've got
a lot of experience at waiting because that's what we mostly do in the Corps.
We're conditioned to waiting. We learn to cope by blanking out our minds for
long periods of time. There's nothing else we can do. Just go blank. That's what
I do, and eventually, finally, I'm able to catch a few winks. I doze on and off.
Sometimes it's hard to tell when I'm dozing and when I'm simply blank. Not
that it makes any difference. Blank or dozing, it's the same. It beats staying
awake and the tension and boredom that come with being awake.

Suddenly, it's morning. The sun pops up over the horizon. *And then there
was light!* We're still circling, still waiting for orders. Betio is still burning. I
wonder how our boat can carry enough fuel to circle—how long is it?—twelve,
fourteen, sixteen hours? (Answer: we were afloat for about twenty hours.
Twenty hours.) Our mouths are dry, our muscles are stiff, we feel haggard and
cruddy. Some guys are sipping from their canteens or nibbling on their rations,
although there's not much eating because we just aren't hungry. Others are
relieving themselves over the side of the boat. Most of us didn't shave yesterday,
which means we have two days' growth of beard stubble. The "real men" among
us have heavy five o'clock (in the morning!) shadows and look like pretty rough
customers. As a matter of fact, they *are* pretty rough customers, all of them,

even the ones who haven't been in combat, even the ones with smooth, boyish faces. They'll prove this to me in just a few minutes.

At about 0530 the LCVP carrying our battalion commander, Maj. Lawrence Hays, chugs up next to our boat. Cupping his hands around his mouth and shouting to make himself heard above the noise of the boat engines, he says, "We're going in at Red Beach 2."

We're dismayed by this news. Red 2 is at the geographical center of the operation, between Red 1 to the west and Red 3 to the east. Two battalions of the 2d Regiment assaulted it yesterday. We had thought that it would be secure by now and that we would land on Red 3 or farther east of that beach, toward the island's tapering "tail," in order to outflank the defenders. Instead we're going to make a frontal assault into the middle of the battle.

Still shouting, Major Hays assures us that Red 2 won't be a problem. The Japanese positions on the beach have been eliminated, he tells us, and our landing will be unopposed. "You'll probably be able to go in standing up."

He actually said that.

The major's boat speeds off to the next boat in the formation. He'll proceed from boat to boat to tell everyone what he just told us; when he has completed this task, he'll lead us on our merry way to assault Red 2. None of us really believe we'll go in standing up. Not that we think Major Hays is feeding us a line; he's a good man, he wouldn't do that. But it could be that he has been misinformed.

Uninformed is more like it. Totally uninformed. Communications with the units ashore are in disarray, and in several instances, functionally nonexistent. Same goes for communications with General Smith and his staff on the battleship *Maryland*, the invasion fleet's flagship. This is due in large measure to the failure of our radios, which are too fragile to withstand the rigors of an amphibious assault. I've got a walkie-talkie strapped over my shoulder, and it's a hunk of junk. I can't even use it to communicate with the other boats, which is why Major Hays had to come by in his boat to shout orders to us.

In any event, we're relieved the waiting is almost over. This business of riding around in boats is for the birds. We want to get ashore and throw some punches.

I'm standing in the bow of our LCVP. Behind me are the thirty-two Marines of my platoon, most of them teenagers, most of them new to combat. I look at them and they look at me. I see fresh, boyish faces and wide worried eyes staring out from beneath their helmet brims. Their helmets all seem a size too big, accentuating their boyishness, making them look as young as, well, as most of them really are. The helmets are jammed down on their heads, the straps pulled tight under the chin. You wear the helmets this way so they don't fall off while you're clambering down the cargo nets of the troop transport into your boat. The helmet is nothing more than a steel pot, heavy and getting heavier the longer you wear it. If it falls off while you're on that net it could hit somebody beneath you; somebody could get hurt. And that's not when Marines are supposed to get hurt. Not during the "boating" phase, as it's called, the phase of the operation when the emphasis is on safety. The getting-hurt part, the part where safety is, one might say, beside the point—that comes later.

For us, for me and the men in my boat, that part comes now.

Did I say "men"? Well, I suppose they are. We call them men; we treat them as men; we expect them to act like men. They are, after all, United States Marines. But, really, they're kids, just out of high school or not even that. Kids with rifles, true; kids trained to kill, also true; but kids nevertheless. To use a term that has long since fallen into general disuse, they're "youths," a state of being between childhood and adulthood. Today's American male, exercising a "lifestyle choice," can and often does loiter for many years in that state. But in the mid-1940s, in a world at war, the state of youth tends to pass swiftly and—do I need to say it?—violently. The youths, the kids on my boat, have got a lot of growing up to do. Unfortunately, they'll be doing a hefty portion of that growing up in the coming minutes and hours. In that period, many—far too many—will undergo all the growing up they will ever experience. They will transition with almost obscene dispatch from youth to adulthood to the grave. At Betio, youth won't be served; it'll be served up and consumed, literally, in fire. These youths will be men only briefly, and then they will be just a memory, forever.

All this sounds as if I'm a grizzled veteran. I am a combat veteran—I fought on Guadalcanal earlier this year—but the fact is, I'm just twenty-three years old, still young, and not at all grizzled in either appearance or temperament. Practically speaking, though, I'm the graybeard of this bunch. Same goes for the platoon sergeant, who's about my age. We're the tribal elders, the warrior chiefs. I'll lead my boys off the boat, and the platoon sergeant, standing in the back, will make sure they follow, urging and cajoling them, yelling at them, maybe throwing in a few choice cuss words—whatever it takes to get them moving.

I'm watching my boys as they watch me. Things begin to happen fast. With the major's LCVP leading the way, our boats break formation one after the other and file off to our line of departure. This is an invisible line about six thousand yards offshore that runs parallel to the landing beaches. When we get there, our boats form up in line abreast, arrayed like a cavalry squadron waiting for the bugle to sound charge. The coxswains rev and gun the engines in neutral gear and the boats are rearing and lurching, champing at the bit; it's as if the coxswains are struggling to rein in warhorses that can't contain their eagerness for battle. Our boat's engine is blasting, the noise almost painful to our ears. We're pumped up, my men and I, we're *really* pumped, the adrenaline is flowing, surging through us. Clutching our weapons, looking over the side of the boat at the island, breathing hard, thinking hard, focusing on the task ahead, steeling ourselves, getting ready, ready, ready . . .

Here we go! The signal is given. Our coxswain shifts out of neutral, pushes the throttle wide open. The engine bellows, belches smoke, the stern dips, the men in the boat rock back slightly as the boat leaps forward. Now we're barreling toward the island—our boat, all the boats, the six hundred men (more or less) of the 1st Battalion, 8th Marines. Water churning, boiling behind the boat, we're bucketing and bouncing, bulling ahead with our squared-off bow muscling the water aside. The boat is throwing spray, soaking us—and we're getting closer, closer to the island.

We're about eight hundred yards from the shore when, *zip, zip, zip,* we hear tiny objects flying past, and those aren't hornets, boys, they're bullets. We're in range of the Japanese machine guns, and good gosh, they're shooting at us! We find this . . . interesting. Bullets zipping by, splatting on the water's surface. Splat, splat here, splat there, splats to the left and right, splats in front of us. "Look, by golly, there's some enemy fire hitting right over there! Look over there!" That's me talking. That's all of us talking. Talking and pointing at the impact circles in the water, little splats, little dots, where the bullets hit. People shooting at *us.* Fascinating!

Realizing that we could get our heads shot off, we duck down into the boat. More bullets are splatting into the water, but none hit our LCVP. We tell ourselves that most are 7.7-mm slugs, which is what your basic light Japanese machine gun fires, and are really nothing much to worry about because they're too small to pierce even the thin-skinned Higgins boats. That's what we tell ourselves, all right, but we don't really believe it. We know good and well that the Japanese are also shooting at us with heavier automatic weapons, big 13-mm machine guns and the even bigger dual-purpose antiboat/antiaircraft guns, which range in size from 37 mm to 77 mm, and they're lobbing shells from 70-mm mountain howitzers.

These weapons can and do inflict considerable damage on our assault teams, killing and wounding hundreds of men, disabling or destroying many amtracs and LCVPs. They're not my chief concern, however, and never mind that they might at any second blow us into eternity. What really bugs me is being hunkered down in the boat where I can't see anything. I can't see where we are, where we're going, where we should be. I can't observe the enemy fire and gauge the resistance we're likely to encounter. I feel as if I'm going into battle blindfolded. This really stinks. How can I do my job if I can't see anything? How can I be sure the coxswain is taking us to the right place?

My men: what are they thinking? They're watching me, watching to see how I'm bearing up. Well, I'm watching them, too, and for the same reason. They look okay. Check that; they look grim and resigned. But that's good. The grim-and-resigned look means they've more or less accepted the situation. Which is also good, because the situation isn't going to change, unless it changes for the worse. This whole thing is on rails; it's a runaway train, and nothing's going to stop it now. If you know this, if you accept it, you can keep your fear under control. And if you can keep your fear under control, you'll do your job; you won't let your buddies down.

So we're doing fine, relatively speaking; the boat is racing toward shore when . . . *crannnnng* . . . scraping bottom, metal grinding on coral, it abruptly stops. We're thrown forward, cursing: we've run aground! All along the reef it's the same, boats grinding to a halt on Betio's fringing reef. I think, *What the heck?* The tide is supposed to be up, the water deep enough to allow the LCVPs to clear the reef. We're six hundred yards from the shore: six hundred *long* yards. This just cannot be!

Wrong. It can be; it is. Though we're not aware of it, we're victims of the same disagreeable tidal conditions that fouled up yesterday's landings.

"This is as far as we go!" our coxswain yells. "We're going to unload!" His passengers are not happy. There are exclamations of astonishment and protest: "Oh, shit!" and "You gotta be kidding!" But he's not kidding. "Yeah, this is as far as we're going to go," he repeats. "We're hung up, we've hit the reef. You gotta get out here." Then he works the controls that release the cables that hold the ramp up. The cables, which are strung along both sides of the hull, unwind with a metallic rasp. The ramp screeches as it opens, drops, splashes into the water. And there before us is Betio in all its hideous glory.

Not to exaggerate or overdramatize, but it is a scene from hell. I mean, one second we're looking at this slab of a metal ramp, then the ramp drops and we're looking at an inferno. Fire and smoke fill our field of vision, framed by the sides and the bottom of the boat. Orange fire, red fire, and black, black smoke, and the fire is shooting up. The smoke is roiling, curling, climbing fast and high. The sky isn't high enough to contain it. You'd think you were looking at a volcano being born. You wonder what could produce so much smoke.

Surely by now everything on Betio that can burn has burned. So where is all that smoke coming from? From the bowels of the earth, it would seem. From somewhere deep underground, under the ocean, from the ever-blazing furnaces of the world. And let's not forget the explosions. There are lots of them, explosions here, there, everywhere: fire and fireballs, tongues of flame, crimson and yellow flashes in the smoke.

So this is Betio, codenamed "Helen," which is the name of that queen of ancient Sparta, reputedly the greatest beauty of her age, said to have a "face that could launch a thousand ships"—ships that took men to war in a faraway place. Betio is not beautiful, and we don't have a thousand ships, but otherwise the codename is apt. The time is 0615, and some six hundred Marines are about to be launched, or rather launch themselves, at Betio-codenamed-Helen.

To our left is the island's main pier, extending some five hundred yards into the lagoon. To our right is the hulk of a freighter grounded on the reef. On Betio I can see palm trees sticking up out of the smoke. Lots of palm trees. Amazing—you'd think they'd all have been blown into splinters by now. Makes me wonder: if palm trees could make it through more than twenty-four hours of bombardment and burning and fighting, what about the Japanese fortifications? Good question. The answer is, the fortifications made it through, too. As did the Japanese who occupy them.

I'm at the front of the boat, the lieutenant, the platoon leader: time for me to lead. A few seconds ago I was deploring the limited protection offered by the thin metal ramp. Now I'm deploring the lack of that limited protection. It was, after all, better than nothing, which is what I've got now. I feel kind of sick. And I'm thinking, *Gosh, why am I in this mess? What am I doing here?* But I'm resigned to the situation. I've got to ride it out whatever happens. No turning back now.

So the ramp hits the water and I run down the ramp, clutching my M1 carbine, waving my guys forward, shouting, "Let's go!" I sense that my men are hesitating but I pay no attention to them. I jump into the water, not knowing how deep it'll be, thinking that I might jump into a shell hole and go all the way under. But I land on coral and sand, solid footing, and it's only thigh-deep. What a relief! And the water feels good. That, incredibly, is my first thought: the water feels good. It's calm and warm, like bathwater, almost soothing, a pleasant contrast to the still-cool morning air. It's murky, though—sand and coral all stirred up beneath the surface; none of that crystalline purity that comes to mind when you picture a tropical lagoon. War comes to paradise and literally fouls it up.

I look shoreward. Only six hundred yards to go.

Six hundred yards, six football fields, just under a third of a mile. If you run that distance on dry land, unencumbered and unopposed, you'll be gasping at the finish line, I don't care what kind of shape you're in. We're in water, we're wearing and carrying sixty pounds or more of gear, and the Japanese are ripping us apart. They've got an absolutely clear field of fire and we have to walk straight into it. Walk, not run—we're in water, remember? Walk slowly, because we can't run, can't even walk fast.

The Marines are the world's experts in amphibious warfare. The Corps has been training for the past two decades to assault and establish a beachhead on a hostile shore. It has developed complex doctrines to guide us in such endeavors. At Betio, on 21 November 1943, all that training and doctrine come to this: We step out of our LCVPs into shallow water and walk slowly across six hundred yards with absolutely no cover whatsoever to make a frontal assault on heavily fortified and defended enemy positions.

Some training. Some doctrine.

We cannot believe the volume of fire coming from that island. The air is just filled with bullets. We can't see them, but we can see where they hit—splat, splat, splat—like raindrops, dotting the water, dot-patterns sweeping back and forth across our line. Curtain of fire, it's called. Curtains of fire passing over us, through us. I realize, *Oh, my God, the Japanese have got this reef zeroed in.* Which means they don't even have to aim their machine guns. They just lock the guns to a predetermined setting and traverse the barrel left and right, left and right. Like shooting fish in a barrel.

Major Hays was right. He said we'd be going in standing up, and that's what we're doing. Not that we want to. But there's no other way. No place to run, no place to hide. Some men crouch in the water. They watch the bullet patterns, the "curtains," trying to figure out when the curtains will sweep over them. It's all a matter of timing; they'll duck underwater at just the right moment to avoid getting shot. It would be a good plan if there were only one or two machine guns firing at them. But there are many, many machine guns firing, creating multiple curtains that meet and intermingle and overlap and crisscross. Bullets are flying every which way. Worse, the guns are aimed to fire just inches above the surface. So if you crouch with just your head above the water, you're likely to get your head drilled. Might as well stand up. That way, you'll get shot in the chest or stomach (usually fatal) instead of the head (almost always fatal). Also, if you're crouching in the water you're not moving, and if you're not moving, you're a stationary target, easy to shoot. You have to keep moving. You've got to get ashore. Get ashore or die.

The concept may be simple, but it's very hard to put into practice. Walking straight into curtains of machine-gun fire is not something that comes naturally. Your instincts oppose it. Every fiber of your being screams in protest, resisting, telling you *no way in hell am I going to do that.* That's why, when I glance over my shoulder to see how my men are doing, I see that many haven't left the boat. A few, most likely those who were next to me in the boat, are in the water, but others are bunched at the top of the ramp, all tensed up to take the plunge but hesitating, unable to make themselves move. I can't blame them for hanging back. But I can't allow it. For one thing, they make a big fat target standing there, crowded together at the front of the boat. They've got to get into the water and disperse before the Japanese machine guns find them and wipe them out with a couple of well-placed bursts. But more important, they've got a job to do. They've got to get off that boat, get ashore, and fight and kill the Japanese.

I gesture at them and shout, "C'mon, you guys, let's go! Get moving! Move out!"

They obey me: they get moving. They're good men, the best. They charge down the ramp, jump feet-first into the water, start wading toward shore. And that's when the slaughter really begins.

Right away, the men around me, my men, are taking hits and falling. I'm very aware of this. I'm hearing cries for help, cries for corpsmen. The wounded are calling out, "Corpsman, corpsman! I'm hit! I'm hit! Over here!" They're calling out as loud as they can. I see men going under, often for the last time. What to do? I keep moving forward, that's what. Cries for help everywhere, and I ignore them. I have to. You get hit, you're just going to have to cope with it yourself, do the best you can, hope for the best.

The sounds of battle everywhere. There are those sweeping, slashing curtains of fire, dozens of machine guns rattling, a cacophony of staccato hammering. Artillery shells exploding in the water, splashing, throwing up whooshing geysers of water, fire, and human body parts. And most especially, most memorably, the shouts and screams of the wounded and the dying.

"OH GOD, I'M HIT!"

"CORPSMAN! OVER HERE! CORPSMAN!"

"HELP! HELP ME, PLEASE!"

Men are dropping everywhere, to the left and right of me, dropping, falling, sinking into the water, going under. Some men don't cry out, hardly make a sound when they're hit: the bullet or bullets thump into them, they grunt, and they're gone. We're not permitted to help them. The corpsmen can come to their aid, but not the rest of us; our orders are to move on, to get ashore as fast as we can. If we stop to help the wounded, we'll get shot too. And we won't make it to the beach, where we're needed.

So we keep wading forward. My men, the men from the other boats, the entire battalion—or what's left of it—struggling through the water, holding their rifles over their heads, pushing toward the beach and into the teeth of all that enfilading gunfire. Their courage is incredible—that word only begins to describe it.

Shells exploding, whooshing geysers, machine guns rattling, splat splat splat, those little dots in the water—thousands of them—moving this way and that. A bullet hits four feet to my right, splat, then bullets hit three feet, two feet, one foot to my right. Sure do hope they skip over me. And they do, this time: splat, they begin hitting to my left, one foot, two feet, three feet, and so on. I got lucky. I literally dodged a bullet, several bullets. How long will my luck hold?

I can't see any muzzle flashes from the enemy guns. The Japanese are invisible, just like their bullets. We're being slaughtered by an invisible force. Nothing to see, nothing to shoot at. Not that we would be shooting even if we could see them. You don't stand in open water shooting at the enemy. You get yourself to the beach, you take cover, and *then* you start shooting. Anyway, my weapon isn't any good for shooting at long and medium ranges. For that matter, it's not much good at close range, either. It's an M1 carbine, a pathetic excuse for a firearm, a weakling with a weakling's punch. I'm holding it at port arms, across my chest, as I wade through the water. Maybe there it will stop a bullet that would otherwise kill me. That's about all the good it can do me.

On I walk, pushing forward, straining to move faster, the water dragging at my thighs. No one ever set a speed record running in thigh-deep water. I've gone about one hundred yards—only five hundred yards to go. We're taking fire from the front, from both flanks, from the rear—

The *rear?* What the hell . . . ?

I hear, above and behind me, the drone of aircraft. I throw a look over my right shoulder. Several aircraft are swooping down on us, strafing, their guns blinking fire. Oh, damn, that's all we need. Then I realize that these are U.S. Navy dive-bombers and they're attacking the wrecked and rusting freighter that sits on the reef about one hundred yards to the right of where our landing craft ran aground. That's where the fire in our rear is coming from. Sometime during the previous night, enemy machine-gun teams swam out to the hulk, boarded it, set up their weapons, and stayed hidden until now. The Japanese are really quite extraordinary, and I might admire them if I didn't want so badly to see them dead. Our aircraft attempt to oblige me in this regard by bombing and strafing the hulk. One bomb explodes on the freighter, others fall wide. The planes zoom past overhead, flying very low over the water, over us. Thanks, guys. But their efforts are in vain. The machine guns on the freighter continue chattering at us.

I return to the task at hand: keep moving to the shore. How long has this been going on? How long have I been out here in the water? I can't say. I have no sense of time. Everything is moving in slow motion. Seconds seem to last minutes, minutes seem to last hours. It just keeps going on and on. Every moment is intense, filled with intense thoughts, emotions, actions. I'm thinking, *How can I protect myself? How can I protect my men?* Someone screams, "Another one of my men is hit." And another. And another. "Help, corpsman!" Some are killed outright, some are wounded, some are—well, it's hard to say. Some go quietly, some go noisily. They fall back into the water, they slip under the water, some flail the water in their pain and panic, howling and shouting. I keep moving. My adrenaline is flowing like an electric current through me, allowing me to do things I normally wouldn't, shouldn't do. If I stopped to think about what I'm doing, I'd freeze up.

I try to track the bullets, the movement and pattern of the enemy's traversing fire. The bullet impacts start to my left, to my right. Bullets sweeping back and forth. I see no pattern. Or, rather, I see too many patterns. Splat, splat, splat everywhere. It's like the enemy is throwing thousands and thousands of stones at us. A pattern of splats in the water comes toward me from the right, sweeps past me, continues to the left. I don't hear the crack of the bullets as they zip past at supersonic speed. That's the problem. They're not zipping past, they're hitting us. They've got our range. I'm in the impact zone, and I have to get through it or die.

I turn to look back at my men. "Let's go!" I call out for the umpteenth time. I turn, facing the shore. Then finally, inevitably, it happens. A sickening splat, like an inner tube snapped across my abdomen, slapping my bare stomach: a sharp stinging sensation. "I'm hit!" I hear myself say. A bullet has struck me nearly dead center below the navel, piercing me above the waterline. I'm gut-shot, one of the worst of all wounds. Oh, God.

I've probably been hit by a small-caliber machine-gun bullet fired from straight ahead on the beach. It didn't make much of an impact, not enough to knock me off my feet or even to stagger me. Later I would learn that it tore right through my body, piercing my intestines, bladder, and sacrum before exiting just a quarter inch from my spinal cord. Lucky for me I wasn't hit by something bigger, like a 13-mm bullet or a 20-mm exploding shell; I would've been killed instantly. As it is, I'll probably die in a few minutes.

I'm scared. I think, *My gosh, this is it.* It often happens that you get shot and you don't know how bad the wound is. But when you're hit where I was hit, you know it's bad. It's a gut wound, and you know it's a pretty sure thing you're not going to make it. Very few people survive gut wounds, even in the best of circumstances. I'm in what are arguably the worst of circumstances. If I had been shot on dry land, I might have been able to crawl to an aid station. Or my buddies might have patched me up. But I'm in the lagoon, so there can be no crawling, and my buddies are forbidden to help me. It goes without saying that there are no aid stations close by. I can try to reach our LCVPs on the reef a hundred yards behind me, but I probably won't make it. I'm dying, is why.

I dump my gear into the water. Off goes my pack, my helmet, my webbing, the walkie-talkie slung over my shoulder. Good-bye, M1 carbine: into the drink you go with never a shot fired in anger. It takes just seconds to shuck my equipment. In those seconds I lose most of my strength. After a few more seconds I'm almost too weak to stand. It happens that fast. The energy is draining out of me. I'm going into shock. The weakness doesn't paralyze me, and it doesn't come from any place in particular; it's an all-over sort of feeling that makes me go heavy and limp. I'm in pain, but it's not too bad, not just yet, and I'm not bleeding very much either, but I'm slipping away, no doubt about it. My biggest worry now is that I'll collapse, sink beneath the surface, and drown. All I want to do is keep my head above water, so I won't drown before I die from the bullet that reamed through me. I know this isn't rational. What difference does it make how I die? Drowning or dying from getting my innards scrambled by a bullet—either way I'm a goner, and soon. But I'm not thinking rationally. I'm thinking, *I've got to keep my head above water.* Period.

Maybe ten seconds have passed since I got shot. That's all. In that time, the man closest to me, Pfc. Thomas F. Sullivan, has hastened to my side. "Lieutenant, where are you hit?" he asks. I tell him. He pulls up my dungaree jacket, checks my wound.

Sullivan is the platoon's eight ball: a nice guy, just a teenager, but he's got a wild streak; he's always getting into trouble. You can bet dollars to doughnuts that when he goes on liberty, he'll raise the dickens, get arrested, and afterward spend a few days in the brig as punishment. This happened in New Zealand before we left for Tarawa. This happens everywhere we go. It's standard operating procedure for Sullivan. You can count on him to kick up a row, to break the rules, to defy authority. That's what he's doing now. He's helping me, a wounded man, and in doing so, he's disobeying orders. Sullivan the incorrigible. What can you do with a guy like that?

In the next moment we're joined by Pfc. John Duffy, also a member of my platoon and also, it would seem, a kid who doesn't know how to follow orders. Instead of following orders, Duffy and Sullivan have decided to save my life.

Sullivan keeps me from going under. He stands behind me, grabs me under each arm, and lifts my head and shoulders out of the water, so that I'm sort of floating on my back. Meanwhile, Duffy snatches my webbing—it's in the water but it hasn't sunk to the bottom yet—and opens the first-aid pouch fastened to the belt. He removes a packet of infection-fighting sulfanilamide powder, tears it open, and tries to sprinkle the stuff directly on the hole in my abdomen. It immediately washes away. So much for that idea. Then Duffy slaps a bandage on the wound. Success. The bandage adheres to my wet skin, the wound is closed.

You'd think I'd be happy about this. I'm not. I'm worried about Duffy and Sullivan. Bullets are striking everywhere around us. The Japanese, you can be sure, have not ceased firing on my account, in order to let me die in peace. It's only a matter of time before Duffy and Sullivan are hit. They've got to leave me, that's all there is to it; if they don't, they'll die too. "Go on, get out of here," I gasp. "Get in to the beach." I know I'm probably done for, and I don't want them or anyone else to get killed in a futile effort to save me.

They ignore me. They're going to save me whether I want them to or not.

Getting weaker now, very weak. I hear Sullivan ask, "Should I take you to the beach or back out to a landing boat?"

Oh, okay, if you insist. "A boat," I answer. I know we'll never make it ashore. Also, the LCVP will take me to *Sheridan*, where, provided I don't die en route, my wound can be treated in that ship's well-equipped medical ward.

Duffy heads off toward the beach while Sullivan begins manhandling me back to the nearest boat at the reef, dragging me backward through the water by my shoulders. After a minute or two he stops. *Uh-oh*, I think, *he's been hit*. It doesn't seem possible, in that hailstorm of bullets, that he hasn't been hit. "Are you okay?" I ask. "Yeah," he replies. "What are you doing?" I say. And he says, "I'm resting. Just resting. I'm all right, I'm not hit. I'm just resting." Then we resume our journey, Sullivan pulling, me being pulled.

It takes about ten minutes to reach the nearest LCVP. The boat is crowded with wounded Marines. Other wounded men are being dragged to the boat by their buddies. Evidently, Sullivan and Duffy weren't the only men who ignored the order to ignore the wounded. The wounded men and their rescuers are clustered in front of the ramp, which is about three-quarters raised. One by one, the wounded men are half-pushed, half-flung over the top of the ramp, after which they roll down the ramp onto the deck. My turn comes. The man next to me is that big fellow with the ravaged face. His wound is terrible, worse than mine. I motion for him to go before me. He is boosted to the top of the ramp. Sullivan lifts me up. I'm groaning like mad. The pain is getting worse, I'm really hurting now, hurting bad. My helpers can't quite get me over the top, though. I'm limp and heavy, a bulky sack of flesh and bone with a hole in it, and they just can't manage to raise me high enough. That's when the Marine with the ravaged face performs his lifesaving deed: one-arming me into the boat.

How did he do that? He must be in torment from his wound, but that didn't stop him from helping me.

I tumble, groaning, down onto the deck alongside the man with the ravaged face. The deck is covered with maimed and wounded men, their bodies bandaged and bloody, many writhing in pain, many groaning just like me. Another wounded man is taken aboard, then the ramp is closed and the boat begins to move. The coxswain, aware that our lives are hanging in the balance, opens the throttle wide, and soon we're going full tilt, racing through the channel in the barrier reef toward *Sheridan*. The journey back to the transport is nowhere near as smooth as the ride out. We're going much faster now, and the sea has developed a rough chop in the interim. Our boat is bumping hard on the water's surface corrugations, crashing from wave top to wave top, and with each jolt I feel as though someone is digging at my guts with a long, hot knife blade. The pain is excruciating, but nevertheless I'm feeling a little bit better about the way things are going. *At least if I die,* I tell myself, *I'll die at sea instead of on the beach.* I don't know why, but this is a soothing thought. I think about my parents. It saddens me to think how sad they'll be if I die. The news of my death will devastate them. But maybe I won't die. I'm beginning to think that I won't die, beginning to hope that I'll live.

The boat pulls up alongside *Sheridan*, and I'm gently lifted into a basket-litter. The litter holds two stretchers side by side, and the Marine on the stretcher next to me is my erstwhile rescuer, the man with the ravaged face. As the litter is being hoisted aboard *Sheridan* by one of the ship's davits, I turn my head to look at my companion. I can see that he's in real bad shape. "Well, we made it," I say, trying to cheer him up. He nods. "You're gonna make it now," he murmurs.

★   ★   ★

Those were the first and only words we spoke to each other. I made it; he didn't. He died shortly thereafter. Duffy didn't make it either. He was killed later that day on Betio. Sullivan rescued several more wounded men from the water, and then, finally, he obeyed orders and went ashore to fight the Japanese. I know he survived the war, and I've often tried to find him in the years since the war ended, but without success. Tom Sullivan, are you out there? I want to thank you for saving my life.

I also want to thank that Marine with the ravaged face. Pulling me aboard the LCVP, with that terrible bloody wound, a wound that had surely taken him to the extremes of suffering, causing him to understand clearly that his death was near. I count this as one of the most heroically selfless acts I've ever witnessed. I can only thank him in prayer, but if there's a heaven, and I believe there is, I know he can hear me. Unfortunately, I can't thank him by name. I don't know his name; I've never been able to learn his identity. At 2d Division reunions I'll ask other Tarawa veterans about him. I'll describe him—big fellow, solidly built—and they'll just shake their heads. "Sorry, Dean, can't help you," they'll say. "Description doesn't ring a bell." I don't tell them that he was a man of extraordinary strength, courage, and self-sacrifice, for that describes the majority of Marines in the Pacific War, those with names that are known to us and those with names that are known only to God.

This story, this memoir of my experiences in the Pacific War, is my way of saying thanks to that valiant man, and to Duffy, and to all the those men, known and unknown, dead and alive. All those faithful warriors who served their country as United States Marines. I began the story in the middle, with the Betio landings, to make the purpose clear and to give it context. Having done that, it's time now to backtrack, to begin at the beginning, before the war, when I first got it in my fool head that I wanted to be a Marine.

Faithful Warriors

CHAPTER ONE

From Spokane to Samoa

In early 1939 a boy from the next block over came home from sea, and I was never the same because of it. His name was Lee Preston, and he was a corporal on leave from the Marine Corps. He showed up wearing his dress blues, creating quite a stir in our quiet Spokane neighborhood. Mostly, I think, the stir was in me. He looked so sharp in that uniform, and his manner, the way he carried himself—at once modest but utterly self-assured—got me thinking about myself and my future. I was only a couple of years younger than Lee, but it didn't seem that way. I was a senior in high school, just a teenager, still a kid, and Lee ... well, he was different now. He had changed. He had left home a boy and had returned a Marine, a warrior, a man.

I didn't know much about the Marine Corps, just snippets of its history. I knew that a Marine contingent had helped defend the besieged foreign legations in Peking during the Boxer Rebellion of 1900. I knew about the Banana Wars, when Marines fought in Haiti, Nicaragua, and other jungly places in the Caribbean and Central America—though I couldn't exactly say what they were fighting for. I had seen the 1926 silent film *What Price Glory?* about Marines in France during the Great War. They seemed to spend as much time fighting each other as they did fighting the Germans.

The Marines of that era were called "Devil Dogs." If you believed the movies, the typical Marine was a hard-nosed, hard-drinking, two-fisted sort: dependably brave and habitually fearless, leathery tough and endlessly enduring, bawdy, profane, perpetually combative, and profusely tattooed; a social misfit, an outcast by choice and inclination, perfectly suited for war and little else. And let's not forget the desire for adventure and the streak of romanticism that such desire implied. You couldn't be a Marine without it, at least according to Hollywood.

Actually, there were a lot of Marines who fit this description. They were the career men, the Corps was their home, and they would leave it only dead or too old and decrepit to work the bolt of their beloved Springfield '03 rifles. These "Old Salts" included officers as well as noncoms and privates, and each was a character in his own right. You can bet they reveled in the Hollywood stereotype. You might say they even promoted it, so much so that it was sometimes hard to tell when and whether they were acting according to their natures or simply acting. I'm guessing that it was often a combination of the two: your typical Old Salt was a true swashbuckler and a genuine eccentric, but he was also something of a ham, one who delighted in playing a role that came naturally to him.

Often enough, though, the theater where the Old Salts gave their best performances was far removed from anything resembling a civilized venue, and their audiences were anything but appreciative. On the contrary, those who saw them giving their most accomplished portrayals were usually their enemies. Not for nothing did many an Old Salt possess an exquisite (if rough) sense of irony, a trait common to professional soldiers of all times and places. There's something intrinsically ironic about a profession in which the only people who see you at your best and who get the best of what you have to give are the same people you're trying your best to kill.

This was an elemental fact of life in the Marine Corps, and every Old Salt understood it intuitively if not on a rational level. And in understanding it he became wise in a way that most people weren't. Not coincidentally, he also became a magnificent soldier. It is thus no exaggeration to say that in the interwar years the Old Salts were the backbone of the Marine Corps, and when the Corps had to flesh itself out to meet the challenge in the Pacific, it did so around the straight and steely spine the Old Salts both provided and embodied.

Lee Preston was not an Old Salt. He was still too young for that role, and anyway, he didn't have the personality for it. He was of another type, what you might call the gentleman Marine, a type in its way equally important to the proper functioning of the Corps. The product of a solid middle-class upbringing in a stable home, Lee was polite, modest, well spoken, and, with that splendid uniform he wore, altogether impressive. He had a noble, knightly air that I found admirable and attractive.

I asked Lee about the Marines, questioning him at great length about his experiences in the Corps. Lee was happy to talk and regaled me with stories. A seagoing, or "fleet," Marine, Lee had served aboard Navy warships, which meant that he got to travel all over the world, stopping at many exotic ports of call, all courtesy of Uncle Sam. His duties had included serving in a 5-inch-gun crew, and he had fired that gun during fleet maneuvers. Lee told me all about it, and I was enthralled. His life was so exciting! I wanted an exciting life, too: a life of travel, a life at sea, living on warships, visiting exotic ports, shooting big guns, wearing Marine dress blues. I decided that I wanted to be a Marine. The Corps would have to wait, however, until I graduated from high school.

Shortly after our talk, Lee Preston returned to duty. I never saw him again. He was captured on Corregidor when that besieged fortress-island fell to Japanese assault on 6 May 1942. He died of beri-beri in a Japanese prison camp in July 1943, four months before I stepped off the ramp of a Higgins boat in Tarawa lagoon.

Semper fi, brother. You are not forgotten.

★   ★   ★

I enlisted in the Marine Corps Reserve in April 1939, six weeks shy of my high-school graduation, joining the 14th Organized Reserve Battalion in Spokane. I was eighteen years old and ready for anything and everything. In September, I would start classes as a freshman at Washington State College (now university) studying engineering, but before that I would spend the summer becoming a Marine.

My reserve unit met one night a week for two hours at the Marine armory on the second floor of a department store in Spokane. In June, I attended my first summer encampment at the Marine base in San Diego, home of the West Coast component of what was then known as the Fleet Marine Force. Designated 2d Marine Brigade, it comprised the 6th Marine Regiment, various support units, and an aviation wing. Our East Coast counterpart, designated 1st Brigade, was based in Quantico, Virginia, and comprised the 5th Regiment plus support units and an aviation wing. Although understrength, the two brigades constituted the USMC's largest combat formations (divisions had yet to be activated), jointly totaling just under five thousand officers and enlisted men—fully 25 percent of the Corps' 19,452 active-duty personnel.

The Marine Corps was still small, but it was growing swiftly, thanks to the foresight of military and civilian planners who recognized that another great

war was in the offing. The reservists who took part in the prewar encampments represented an early response to the threat of global conflict, forming
the cadre on which the Marine Corps would build, eventually expanding to
nearly a half-million men and women of all ranks before Japan's capitulation
in September 1945.

★   ★   ★

In July 1940 I attended my second summer encampment of the Marine Reserve,
this time at Bremerton, Washington. In September, I returned to Washington
State College for the start of my sophomore year. On 8 September, seven days
after the Germans invaded Poland, President Franklin D. Roosevelt declared
a limited national emergency. At the start of November, with my fall semester
not even half completed, the Marine Corps Reserve was mobilized and I was
called to active duty.

My unit was assigned to the new Marine Corps training facility at Camp
Elliott, just outside San Diego. On arrival the 14th Reserve Battalion was
deactivated and absorbed by the 1st Battalion of the 8th Marine Regiment,
initially comprising about 50 percent of the regiment's strength. Organization
continuity was maintained by keeping our companies more or less intact, and
thus, Company B of the 14th Reserves, to which I belonged, became Company
B in the 1/8. The 8th Marines were in turn made part of the San Diego–based
2d Marine Brigade, soon to become the 2d Marine Division. The same process
was under way on the East Coast at Quantico, which was receiving a continual
influx of reserve units and recruits to build the 1st Marine Brigade into the 1st
Marine Division.

★   ★   ★

In November 1941, after a year of intensive training, I was promoted to
corporal, an important step in my Marine career. In a letter to my parents
informing them of my promotion, I remarked, "It's kind of peculiar, because it
was only 2 weeks ago that I was drawing $49 a month and now it is $64, nearly
twice as much as before. I ought to be able to save a lot of money now."

I also noted an ominous development: "I hear that leaves have been canceled
and there are strong rumors that there will be a dummy run getting on board
the transports. It looks as if it might be only a matter of a few days before we
leave San Diego. It probably depends on the Japanese situation as to what is

going to happen though. I am going to leave my equipment packed until I find out just what's going to happen the next few days. It might blow over too."

In the meantime, I began attending scout-sniper school, which was held just north of San Diego in Mission Valley, at that time a remote area. The commander was Chief Marine Gunner H. P. "Jim" Crowe, soon to become an officer and, not incidentally, a legendary figure in the annals of Marine Corps combat history. It was supposed to be a six-week course, but the school was closed down after just one week as a result of the aforementioned "Japanese situation": the 7 December attack on Pearl Harbor.

In the hours following the attack, all leaves were canceled. Some of us were put to work loading machine-gun belts, others were detailed to walk the ocean-front along the Southern California coast to guard against Japanese landings. Guard details were dispatched to Miramar Naval Air Station to guard fighter aircraft flown in from the East Coast. We heard that Japanese submarines surfacing just off the West Coast had shelled the mainland with their deck guns. Would the Japanese follow up with a carrier attack—or even an invasion? We were only too aware that we had a very long coastline to protect and that our forces at hand were inadequate for the job. Orders were issued sending us here, there, and back again. Nobody knew what was going on.

The confusion soon subsided, and we began preparing in earnest for overseas deployment. Subsequently, the 2d Marine Brigade was reconstituted as a Marine Expeditionary Force totaling 4,798 men and loaded aboard the Matson liners *Lurline, Monterey,* and *Mariposa.* The 8th Marines, who boarded shortly thereafter, were quartered aboard *Lurline.* Our ships weighed anchor on 6 January. On reaching blue water we formed a convoy with the aircraft carrier *Enterprise* and a number of cruisers and destroyers and headed west by southwest across the Pacific.

We arrived at the port of Pago Pago on Tutuila, the largest island in the American Samoa group, on 19 January and began moving into defensive positions in and around Pago Pago previously occupied by a 417-man force comprising the 7th Marine Defense Battalion and the 1st Samoan Marine Battalion. In due course, we deployed inland and to outlying beaches, until the brigade was spread throughout the island. Our immediate and most urgent task was to prepare the island's defenses for the attack everyone believed was imminent. Just seven days before our arrival, a Japanese submarine had shelled Pago Pago with its deck gun—a harbinger, we thought, of things to come.

The challenge facing us was daunting. Tutuila is relatively big and very rugged—fifty-two square miles of mostly jungle-covered mountains. Its long and irregular shoreline has numerous sandy beaches ideally configured for amphibious assault. If and when the Japanese made a determined grab for the island, we would be hard-pressed to stop them.

We quickly established defensive positions on the various remote beaches where the enemy might land. The 1st Battalion was assigned to defend the southwest coast. My unit, B Company, was responsible for a sector south and west of Pago Pago extending west to east along the coast from Leone Bay to Fagaleo Point, and inland to the village of Pavaia.

Our defense scheme was simple. When the Japanese attempted to land, we would hit them on the beaches with machine-gun fire—lots of it—holding them for as long as possible. Then, at the last minute, with the Japanese threatening to overrun our position (we expected to be outnumbered), the main body of the defending unit would withdraw along the trails we had cut for this purpose, leaving a rear guard to delay the enemy. The main body would set up in a pre-prepared fallback position, after which the rear guard would break contact and withdraw beyond the main body to another fallback position behind it. We would continue these retrograde leapfrogging movements, fighting every step of the way into the mountains, until reinforcements arrived or until we were backed into some jungle corner and wiped out.

This scheme was not universally applicable. A few beach positions were isolated by impassible terrain, completely cut off from the landward side, with the sea providing the only way in and out. These positions were kept supplied by boat. The men who occupied them understood that in the event of an enemy attack, there could be no retreat. Their position would be the site of their first and last stand.

Company B's Weapons Platoon, to which I then belonged, was dispatched to a remote beach on Fagalua Cove in Larsen Bay, just northeast of Steps Point. From Fagalua Cove the machine-gun squad I commanded hiked up and over a steep ridge and then down to an even remoter beach on Fogama Cove. Situated on a body of water approximately 150 yards across and nestled between two rugged, jungle-covered promontories, the beach was a place of surpassing beauty, at once spectacular and restful in aspect. As such, it could not been more alien in spirit to the war that might soon come to it.

This was our home for several months. Most of that time was spent building fortifications and shelters and training with our weapons, especially our machine guns. We dug in, wired in, and settled in to await the enemy.

We waited. And waited. And waited. And the Japanese never came. The days passed, and the weeks lengthened into months. The war went on elsewhere, badly. The Japanese conquered the Philippines, Malaya, Singapore, the Dutch East Indies. There was one ray of hope: in the Battle of the Coral Sea (4–8 May), the U.S. Navy scored a strategic victory that turned back a Japanese invasion of Port Moresby and probably forestalled enemy operations against the Fiji and Samoa groups.

Then came the real stunner: the Battle of Midway on 4–6 June. We heard about Midway on the radio. We were both jubilant and relieved, because we knew that Samoa was no longer in danger of being invaded. We knew as well that we would soon be going on the offensive and carrying the fight to the enemy. We were ready to take the offensive. We were tired of sitting on our butts, tired of defending.

As it happened, on 3 May, just one day before the Battle of the Coral Sea began, the Japanese landed on Tulagi Island in the Solomons group, a few hundred miles north and east of the battle area. Tulagi is just twenty-two miles to the north of the much larger island of Guadalcanal. American military leaders took note. A chain of events had been set in motion, and it would eventually lead to the offensive that we were then so eager to undertake.

On 7 August that offensive became a reality when the 1st Marine Division—including our 2d Regiment—landed on Guadalcanal, as well as on Tulagi and the neighboring islands of Florida, Gavutu, and Tanambogo. At last! The fat was in the fire now, and the Marines on Samoa knew that it was only a matter of time before we would be joining or replacing our brother Marines in the Solomons.

★   ★   ★

Toward the end of August I enrolled in a machine-gun leadership training school. I welcomed the assignment for what it was: an officer candidate school for noncommissioned officers. Most of those selected for the school outranked me, so I considered the assignment an honor as well as an opportunity for advancement.

I was sent to the school to get leadership training as an NCO, preparatory to receiving my sergeant's stripes. By the time I completed the program, however, I had been selected to receive a field commission to second lieutenant. Advancing from corporal to second lieutenant in one big jump was no mean feat, especially in light of the fact that several men who started the program as officer candidates failed to make the grade. It was an achievement attributable in large measure to my attitude and performance, both deemed excellent by my instructors.

But I also benefited from the rapid expansion of the Marine Corps and the concomitant shortfall in second lieutenants. Men who arrived in Samoa as second lieutenants were promoted to first lieutenant a couple of months later and to captain shortly thereafter, whereupon they were transferred to units then forming in the States. Replacing these men as second lieutenants were noncoms such as myself. Most had little or no college education, and some had not yet graduated from high school. We would learn to be officers and gentlemen, as it were, on the job. We were called "Mustangs," after the Spanish-named *mestengo,* a wild horse known for its fiery spirit, fierce courage, extraordinary powers of endurance, and sometimes unruly behavior. It was a name we bore with pride.

I swore my oath as a second lieutenant on 16 October 1942. Secretary of the Navy James Forrestal, who visited our school during an inspection tour of the Southwest Pacific, signed our commission certificates and addressed the graduating class. Lieutenants' bars being then unavailable on Tutuila, I asked a friend stationed at the airfield to fashion my badge of rank from brass bullet casings. After cutting the bars to the proper size and shape, my friend soldered a safety pin on the back. I pinned the bars it to my blouse, and voila! I was a second lieutenant (temporary grade) in the United States Marine Corps.

I was assigned to the same company I had left as a corporal, temporarily attached to company headquarters. Around this time, most of the Marine Corps units were pulled off the beach defenses and replaced by detachments of Samoan Marines. Our formations were reassembled, and we trained and operated as units again instead of being dispersed around the island in small elements.

Although we felt pretty good about our prospects, we were under no illusions about what we would be going up against. The Japanese were experienced soldiers, battle-hardened veterans made confident by victory. Reports of the fighting on Guadalcanal further confirmed what we already knew: the Japanese were formidable opponents. For example, we were told (and would soon learn firsthand) that they were excellent night fighters, extremely adept at infiltrating, probing our defenses, and determining the location of our weak points. And they were extraordinarily persistent—they'd keep coming at you regardless of how many of their men they were losing in the process.

We were also told that the Japanese were not flexible in their tactics. This proved to be true as well. When, in actual combat, we saw how they often threw away their lives quite unnecessarily and to no good purpose, we realized that there was a flaw in their battlecraft, a flaw we could exploit.

The 8th Marines' nine-month Samoan sojourn ended on 25 October 1942 when the entire regiment boarded troop transports in Pago Pago harbor. Some said we were headed for New Zealand. Most thought we were going into combat, destination unknown. We were fairly certain that Guadalcanal was not our destination. Hadn't the Marines completed their mission on that island? In three months of hard and sometimes desperate fighting, the Marines had seized and secured the beachhead and nearby airfield, repelled numerous counterattacks, and pushed the Japanese back into the hinterland. It was time for the Army to come in and finish what our guys had started, freeing the Marines to conduct another amphibious assault against another enemy-held island. That was how the system was supposed to work.

As usual, the system didn't work as planned. We were going to Guadalcanal.

CHAPTER TWO

Guadalcanal

THE 8TH MARINES AND ATTACHED UNITS sailed to Guadalcanal on three ships: *President Hayes, Hunter Liggett,* and *Barnett.* We were confident but concerned by our lack of unit cohesion. The 8th Marines was not the same regiment that had shipped out from San Diego in January. In Samoa it had undergone continual changes: privates became noncoms, noncoms became officers, and many new men—recruits straight out of boot camp and recently activated reservists, officially Marines but hardly more than civilians—had arrived to fill the ranks vacated by those promotions. Integrating the new men into their units was a difficult task. It wasn't just a matter of training the newly made noncoms and officers to do their jobs. "Mustangs" like me—noncoms who had received field commissions—had much to learn about the art of command. And everyone had to learn to pull together as a team. This had been a primary goal of our training on Samoa. We needed more work, but we had run out of time. Ready or not, we were going to war.

But it was high time, we told ourselves. We wanted to get into the fight; we wanted to prove ourselves. We felt we were up to the task. Historians writing about the early stages of the war have made much about the "myth of Japanese invincibility" as a factor in our preinvasion calculations, if only to show how we subsequently "exploded" that myth at Guadalcanal. But this implies that there was a time when we believed the Japanese to be invincible. Nonsense. I never thought that the Japanese were invincible, and I don't know anyone who did, or at least who would admit to thinking that way.

But we were apprehensive. We knew the Japanese were superb soldiers and very tough. We thought we were tough too, but we had yet to prove it. We

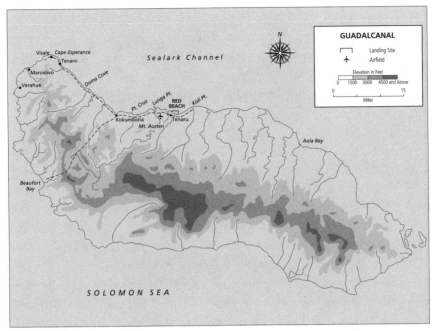

Guadalcanal.

were well trained, we were highly motivated, and we had plenty of esprit—but we had no combat experience. The Japanese we would be facing had plenty of combat experience, and even now, some three months after our forces invaded Guadalcanal on 7 August, they had good reason to believe that victory was well within their grasp.

They still controlled most of the island. Guadalcanal is about ninety miles long and twenty-five miles wide on average—approximately twenty-five hundred miles square. The American lodgment, situated almost exactly in the middle of the island's north coast, occupied no more than fifteen square miles. The size and configuration of our lodgment, marked on maps of dubious accuracy by a roughly oval twenty-two-thousand-yard-long line known as the Lunga Perimeter (because it was more or less centered on Lunga Point), had not changed appreciably since the initial landings. The line had moved outward in some places, inward at others, and not at all in most. Ground had been won and lost by both sides, resulting in expansions and contractions to the perimeter that were on the whole minor, localized, and insignificant in the sense that they had little effect, for better or worse, on the position either force held in relation to its foe. Nobody was winning, nobody was losing, and everyone was suffering.

Situated within this so-called Lunga Perimeter was Henderson Field, the base of air operations for what became known as the "Cactus Air Force" (after Guadalcanal's codename, "Cactus"). Named in honor of Maj. Lofton Henderson, a Marine aviator killed in the Battle of Midway, the field had a single runway, covered with Marsden metal matting, just 3,378 feet long and 150 feet wide. At this juncture in the war it was arguably the most important airfield in the Pacific. We had taken Henderson Field, and the Japanese wanted to take it back. For the better part of six months everything that happened on and around Guadalcanal boiled down to a battle for the airstrip's ownership.

★   ★   ★

We arrived off Guadalcanal on 3 November, nine days after leaving Samoa. In the predawn darkness our convoy quietly slipped into the placid waters of Sealark Channel, also known as "Ironbottom Sound" because of the many ships that had already been sunk there. The "Canal" loomed before us, rearing from the sea, mountains silhouetted against the starlit sky. No lights, no sounds, no flashes of gunfire from that land mass. Guadalcanal was quiet.

Our transports anchored just east of Lunga Point in mid-afternoon and we geared up and prepared to board the LCVPs that would take us ashore. Then we learned that our landing had been delayed until the next day in response to events unfolding simultaneously on opposite sides of the perimeter. To the west, Marine and Army units were advancing beyond the Matanikau River, driving past Point Cruz toward Kokumbona. Meanwhile the Japanese had landed reinforcements at Tetere Cove, thirteen miles east of Lunga, and were pushing inland and along the coast past Koli Point, forcing the defending 2/7 Marines to withdraw across the Nalimbiu River. The brass decided to halt the Kokumbona operation temporarily and put us ashore the next day to counter the threat from the east.

So we stayed aboard ship. We hung out on deck and studied the island. There wasn't much to see. Sandy beaches, palm trees, jungled ridges, and green mountains beyond the flat coastal zone. Clouds clung to the higher peaks, the cones of dormant volcanoes, some reaching altitudes above seven thousand feet. We'd seen it all before on Tutuila: your basic tropical paradise.

Next morning, 4 November, we assembled on deck preparatory to boarding the LCVPs that would take us ashore. The cargo nets had been lowered, and the LCVPs waited, bumping gently against the ship's hull, diesels growling. Muffled clanking sounds as we got our gear squared away, adjusting packs and webbing, checking our weapons, working the bolts on our Springfields, *clack-clack, clack-clack,* making sure the action was smooth. Talking softly with each other, as if out of respect for the morning hush. Butterflies fluttering in your gut. *Let's go, let's get on with it.*

Then came the order to disembark, and over the side we went, clambering down the nets, hopping into the little boats. The coxswains worked their throttles with business-like detachment, holding the boats steady as we boarded. Someone had said that Japanese planes were en route from—where? *Rabaul, right?* We were told this was no big deal. The Japanese bombers, when they came in force, never arrived until 1100 or thereabouts. Plenty of time to get ashore.

I remember thinking as my LCVP chugged toward the beach that my time had come, and that it would be a time of testing when I would get to show what I was made of. At last! Even so, a part of me wished I were somewhere else. What if I failed the test? I was assigned to the headquarters section of B Company, 1st Battalion, an "extra" second lieutenant with no specific duties other than to follow whatever orders I was given and make myself useful in whatever way possible. The regiment was actually above full strength, with junior officers to spare. It was an unusual circumstance, and I knew it would soon change because junior officers typically suffer the highest casualties relative to other ranks. Attrition would quickly and inevitably take its toll. Lieutenants in command of line units would get killed, wounded, injured, sick. "Extras" like me would replace them. Inevitably, too, a few junior officers would be relieved for incompetence or cowardice. I prayed that I wouldn't be one of them, that I wouldn't turn yellow and let my buddies down when the going got tough—a fate worse than death.

As for death itself: no worries there. Getting killed was something that happened to the other guy.

And then: arrival. Our LCVPs came to a gentle halt at the waterline, nosing into the sand of Beach Red, between the Tenaru River and Lunga Point. We climbed over the sides—there were no ramps on these early-model Higgins boats—and walked onto Guadalcanal. We hardly got our trousers wet. We had experienced rougher landings during amphibious assault exercises outside San Diego.

★ ★ ★

Positioned near the beach where B Company came ashore were sandbagged emplacements for antiaircraft guns and machine guns. We filed past them, noting the relaxed, almost languid demeanor of the gun crews—reclining with their backs against the sandbags, smoking, snoozing, talking softly, uncon-cerned that Japanese aircraft were en route. We stared at them with intense interest. They looked back at us with blank, haggard faces and empty eyes. Neither scornful nor arrogant, they just didn't give a damn about us. A few words of greeting were spoken—nothing effusive, but no razzing or heck-ling either.

Probably, if they thought about us at all, they were thinking we looked kind of funny. With our flat 1917-model helmets and our Springfield bolt-action rifles we were virtual throwbacks to the First World War. On Samoa we had been at the end of the logistics pipeline, and very little of the new gear then being issued stateside had made its way to us. The Marines of the 1st Division who had invaded the island and the GIs of the Army battalions sent recently as reinforcements were generally better outfitted and equipped than our regi-ment. The majority of 1st Division Marines wore the new bucket helmets and herringbone-pattern olive-drab fatigues (ODs), and the Army troops were armed with the M1 Garand semiautomatic rifle.

After forming up on the beach, we headed inland to a bivouac about a mile from Henderson Field in a coconut grove on the Lever Brothers plantation. Somewhere off in the distance a machine gun stuttered briefly and artillery thudded. The shells exploded nearby but not close enough to concern us. The grove was a mess, torn up by Japanese shells and bombs and littered with coco-nuts, coconut fronds, and blasted-down trees lying next to splintered stumps.

While deploying we saw more veterans of the fighting, Marines of the 1st Marine Division and GIs of the Army's 164th Infantry Regiment. What a hard-bitten lot they were: gaunt, sallow-skinned, and grimy, their clothes in tatters—scarecrows in green. Many sported scraggly beards. Many didn't, and couldn't—teenagers with peach fuzz still looking forward to their first shave. All gazed at us with thousand-yard stares—at once haunted, detached, and pitiless, old beyond their years, wise in ways we could only imagine.

We chatted with some of them, buttonholing them with questions, wanting them to tell us about combat. They didn't have much to say, or, more likely, they didn't want to say much. Typical reply: *Well, you know, we had this battle over there, by this river; it was a dilly, we fought them hand to hand.* Brief and to the point. Just kind of letting us know, in a casual way, that they had been through a firestorm and could handle the Japanese. Unimpressed with themselves, unimpressed with their accomplishments, but I was impressed. They were still just kids, most of them, but they were something else too, something more, something different. They were salty, they knew their business, they were calm and confident. They were warriors.

That night we received a visit from Washing Machine Charlie, a Japanese twin-engine bomber that often overflew the perimeter after sundown, mainly for the purpose of annoying the hell out of us. His engines churned like the agitator of an overloaded washing machine, hence his name, hence the reason why we found him so annoying. At this stage of the campaign, he conducted his nocturnal forays with impunity, because we didn't have night-fighter aircraft to oppose him, usually dropping a few small bombs that rarely hurt anyone. In terms of attack from the air, we had more to fear (far more, as it turned out) from mosquitoes. But we had yet to learn that Charlie was essentially harmless, and so we hunkered down in our foxholes while he puttered around above us.

Technically, Washing Machine Charlie's antics constituted our baptism of fire.

★   ★   ★

Next day, 5 November, B Company was ordered into action east of the Lunga Perimeter as an attachment to the Army's 164th Infantry. Moving in separate columns on the same axis of advance, Company B and the 2d and 3d Battalions of the 164th were to thrust east beyond the Nalimbiu River and then swing north, sweeping around the enemy's inland flank and driving into his rear at Koli Point. At the same time, the 2d Battalion of the 7th Marines (2/7) would counterattack across the Nalimbiu along the coast. Joining the 2/7 in this action was the 1st Battalion of the 7th Marines (1/7), commanded by the redoubtable Lt. Col. Lewis B. Puller, better known as "Chesty," already a Marine Corps legend.

We boarded trucks at daybreak and rode to our jumping-off point on the west bank of the Ilu River. There we dismounted, deployed in column of march, and crossed the river, entering enemy territory. The Nalimbiu, our immediate objective, was seven miles distant as the crow flies. But we were not crows. We were ground-pounding Marine infantrymen who were shortly to discover that seven miles on Guadalcanal is a very long and difficult way to go, even if you are "acclimated" to the tropics, as we were said to be by virtue of our service on Tutuila.

It was slow going from the start. We waded through fields of waist-high kunai grass in the molten heat of a relentless sun that scorched our helmets and baked our brains. Toward the end of the day the fields gave way to swamp and then jungle, where the heat was not so much lessened as it was changed in nature. We shoved and hacked through dense foliage and an even denser atmosphere: air so steamy and close that you could almost feel it pressing in on you, heavy with the smells of vegetation in various of stages of growth and decay, floral perfumes mingled with the stench of organic rot. You couldn't see much past the man you were following, and so you kept your eyes on the back of that man, who was presumably in visual contact with the man in front of him, and so on up and down the line. The column moved fitfully, extending and contracting like an accordion, starting and stopping, starting and stopping. All the while birds screeched in the trees, mosquitoes whined in our ears, and some strange creature (a species of lizard, as it turned out) barked at us like a dog from the underbrush.

We made a lot of noise too, the kind of noise a company of Marines will unavoidably make when you can't see much of anything and every step you take places your boondockers in the morass of the jungle floor with its tangled growth: roots and creeping vines, branches and deadwood. The rustling sounds of men toiling through the bush, the clanking of loose gear, brush crackling underfoot, twigs snapping, and every now and then the muffled thump of someone stumbling or falling followed by a curse, no less vehement for being uttered sotto voce. We communicated in whispers when we communicated at all, brief statements and exclamations, questions and answers:

"Dang, this is hard."

"Ouch! That was my foot, you moron!"

"Screw you, mac."

ARF! ARF!

"Hey, where's the dog?"

"That ain't no dog, you numbskull."

"Why're we stopping?"

"I dunno."

"Cripes, it's hot."

"Shhhh!"

ARF! ARF!

"What the hell?"

Whisperings, murmurings . . . but mostly grunts and gasps, panting and puffing, the labored breathing of intense physical effort.

We tried to be quiet but not silent. This was not a reconnaissance patrol requiring stealth—when you want to find the enemy without disclosing your presence. This was a combat sweep, and our goal was to find the Japanese and kill them. Well, that was our mission objective. Our real and immediate goal was simply to keep moving. Somehow, and despite mounting weariness, we had to find a way to push on through this dark and miserably wet, stinking, mosquito-infested, energy-sapping jungle.

Then the column halted and stayed put. We were lost, sort of. Our commanders didn't know our precise location or the location of the Japanese. Fortunately for us, the Japanese, wherever they were, apparently didn't know we were in the vicinity. "Ignorant armies that clash by night." Except we weren't clashing. We were blundering around in the jungle, clueless, going somewhere and nowhere at the same time. We had no idea what the Japanese were doing. Whatever it was, they were doing it somewhere else.

In the circumstances our commanders decided that our best course of action was to take no further action at all. Word came down the line: we were staying put for the rest of the night. At daybreak our commanders would, presumably, be able to determine our coordinates and the direction in which we should be moving.

Well, okay, if that's what they want. And so, remaining in column, we posted guards and made ourselves as comfortable as we could, sitting and lying down, helmets off, rifles at the ready. Many Marines took the opportunity to grab some shuteye. Not me—too tense, I suppose. Instead I sat on the bank of the Nalimbiu River, my feet dangling just above the surface, watching the murky water flow sluggishly toward its outlet at Koli Point. No combat tonight.

Maybe after a little while I dozed off, too. I can't remember. Probably I did. Lord knows I was tired enough. And apart from the fact that we were in fairly close proximity to thousands of Japanese soldiers, it was a pleasant spot.

Not everyone was so fortunate. First Lt. John Murdock, the company's executive officer, was bringing up the rear of the column with two or three others, and they were still in the river when the order to halt came down the line. Our company commander, Capt. O. K. LeBlanc, being near the head of the column did not know this, nor did he think to send someone back to check on them. And so they remained standing in the river for the rest of the night.

Which was not a difficult proposition, on the face of it. The water was only knee-deep, the current was slow, and dawn wasn't too far off. But it was so quiet, so dark. No one spoke and Murdock couldn't see anything. In effect, he was alone with only his own thoughts and the mental images they formed to keep him company. Bad company, as it turned out. The water gurgled softly as it eddied and swirled around his legs, which was okay, but something nearby was making a strange kind of swishing or rippling sound, which was not okay. He remembered a briefing aboard the *Hayes* from Ty Wilson, the regiment's intelligence officer, concerning Guadalcanal's flora and fauna. The island,

Wilson had said, abounded with many species of exotic creatures. There were poisonous snakes, spiders, giant stinging centipedes, and scorpions; there were sucking insects of all kinds, white ants, swarms of flies, and clouds of malaria-bearing mosquitoes. There were leeches, bats, and fiddler crabs; there were feral pigs, mean as junkyard dogs, and those strange barking lizards that sounded like dogs. And there were crocodiles.

Question: Are those *man-eating* crocodiles?

Answer: Are there any other kind?

Murdock's imagination ran wild: "I was scared to death because I could hear the water rippling, and I thought it was a big crocodile. I was scared shit-less! I was more afraid of the crocodiles than the Japanese!" Even so, he stayed put. His imagination might run wild, but he wouldn't. Better to be eaten by a crocodile than to show your men that you were afraid.

Came the dawn, grayish light filtering into the jungle, penetrating the thick white mist that hung over the river, and Murdock saw that the rippling sound was made not by a swimming crocodile but by water flowing around rocks and logs. He had endured; he had mastered his fear. And make no mistake, it was a signal victory, even if his enemy was only imaginary. Because when it comes to holding your courage, imaginary enemies can sometimes be the worst.

★   ★   ★

We were on the move again at dawn. Emerging from the jungle, we followed a track that took us roughly along the river but through more open terrain: groves and fields, coconut trees and kunai grass three to four feet high. At length we came to a place where the grass was beaten down and wet with dark blood—as though several large animals had fought and been slain there, bleeding to death, thrashing and writhing, trampling and staining the greenery in their death throes. We learned that the two Army battalions taking part in the sweep had briefly battled each other in what was euphemistically known as a "friendly-fire incident."

It had happened the previous night. The GIs of the 3/164 were crouched in their foxholes, alert for trouble, when a large group appeared to their front, shadowy figures moving through the darkness toward their positions. Since no friendly units were known to be operating in the vicinity, the GIs assumed the intruders were Japanese. Without hesitation they threw grenades at them and opened fire with everything they had. It was all over in seconds. And then they made the anguished discovery that their putative attackers were Americans belonging to a unit from their own regiment, the 2d Battalion of the 164th. The toll: seventeen wounded, three dead.

We were horrified. You're not supposed to get killed by your own people. And there was so much blood. Twenty guys shot and blown apart can pump out a lot of blood. We had never seen anything like this. I had been a Marine since 1939 and had been at war for the better part of a year, but I had not yet experienced war, not really. In all that time I had been practicing for war, preparing for it—or so I thought. But I wasn't prepared for this. It was an ugly, ugly sight, just sickening.

Murdock was similarly affected: "That's the first time I smelled blood. They were carrying the wounded guys back: you'd walk by, and it was so hot there, and you'd get that odor. I'd never smelled it in my life before. That made you stop and quiet down. And everybody's thinking, *Oh, shit*. Not a man said a word. They just looked. We were really shocked. There were these people on stretchers that they were carrying through, and we were standing there and looking down at them. Some of them were alive. I could see it was horrible."

We moved on. Moving, stopping, moving again: hour after hour. And still no sign of the enemy.

Finally, with daylight fading, we halted and dug in at the edge of a densely jungled swamp. Then we crawled into our holes, the entire company disappearing into the earth. Movement ceased. One minute you had a hundred-plus men burrowing into the ground, setting up machine guns and mortars, gobbling field rations, pissing or squatting to relieve themselves; the next minute—nothing. We're gone. Well, not quite: round helmet tops poked above the rim of each hole. But that's about all. The goal was to become invisible. We tried to achieve invisibility by hunkering down, silent, motionless.

To no avail. The jungle saw us, and it was amused. When darkness came, the jungle started to play tricks on us. The tangle of vegetation in front of Murdock's foxhole quivered slightly and emitted the kind of furtive little scraping, scrabbling, slithery sounds that might be made by a man who is creeping up on you and trying very hard not to be heard. Slowly withdrawing his KA-BAR from the sheath on his belt, Murdock raised the knife up behind his ear and held it there for many long seconds, his arm cocked and poised to strike at the enemy the instant he emerged from the brush. When that instant arrived, however, the foe turned out to be a land crab, not a Japanese soldier. Crawling out from under the foliage, the crustacean lumbered insouciantly past the rim of the foxhole with Murdock watching it, mouth agape. His arm was still locked in its murderous pose, made rigid by the paralyzing effects of unappeased fear and unreleased excitement, while his brain processed this very strange episode. *Okay, you dummy, you can relax now.* Whereupon, finally, Murdock found himself able to lower his arm.

But the night was far from over, and the jungle would not let us off so easy. It made a lot of noise: insects buzzing and ratcheting, birds shrieking, and larger creatures—wild pigs and dogs—snuffling and rooting and snorting. It showed fleeting movement, glimpsed from the corner of the eye. Leaves stirred and branches cracked, and the resulting adrenaline rush hit like an electric shock. *What the hell was that?* Ghoulies and ghosties, long-leggedy beasties, things that go bump in the night—this place is full of them. *What else is it full of?* Maybe your ears picked up a faint murmuring, a breathy sound, probably the wind in the trees, or possibly Japanese soldiers whispering to each other. Maybe you saw a shape in a thicket just yards in front of your foxhole, the shape of a man, utterly motionless, and you looked at that shape, you looked at it hard and long without blinking. *Is that what I think it is?* You wondered whether you should shoot it or throw a grenade at it. But you don't want to be wrong . . . if it's just your imagination . . . you don't want to make a fool of yourself . . .

And then: BANG!

Someone yelled; another shot followed. And then another and another. Several shots in quick succession, all from our foxholes. More shots all at once, and just that fast the whole company was shooting, firing every which way, shooting and shouting. Grenades were thrown, bursting left, right, front, and to my rear. Explosions and muzzle blasts lit the area like popping flashbulbs.

Cpl. Paul Lane was hit in the arm, a minor wound, but he didn't think that it was minor. In a panic he shouted to 1st Sgt. Whimpy Wright, "Top, my arm's shot off!"

Since Wright and Lane were best buddies, a show of concern from the first sergeant might in the circumstances have been expected and would certainly have been warranted. But Wright, an Old Salt who was as crusty as they come, was not practiced in showing concern, even to best buddies who had been wounded in combat.

Muttering just loud enough to make himself heard above the racket (and I heard him too), Wright replied, "Shut up, you fool—you wanna let 'em know where I am?"

The shooting continued. More grenades exploded. Pfc. Harold Park, a BAR gunner with the 1st Platoon, realized that several men just to his left were "throwing hand grenades all around the darn place. The guys were having a little hand-grenade war with each other."

Maybe the Japanese were out there too, tossing a few grenades of their own, but Park didn't think so. He stayed low and didn't fire his weapon. "I didn't figure it would do any good even if there were Japanese. You couldn't see nothing, and all you could do was go by sounds. So I just hunkered down in my hole and said, 'The hell with them.' That's the best thing you could do. There wasn't no use making it any worse than it was."

Harold, it should be noted, had a better reason than most to keep his head down. Born in Chicago to an Irish-American mother and a Korean father, he took after his father in looks. Which is to say, he looked more Asian than Irish. To us, at the time, he looked all Asian, and since we couldn't distinguish between Japanese, Koreans, Chinese, or what-have-you (they all look alike, right?), he also looked all Japanese to us.

Not that it mattered in the present circumstances. In the darkness everyone looked Japanese—and was treated accordingly.

Which is why I stayed down in my foxhole too. Like Park, I suspected that the Japanese were absent from this "battle." I couldn't be sure. But I was certain that if I got of out of my hole to find out what was really going on, I would be dead in seconds.

Then I heard something thrashing nearby: it was Pfc. Barney Ross, lunging from his foxhole, stabbing into the foliage with his bayonet. Ross, a former lightweight and welterweight world-boxing champion, was very quick with his hands—but not quick enough to kill phantoms, which is what he was attacking. He did manage to impale a large banana leaf that he mistook for a Japanese soldier. Give him credit: he killed it dead. That banana leaf would never again threaten the Marines of Company B.

On and on it went. The volume of gunfire and grenades exploding waxed and waned for no appreciable reason. Sometimes a lot of shooting and grenading, and then, suddenly, silence. After a few seconds it would start up again: a few shots instantly escalating into a fusillade of gunfire and grenade explosions.

LeBlanc and Murdock were in separate holes but close to each other. The company commander called out to his exec: "Murdock, get out there and stop that!"

Murdock's reaction: "I thought, *Screw you*! No way I was going to go out there! I stayed down. But I yelled: 'Cease firing! Cease firing!'"

Eventually, they did cease firing, this time completely—and, again, for no appreciable reason. The whole episode had lasted about ten minutes.

In another hole near Murdock's, someone cried out, "I'm shot! I'm shot!" Murdock recognized him: a kid named McGuinness. Murdock emerged from his hole and scurried across open ground to help the wounded man, a very brave thing to do.

"Lieutenant, I think my pecker's shot off," McGuinness wailed. "Tell me, is it shot off?"

Murdock said, "Just wait a moment. I can't see a thing."

He threw a poncho over himself and the wounded man, lit a cigarette, and inspected the private's privates in the faint glow of the burning ash. He found that the tip of the man's penis had been nicked and slightly shredded but was otherwise intact. "Good news, kid," he told McGuinness. "You're still a man. Better still, when you go home you'll have a built-in tickler to make the ladies happy."

But there was bad news too. The bullet that had nicked McGuinness' penis had penetrated his abdomen, and Murdock thinks he had taken a second bullet in the same place. Murdock didn't tell him that he was gut-shot, and McGuinness was as yet unaware of it; he was in too much pain from the wound to his penis to feel or think about anything else. A corpsman poured sulfa on the little holes in his abdomen and placed a bandage on them, and McGuinness was sent to the rear for treatment that may or may not have saved him. I don't know whether he survived, but the odds were very much against it.

★   ★   ★

We reached Koli Point on the morning of 7 November and linked up with the Army and Marine battalions, which had arrived ahead of us. All units then advanced a short distance east along the shore, halting and digging in on the beach about one mile west of the Metapona River. There we spent the night waiting to repel an amphibious assault that never came. So far in this operation the enemy had been notable by his absence, especially from B Company's standpoint. The 7th Marines had done a measure of fighting. Otherwise the enemy had offered scant resistance to the Army units and none at all to B Company. But why should the Japanese bother to attack us as long we were doing such a good job of attacking ourselves? The Japanese had in fact withdrawn east of the Metapona River to Tetere, and a cynic might have thought they had done so in order to give us all the freedom of space and action we needed to further destroy our own ranks.

Actually, they were trying to get away from us. We had them on the run. The next day, 8 November, the 7th Marines and the 2/164 crossed the

Metapona and began maneuvering to encircle the enemy force at Tetere. At this juncture the high command, judging the situation at Tetere to be well in hand, ordered B Company and the 1st and 3d Battalions of the 164th to the opposite side of the Lunga Perimeter to resume offensive action west of the Matanikau. The entire 8th Marine Regiment—infantry, artillery, and support units—would participate in the effort and was assembling for that purpose just east of the river. Trucks using the unpaved coast road would take B Company to the assembly area, there to rejoin its parent unit, the 1/8. The Army units would journey to their respective assembly areas by trucks and LCVPs.

My unit pulled back a short distance from the front line and gathered at the side of the coast road to await the trucks. As we were standing around, several low-flying Bettys suddenly appeared, zooming overhead just above the treetops. We scattered and dove into the sand. The bombs hit close—we could hear them whistling as they fell—then the explosion, the ground shaking, dirt and sand pelting our backs. No one was hurt, but we were all plenty scared. We felt so helpless, so naked and unprotected, lying on the ground, while a couple hundred pounds of metal and high explosive fell from the sky.

After getting up and dusting myself off, I thought I might grab a quick bite to eat and started to open a C-ration can. In the process, I somehow managed to cut my thumb to the bone. Blood gushed from the wound, and I spent some frantic moments applying a field dressing to stanch the flow. The noncoms and enlisted men watched me, probably trying hard not to laugh and certainly thinking, *Second lieutenants are idiots.* Hard to argue with that assessment, which the lower ranks held as virtually axiomatic, and I had just given them another reason for their certitude. How humiliating! (And annoying: the cut would not fully heal as long as I remained on Guadalcanal, and I still bear a scar from it.) Thus far, the chief dangers Guadalcanal had posed to my well-being had come from: (1) my buddies (via friendly fire) and (2) myself. The Japanese in comparison had been a relatively benign presence.

About the same time that I sliced my thumb, a kid from the 1st Marine Division ambled by swinging a length of rope weighted with the bleached skull of a Japanese soldier. His clothes were in the usual tatters, and he was of course emaciated, but also cheerful. We gaped at him and at his grisly trophy, and when he saw us staring, he grinned and twirled the skull over his head. A real nut case, right? Well, yes—and no; mostly no. Later, but soon, we would understand that the kid was doing just fine, in the circumstances. He had found a way to keep his spirits up. He had "acclimated" to conditions on Guadalcanal.

Battles on the Matanikau

THE RENEWED MATANIKAU OFFENSIVE kicked off at 0630 on 10 November, an auspicious date: the 167th anniversary of the founding of the Marine Corps. But we were too busy to celebrate. Following a preliminary artillery bombardment, the 1/164 Infantry attacked along the coast while the 2/7 Marines drove forward on its immediate left and the 2/2 Marines, operating on the extreme left, maneuvered to protect our southern flank. The 8th Marines were held in reserve behind the Matanikau. Separating our forces from their geographical objective, the coastal village of Kokumbona, was some four miles of exceptionally rugged terrain—grassy ridges falling away steeply to jungle-choked ravines—and several thousand Japanese infantrymen, also exceptionally rugged. Our mission objective was to engage, defeat, and destroy the enemy formations in our path.

Our assault units advanced slowly but steadily against determined resistance. The 8th Marines, ordered to move up in column behind the 2/7, filed across a narrow pontoon bridge over the Matanikau and continued a short distance before halting for noon chow. As before on the sweep to Koli Point, we encountered no Japanese—the attacking units had driven them off—but we suffered casualties just the same. The weather was, as usual, ungodly hot, and we lost several men to heat prostration. Quite possibly some were also overcome by the stench from hundreds of putrefying Japanese corpses that lay scattered about, killed a week earlier in a sweep by the 2d and 5th Marines. This too was something new to us: the reek of mass death. Never mind the heat, the smell alone was enough to drop a strong man in his tracks.

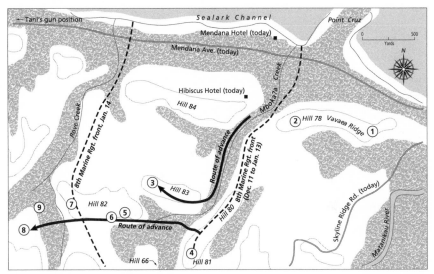

The Point Cruz Area of Operations.

Notes:

1. Author led several recon patrols along this ridge in mid-November 1943. Author's unit killed three snipers in tree above Army 182d Regiment command post. Catholic church now located at this site.

2. Author shot a sniper in banyan tree beachward from this site on 18 November. National boxing champion Barney Ross, Myron Guarnett, and Joseph Washvillo received Silver Star for holding a position here after being cut off during the fighting.

3. Author's platoon was repulsed attempting to capture this ridge 23 November. McCoy Reynolds, Walter Kuss, and James Bell killed here; Harris, McBernie, and Manderville wounded.

4. Location of author's foxhole 11 December 1942–13 January 1943 on front line that extended along this ridge to Point Cruz.

5. The 8th Marines killed enemy soldiers in their gopher-like foxholes along creek bank. Author took personal effects off dead Japanese soldier, returned them to his family after the war.

6. A dud enemy grenade landed by author's legs here 13 January. Nelson, Isabelle, and Kuykendal wounded here.

7. Marine Gunner Otto Lund, leader of platoon adjacent to author's, killed here 14 January.

8. Author rested here with George Stein, Weapons Platoon leader, when a bullet struck between them.

9. Silver Star recipient Washvillo killed here.

Ignoring the stench, I got in the chow line and shuffled forward with my mess kit in hand, eager to eat the hot slop our cooks were dishing out. A few hundred yards ahead, maybe half a mile or so, machine guns rattled, mortars thumped, shells exploded, the sounds muffled by distance, terrain, and jungle. No big deal, nothing to get excited about. Nearby I saw a booted foot sticking out of the ground: the single-toed boot of a Japanese soldier, his body partially exposed. A thin layer of dirt had been thrown over the corpse, not enough to cover it entirely. I ignored this too, and I also ignored the news that Japanese bodies had been spotted floating in the Matanikau just upriver from where we had recently filled our canteens. I drank from my canteen just the same.

Like that kid twirling the skull, I was acclimating to conditions on Guadalcanal. I had been on the island seven days.

After chow, 1st Battalion formed up and headed off a little toward the left to relieve an Army unit on a bare knoll that was part of the front line. We reached our destination around mid-afternoon and occupied foxholes the GIs had dug just below the top of the ridge. All was quiet—no sign of the enemy. But we knew the Japanese were nearby, presumably ahead of us, on the reverse slope. They soon made their presence known: later that day an enemy unit penetrated our line and ambushed Weapons Platoon, killing three Marines with a burst of machine-gun fire.

This happened some distance down the line from our position (I was still attached to Headquarters Platoon). I had heard no shooting and did not learn about the incident until the next day, 11 November. By then, 1st Battalion, along with every other unit involved in the offensive, had received orders to pull back behind the Matanikau. The entire offensive had been suddenly called off. And not only that: we were going to give up the ground we had taken, relinquishing it to the Japanese. *What the hell?* we thought. We were winning, making good gains toward Kokumbona, and now we were withdrawing. *What the hell?*

I had served in Weapons Platoon in Samoa, and I knew the men who had been killed. They were my friends and had served under me. One of those killed was Pvt. Howard Schlesinger. Another, Sergeant Smith, had been my senior NCO after I made corporal; a third, Corporal Asher, had a younger brother who would join our unit after the Tarawa campaign. They were B Company's first KIAs, and their deaths hit us all very hard. A real shock: the first friends to die in combat. There would be more, many more. But these were the hardest to take.

We were supposed to pull back immediately, but their bodies still lay on the battlefield. Sergeant Spell, the platoon sergeant for Weapons, called for volunteers to recover the bodies. "We don't leave our dead unburied," he growled. "Maybe the Army does, but we don't. We go up and get our wounded and bring 'em back. If they're dead, we bury 'em."

Spell got his volunteers, and they retrieved the bodies of their fallen comrades. Then, and only then, did B Company withdraw.

★   ★   ★

The 8th and 2d Marines passed through positions held by the 1/164, which covered their withdrawal, and crossed back to the east bank of the Matanikau. I didn't take part in this movement. Instead I led a patrol in the area we had evacuated to ascertain whether the Japanese intended to pursue our forces across the river. They didn't. My patrol poked around for a few hours and saw no one. The land was empty and silent, and scary for just that reason. I was sure that Japanese patrols were also poking around the area, and the thought that the enemy might be somewhere close by, present but invisible, really spooked me.

Meanwhile the 8th Marines crossed the Matanikau and deployed east of the river, with 1st Battalion on a ridge overlooking the channel, 2d Battalion to our immediate left, and 3d Battalion on the far left, with the flank refused. All three battalions of the 2d Marines occupied positions around Henderson Field. When the Marines had completed their passage through the 1/164's lines, the Army unit crossed the Matanikau and moved to the rear as the reserve force.

In mid-afternoon and again later in the day, large formations of Japanese bombers attacked our ships in Sealark Channel. I didn't see either raid, because I was still on patrol west of the Matanikau. Finally, near dusk, my patrol crossed the river and joined the battalion on the ridge. Shortly thereafter, Army engineers dismantled the bridges over the river. An ominous sign: you don't dismantle your own bridges unless you're expecting the enemy to come across them.

Something big was coming: we could feel it in the air.

It so happened that an enemy task force that included the battleships *Hiei* and *Kirishima* had already left their bases in the northern Solomons and Rabaul. Also en route was a convoy with eleven transports carrying some ten thousand fresh troops plus munitions and assorted stores, to be landed at Tassafaronga west of Point Cruz. American intelligence had been informed of this activity

by coast watchers, the clandestine network of British and Australian plantation owners and civil servants who had stayed behind on islands occupied by
the Japanese to monitor and report on enemy naval and air activity.

Communicating by radio, the coast watchers flashed news that large
groupings of enemy ships were steaming southeast down the "Slot," the
long waterway (formally known as New Georgia Sound) that ran through
the Solomons to Guadalcanal. Air reconnaissance and decrypts of Japanese-
coded radio traffic confirmed these sightings, which convinced our high
command that this was no ordinary run of the "Tokyo Express," the term
given to the frequent attempts by the Japanese navy to deliver reinforcements
to Guadalcanal and harass our forces in the region. The Japanese, the brass
concluded, were winding up to deliver a knockout blow.

Now it also happened that American transports carrying some fifty-five
hundred troops, including those of the Americal Division's 182d Regiment
(sister regiment of the 164th), had arrived off Lunga Point on 11 November
and were scheduled to unload on the twelfth—the same day the Japanese
armada was expected to arrive in Sealark Channel. Accordingly, the covering
force of warships for our troop transports was placed on alert to intercept the
enemy fleet.

Of course, we—the lowly riflemen of the 8th Marines—weren't aware of
these developments. The brass had issued a "condition black" advisory, however,
which meant that an enemy attack was imminent, and we had been put on
notice to repel a Japanese amphibious assault that might take place on the
beach extending east from the mouth of the Matanikau to Kukum. More than
that we didn't need to know. We could guess the rest. All hell was about to
break loose.

We received a foretaste of things to come in the form of a bombardment by
enemy heavy artillery collectively known as "Pistol Pete." The bombardment
was brief and ineffectual: no casualties. Night was coming on. We hunkered
down in our foxholes and awaited developments. *What next?* we wondered.
Will our luck continue to hold? For the superstitious among us (which was
everyone: all soldiers are superstitious) it was an appropriate night to think
about luck. Tomorrow was Friday the thirteenth.

★   ★   ★

Nightfall. We waited and watched, staring out to sea, into blackness. The
hours passed; midnight came and went. Lightning forked in a mostly

overcast sky, and thunder rumbled distantly as rain squalls swept through the area. Otherwise all was calm and quiet. And then—

The battle between the American and Japanese surface fleets began a little before 0200 like a suddenly breaking storm of cataclysmic size and power. In the language of naval tacticians, the coming together of two fleets in Sealark Channel constituted what is known as a "meeting engagement"; but "collision engagement" is a better term for describing what happened. Steaming more or less blindly into the channel, the fleets ran into each other at oblique angles. Their ships quickly became intermingled, resulting in a close-quarters melee that saw the combatants charging madly about, their big guns flashing and booming, hurling red-hot shells in high, flaming arcs above the channel. The thunder of the guns rolled across the black water, a steady pulsating roar, and the molten projectiles streaked like meteors, crisscrossing the sky with fiery tails, rising and falling and crashing into ships and exploding in massive fire-balls. Violent secondary explosions caused by ammunition cooking off in the intense heat of the detonating shells rocked some ships and set them furiously ablaze, burning like roman candles, fountains of fire sparking and shooting flames and blasting big chunks of steel in every direction. All the while, star shells and flares burst high above the channel and then faded like dying galaxies as they drifted down at the end of their parachutes into the extinguishing water. The canisters that had held the flares periodically flew over our positions, chugging like locomotives. Searchlights probed the lower darkness with their long, brilliant beams, sweeping back and forth above the surface, bisecting, fixing on some hapless ship, bringing the blazing shells down on it. Streams of tracers from automatic cannons and machine guns curved through the middle air. Every now and then an errant torpedo slammed into the beach below us, twenty-five hundred pounds of explosives blasting a big crater at the waterline.

We watched all this from our foxholes on the ridge, front-row seats to a spectacle that John Murdock likened to "all of the Fourth of July's I ever saw in my life, all put together at once." We were a vocal audience, awestruck and profane. A ship would explode, and all up down our line you'd hear men exclaiming, "Jee-sus Christ!" and "Holy shit" and "Oh, my fuckin' God, did you see that?" It was thrilling, really; you couldn't help feeling that way. But I also couldn't help wondering which ships were ours and how they could distinguish friend from foe. I thought of the many men who were losing their young lives right before our eyes. I felt very fortunate to be safe in my foxhole. And I wondered: *Who's winning?*

It was all over by dawn. In Sealark Channel the early morning light sparkled on placid waters, revealing derelict warships and countless sailors, black with oil, afloat in their life jackets and swimming to the beach. Just offshore, the cruiser *Atlanta*, now a charred wreck, was slowly sinking. Another American cruiser was shelling abandoned hulks, finishing the job guns and torpedoes had started. A crippled Japanese battleship (it was *Hiei*) stood just off Savo Island, listing precipitously. Higgins boats scooted among the swimmers, the crews hauling them aboard if they were Americans and usually shooting or abandoning them if they were Japanese.

★   ★   ★

Thus ended the so-called Friday the Thirteenth Battle, the first phase of the Naval Battle of Guadalcanal. It was a tactical draw: despite being badly mauled, our fleet had prevented the Japanese force from achieving its primary aim of bombarding Henderson Field and thereby rendering it unusable. Throughout the rest of the day our aircraft, joined by fighters and bombers from the carrier *Enterprise*, sortied continuously from Henderson against enemy warships, particularly *Hiei*, which was mortally damaged and was eventually scuttled.

That night two Japanese cruisers steamed into Sealark Channel to bombard Henderson Field, throwing nearly one thousand 8-inch shells at the airstrip without hitting anything important. On the fourteenth, our aircraft attacked the convoy of enemy troop transports, which had recently arrived in the battle zone. Six transports were sunk, one returned to Shortland, and the remaining four were run aground near Kokumbona. Most of the ten thousand troops embarked on the transports made it ashore, but without their supplies, which were lost along with the ships that carried them.

On the night of 14 November, in the waters around Savo Island, an American naval task force centered on the battleships *Washington* and *South Dakota* met and defeated a Japanese task force that included the battleship *Kirishima*. The latter was sunk in that action, which proved to be the final engagement of the Naval Battle of Guadalcanal. We had won the battle decisively, turning the tide of the Guadalcanal campaign—and, arguably, the Pacific War itself—irrevocably in our favor. Of course, this was not evident at the time, either to us or to the Japanese. Both sides still had a lot of hard fighting to do before anyone could be certain of the outcome.

★   ★   ★

November 18. Another day, another offensive west of the Matanikau. The Army kicked things off by sending the 182d Infantry's green 2d Battalion across the Matanikau on a newly built footbridge some seven hundred yards inland from the river's mouth. Most of my regiment was deployed along the east bank to support the 2/182 should it meet up with any Japanese. But the enemy had abandoned the west bank, and the Army battalion crossed the river unopposed. It then ascended the ridge just beyond (known today as Skyline Ridge) and headed southeast to seize Hill 66. The 8th Marines stayed put for the night, and B Company was put on alert for movement on the morrow.

Early the next morning B Company crossed the river to spearhead the attack by another green Army battalion, the 1/182, along the coastal flat toward the base of Point Cruz. The company was to advance ahead of the 1/182 on a line extending from the shore to the top of Vavaea Ridge, which lay adjacent to the coast road and ran parallel (east to west) to the sea. The 2d Platoon was tasked to climb the ridge and advance along its crest to Hill 78 at the west end. The lieutenant commanding the platoon proved unequal to the job of leading his unit in combat; put bluntly, he was a coward. Captain LeBlanc acted with dispatch: "Dean," he told me, "take over that platoon." And I did. Just that fast I quit being an "extra lieutenant" and became a platoon commander.

Whimpy Wright was the company's first sergeant. He was a tough Old Salt, short and stocky, late thirties or early forties, old enough to be my father—old enough, for that matter, to be the father of quite a few of the lieutenants in the regiment. He was going on twenty years in the Marine Corps and had served in China, Nicaragua, and Haiti. He was no newcomer to war, no stranger to combat and getting shot at. He possessed a commanding voice, which he used in a full-throated bellow when reading off one of his charges for doing something stupid. On Samoa, before I was commissioned, I had been one of his charges and had more than once (deservedly) been on the receiving end of one of his harangues. But now I outranked him.

I was at first uncomfortable with our new relationship. I found it hard to imagine giving orders to a man who not so long ago had been shouting in my face and giving me a dressing-down, the likes of which I had never before experienced and never would again. It wasn't that I was afraid of him; rather, I respected him too much and knew too well that he was a great Marine to think that I could or should be telling him what to do. And I thought that he might resent my status and, just to be cantankerous, make things difficult for me.

I needn't have worried about Wright. A consummate professional, he supported me fully and sincerely. I have should expected that. After all, it was because of his recommendation that I had received my commission. He looked on me as his protégé, and he wanted me to succeed in part because my success would reflect well on him but mainly because he was genuinely proud of me. Also, because I was a known quantity whom he had personally mentored, he much preferred for me to be giving orders rather than some ninety-day wonder fresh out of officer training in the States. Since he had taught me everything I knew, he was confident that in combat together we would more or less be thinking along the same lines, an important connection for a top sergeant to have with his platoon leader. Nor would he brook the slightest insubordination toward me from anyone else in the platoon. "You obey your lieutenant or you'll have to answer to me," he growled at my guys, and you can be damn sure they did. Nobody wanted to have to answer to Wright.

★   ★   ★

We walked the length of the ridge without incident and halted at the top of Hill 78. Of this episode the Army's official "Green Book" history of the Guadalcanal campaign states that "B Company . . . met enemy fire west of Point Cruz and withdrew to the vicinity of Hill 78 to take cover." Another historian wrote that "Company B traversed the entire ridge and stepped down from its western end (Hill 78), only to be forced back by enemy fire." Both are wrong on several counts. In the first place, 2d Platoon, which I now commanded, was the only element of B Company on the ridge. The rest of the company was spread out below and to our right in the alternating terrain of field and foliage extending from the lower slope of the ridge to the coast road and the shore a few yards beyond. We did not "step down" from Hill 78, nor did we meet enemy fire that caused us to be "forced back." Our halt at the top of Hill 78—and the west end of the ridge—was planned and deliberate, a function of our role as the anchor and guardians of 1/182's left flank.

So far the enemy had been conspicuous by his absence. And then, suddenly, I glimpsed movement below in the ravine at the northwest base of the hill: four men, maybe a hundred yards distant, running away from us across open ground, making for the nearby jungle and glancing up and back over their shoulders at us.

"Japs!" I shouted, raising my rifle to my shoulder.

Standing next to me was one my squad leaders, a kid named Allen. He said, "No, sir, those aren't Japs; those are Marines!"

I hesitated for an instant, and they disappeared into the trees. I should have fired. They were Japanese, no doubt about it. I looked at Allen. He shrugged. Probably we were both reluctant to shoot at anyone we couldn't positively identify; the friendly fire incident near the Nalimbiu River was still fresh in our thoughts. An opportunity had passed. Many more would come.

★　　★　　★

While 2d Platoon made its way west along Vavaea Ridge, the rest of B Company advanced in the same direction on our right. They had gotten off to a late start, however, because the preliminary bombardment of the area immediately in front of the company's jumping-off positions failed to lift and roll forward as planned. With the company all set to go, some of our guns kept pounding their initial target grids. The Marines, understandably reluctant to walk into their own shellfire, had stayed in their jumping-off positions until the errant batteries corrected their aim.

By then Japanese units were filtering into the battle zone, the lead elements of a major offensive the enemy launched simultaneously with our own. The Japanese had also landed reinforcements during the naval battle of 13–15 November too (they had debarked from the transports beached at Tassafaronga Point), and they too were using their newly arrived troops to fight what they hoped would be a decisive battle in the Point Cruz–Matanikau sector. That both sides should attack each other at the same time might seem coincidental, but the logic of the situation pretty much ensured that it would happen. The Japanese were getting desperate, but if they managed to break through on the Matanikau, we would be hard-pressed to stop them from overrunning Henderson Field. And if we lost Henderson Field we would lose the island.

The two armies approached each other warily, since neither knew quite what the other was up to or where, precisely, his units were located, and also because units from both sides quickly became fragmented in the rough and variable terrain. In this land of steep ridges and plunging ravines, of alternating patches of dense jungle and open ground, big formations could not cohere. Inevitably, units advanced at different rates and became separated and scattered. As a result, the meeting of the armies occurred in piecemeal fashion with small groups blindly stumbling into each other and fighting in isolation from their parent units.

B Company was to advance to a point that would put its units roughly on a south-to-north line extending from the western base of Hill 78 to the sea. There the Marines would stand fast while the 1/182, coming up behind them, passed through their line and continued attacking toward the base of Point Cruz and beyond. B Company would then retire and go into reserve behind the Matanikau.

The men of 1st Platoon, advancing on the extreme right flank along the sea, reached their designated stopping point and stood in place, waiting for the Army to come up. Harold Park and his squad occupied the ground on the coast road's seaward side, a brushy strip some forty or fifty yards wide from the road to the waterline. The rest of the platoon was deployed in the brush on the inland side of the road. There was no sign of enemy activity in the immediate vicinity.

Picture the scene: Harold is standing at the edge of the road next to a big clump of bushes; his long, heavy BAR is hanging from a shoulder strap and he's holding it at his waist with the barrel pointed straight out in front of him and his finger resting lightly on the trigger guard. He's alert but not expecting any trouble. Up ahead, around Point Cruz, he can hear gunfire and explosions, but in his little corner of the island all is quiet, even tranquil. Insects buzz and hum in the thickets and tall grass on either side of the road; a calm sea gently laps the shore; the hot sun beats down on his World War I helmet. He waves mosquitoes away from his face, and he shifts his weight from one leg to another. The Army will come soon and he'll go back to the Matanikau. So far, so good.

Well, not entirely. Harold noticed that his assistant, who carried six extra magazines for the BAR, had drifted away from him. Annoyed, Harold called him over and got on him just a bit for wandering off. No doubt it was a very mild reprimand, because Harold was and is a very mild-mannered fellow, reserved and soft-spoken, modest to a fault. "We were talking about it," is how Harold puts it. His assistant nodded contritely, saying, "Okay, okay."

"Then all of a sudden I heard somebody walking on the road. You know how it sounds when you've got sandals on and you walk over the beach? I turned around and there were these two Japanese point men for a bigger unit. All of sudden they were right there in front of me."

The two enemy soldiers carried rifles with bayonets fixed, and they wore helmets with cloth covers emblazoned with a red star. "I would say they hadn't been in combat for long," Harold added. "Their uniforms looked fairly good." Very probably they were reinforcements who came from the ships beached at Tassafaronga.

"They were standing there along the road. They're looking at each other and at me too. I was just off the road a little ways, and this big bush was between my assistant and the Jap on my side of the road, and there was only about six or seven feet between them—my assistant couldn't have been six feet from his rifle. The Japanese guy on the other side of the road was maybe ten feet from me at the most."

Harold was dismayed: "I thought, *Jeez, how come we didn't hear them or know they were coming?*"

The two Japanese just stood there staring at Harold, at his Korean face. "They looked sort of flabbergasted. I think maybe they thought I was Japanese."

Harold reckons that this standoff lasted for all of about two or three seconds. The Japanese looked at him and at his assistant and then looked at each other. Harold and his assistant looked at the Japanese.

"Then one of them sort of turned around to look back down the road where his unit was, and yelled something like, 'Banzai!'"

The man's battle cry jolted Harold out of his momentary trance. "Then I just knew I had to get the guy on our side of the road."

Harold was locked and loaded. "I was all ready. All I had to do was just pull the trigger."

But the Japanese soldiers fired first: "They both got off a couple rounds. The one guy on my side of the road killed my assistant and the other guy was trying to get me." In the next instant Harold fired a burst from the hip—"they were too close to raise the BAR to my shoulder." He cut down the man on his side of the road, the one who had killed his assistant.

> Then I made a quick turn and got the other guy on the other side of the road. The guys I had knocked down, I made sure they were dead. I walked over there and took a look at them. Then I looked down the road and there was a whole damn column of Japs. But when the shooting started they had jumped off the road.
>
> Right after that the staff sergeant we had on the other side of the road, he came running over and he said, "Hey, Park! What the hell are you doing? Knock it off! You're killing our own men!" He just couldn't believe there were any Japanese so close. I guess he figured I was doing all the shooting. So I pointed at the two Japs lying on the side of the road, and I said, "Do these look like our own men?" And he said, "Oh, God!" And he took off. That was the last I saw of him that day.

Just then Barney Ross came running across the road. Too late to take part in the fighting, he stayed with Harold for a minute or so, talking about what had happened, then both men rejoined their units. Harold withdrew with his squad toward the Matanikau. He would see no more fighting that day. As for the enemy unit behind the point men Harold had killed: it never did come down the coast road. The Japanese must have gone back the way they came, figuring that the road was blocked by a force greater than their own.

They were right. His name is Harold Park.

★   ★   ★

Meanwhile, on Hill 78, the 2d Platoon was dealing with a lone sniper who had opened fire on us from the trees on the coastal flat below. He was high up in one of those trees, high enough to place him a little above the hilltop, allowing him to shoot down on us at a shallow angle. We went to ground and sought cover wherever we could find it. This mainly entailed moving back a few yards behind and below the crest and keeping our heads down. Maybe this is what that historian meant when he said we were "forced back by enemy fire." The sniper bided his time, choosing his shots carefully. Movement drew his fire; if we didn't move and stayed low, he generally didn't shoot. So we didn't move—not much, anyway—and we pretty much stayed low. Now and then one of us scrambled to another position or rose up on elbows for a quick look-see and got shot at in return. Sometimes, though, the sniper shot at nothing in particular—just throwing bullets at the hill to keep us honest.

He potted at us for the better part of four hours, all through the heat of the day, effectively pinning us down in the open beneath the broiling sun. He didn't hit anyone, but after four hours or so of getting shot at and baking in the heat, we were getting pretty cranky. At the same time, a sizable battle was being fought below and to the right, on the coastal flat near Point Cruz. We couldn't see the battle but we could hear it, small-arms fire punctuated by the thump and thud of heavier ordnance. Our aircraft swooped and dove over the combat zone, bombing and strafing enemy positions. The Japanese responded aggressively: their artillery, recognizable by its distinctive sound, pounded the Army troops. The Japanese had launched their own offensive on the coastal flat, meeting our offensive head-on. The green 1/182 was receiving its baptism of fire in a big way.

★   ★   ★

When the 182d Regiment came up to the line, John Murdock volunteered to stay and help the regiment's colonel get situated. The colonel began setting up his command post (CP) in a spot previously hit by Japanese artillery. Murdock said, "Hey, Colonel, I don't think you should set it up over there. Come over this way." But Murdock was just a lieutenant—a *Marine* lieutenant—and the Army colonel was not about to take his advice. He said, "I'll run my outfit the way it should be run."

Murdock was disgusted. "I'll never forget the guy. I think he was from Lowell; he had an accent from lower Mass., which is an area I know quite well. And I said to myself, *Screw you. I'm not going to stay with you tonight.* And I walked down the road a way, and some kid was digging a hole, and I said, 'Dig that deeper. The two of us are going to sleep here tonight.'"

Murdock and the Army private were safe in their hole when, later that night, the Army CP was hit by shellfire, killing one man and wounding several others.

Back on Hill 78, the sniper continued to bang away at us in his occasional fashion, and we got hotter and crankier by the minute. Bye and bye, and much to my astonishment, a lieutenant I didn't recognize came strolling along the ridge, fully upright, fully exposed to the sniper, smirking at us. I was lying on my belly in the grass, and he approached me, saying, "Ah, whaddya worried about? That sniper can't hit anyone." In the next instant a shot rang out and a bullet winged his arm.

Serves you right, I thought.

The wounded lieutenant, no longer smirking, scurried off. I didn't much care where he went or what happened to him—I wanted to get that sniper. I pulled out my field glasses and scanned the trees below our position. As luck would have it, I spotted the sniper almost at once; that is, I spotted his puttee-wrapped legs and booted feet dangling from the limb of a huge banyan tree about 150 yards from my position. I lifted the field glasses a notch to the clump of leaves above those legs. I couldn't see him, but he had to be there: Japanese legs are always attached to Japanese bodies.

Just then he took a shot at me. He must have seen me looking at him. Maybe my field glasses glinting in the sun had given me away. His bullet hit the ground just inches from my nose, spraying dirt in my face. I dropped my field glasses and snatched up my Springfield. Firing from the prone position, I unloaded the entire clip at the clump of leaves above his feet, five shots one after the other, working the bolt quickly, but smoothly, so as not to spoil my aim—just as I'd been taught to do and just as I had practiced doing on Marine Corps rifle ranges. I didn't think about it. I didn't have to think. All that training just kicked right in, and I killed the man who had been trying to kill me. He didn't drop from the tree, he didn't drop his rifle. But that was to be expected. Japanese snipers customarily tied themselves and their rifles to their trees. Bottom line: he didn't shoot at us after that. He was dead, all right—the first man I had killed.

Late that afternoon B Company received orders to withdraw. I pulled my platoon from the ridge, descending the east end to the coast road, where the company was assembling before crossing back over the Matanikau to rejoin the regiment. For some unfathomable reason, no unit was sent to replace 2d Platoon on Hill 78, and the enemy promptly emerged from the ravine to occupy our former positions. These they used to good advantage, firing down on the 1/182, which was, as told, then under attack by a Japanese force advancing from the west.

My platoon arrived in B Company's assembly area to find elements of the 1/182 retreating in disorder—practically running—toward the river. The inexperienced Army battalion was taking a beating, and the young GIs were starting to crack under the pressure. Making matters worse, the soldiers carried heavy packs, fully loaded—a big mistake. Normally these would have been left in the rear, and their owners would have gone into combat stripped to the bare essentials of water, ammo, and rations. Overburdened by too much gear, enervated by the climate, and beset by the Japanese, many of the soldiers had acquired the wild-eyed expression and the sickly pale, green-at-the-gills pallor that signaled the onset of panic and heat exhaustion. One of the fleeing soldiers hotfooted past Captain LeBlanc, who asked him where he was going. "I'm trying to catch up with my corporal!" came the breathless reply.

But not all of them broke. Murdock encountered a far more stalwart GI.

The Japs were coming at us: you could see them probably a hundred yards off; they were moving up, a whole line of them. And I saw one Army kid there with an air-cooled machine gun, and he was sitting there firing like mad. I grabbed him and said, "Where are your officers?" He said, "They're gone."

"Where're your NCOs?"

"They're gone."

I said, "You oughta go too! Get your ass out of here!"

He was by himself. Everybody had taken off. He slowed the Japs down long enough for me to get out of there. He should have gotten a medal.

★   ★   ★

With night coming on, the situation was growing increasingly confused. Japanese and American elements were groping about and running into each other. No one knew quite what was happening. A small group from B

Company stumbled on a Japanese machine gun, which opened fire on them. Only a few survived the initial burst. One of them was Barney Ross; the others were Myron Guarnett, Dick "Heavy" Atkins, and Joseph Washvillo. Cut off from the rest of us, they now had to decide whether to chance the withering machine-gun fire or to remain where they were and dig in for the night. They decided to stay. Subsequently they beat back several attacks on their position. In doing so all four were wounded, Atkins most seriously.

Murdock, who liked Barney Ross because he always let the "kids" win at poker ("he could have beaten them every time, taken every cent they had, but he didn't"), organized and led a group across an open field to rescue the beleaguered Marines. On reaching their position, he and Ross made a stretcher for Atkins using tree branches and their dungaree jackets. "We put the branches through the sleeves to make the stretcher. I'm carrying the front end, Barney Ross is carrying the back; and here I am in a bright, white, clean skivvy shirt that had been issued to me the day before. The Japs saw it and began shooting at us. I could hear the bullets whizzing all around. Washvillo yelled, 'Lieutenant, get rid of that goddamned skivvy shirt!' I didn't even have to think about it; I pulled it off and threw it away."

Ross, Guarnett, and Washvillo subsequently received the Silver Star for their actions. The press soon learned about the incident and singled out Ross for special attention because of his prewar fame as a boxer. Newspaper accounts made him out to be a hero who almost singlehandedly prevented the Japanese from overrunning their position by throwing some twenty grenades at the enemy and otherwise setting an example for his buddies to follow. Ross was ordered home, where he was much celebrated and became a featured speaker at war-bond rallies.

In his postwar writings, including his autobiography, *No Man Stands Alone,* Ross basically reiterated this version of the events—but he didn't mention Murdock. Murdock has no hard feelings about this. But most of those who were in B Company at the time will tell you that Ross' version of events is about three parts baloney and one part truth, and that Guarnett and Washvillo were the real heroes. Ross was certainly brave—and I liked him personally—but those two did most of the fighting, and everybody in B Company knew it.*

* While being treated for his wounds, Ross became addicted to morphine and developed a habit that almost destroyed him before he quit by going cold turkey in a federal drug treatment facility. In 1957 Hollywood released a movie about his trials and tribulations as an addict; it was called *Monkey on My Back.* Ross, unhappy with the way he was portrayed, sued the producers for defamation of character. He lost.

After nightfall on 20 November the 1st and 3d Battalions of the 164th Infantry entered the battle, driving between the 1/182 on the coastal flat and the 2/182 on Hill 66. The 8th Marines stayed in reserve behind the Matanikau.

That didn't mean we were idle. On 20 or 21 November I led reconnaissance patrols back across the river and into the Vavaea Ridge–Hill 78 vicinity. On the return leg of one of those patrols my men and I happened upon the 182d's regimental command post, newly established on Vavaea Ridge, where a Catholic church now stands. The regiment's commander clearly resented our presence—that is, the presence of Marines—in that sector, *his* sector. "What were we doing here?" he asked peevishly. I replied—respectfully, because of his rank—that we were conducting a reconnaissance patrol. He said, "Well, you don't have to be here anymore. We're taking care of it now." But we had not completed our patrol circuit and could not leave the area until we had. I had my orders and intended to obey them. I let him know—carefully, to avoid even a hint of insubordination—that this was the case. Although visibly annoyed, he didn't argue the point, and we continued on our designated path.

A few minutes later, as we ascended the slope of a nearby ridge, a runner from the CP caught us up with a message from the colonel informing me that we were skylined on the crest and thus dangerously exposed to the Japanese. "The colonel wants you to get off the ridge ASAP," said the runner, "before you draw enemy fire on us."

Now it was my turn to be annoyed. I knew my business, and I knew we weren't skylined on the ridge, at least not from the enemy's perspective. I had made sure of that. I realized, however, that we were skylined from the colonel's perspective. *What an idiot,* I thought. *Typical.*

Just then, one of my guys came over to me and said, "Lieutenant, we've spotted some snipers in that large tree next to the CP—what should we do?"

The tree in question stood a few yards from the command post; the CP had been set up in the shade of its spreading branches. I looked at the tree. Sure enough, perched in the branches—well camouflaged but nonetheless visible to the naked eye—were *three* Japanese snipers! Why they hadn't already fired on the CP is beyond me. With just a few shots, easily placed at such a close range, they could have taken out the 182d Infantry's top command structure. Maybe they were waiting for nightfall, when they might shoot up the command post and escape under cover of darkness. Maybe they were paralyzed with fear. We'll never know.

I had been asked, "What should we do?" I replied without hesitation, "Shoot them."

Whereupon my men cut loose at the tree, sending a fusillade of bullets into the branches and killing the snipers.

The colonel and his staff came running out of the command post, astonished and angry, demanding an explanation. Calmly, and maybe a bit condescendingly, I told the colonel about the snipers and pointed at their bodies dangling limply from the branches to which they were tied. The colonel brushed the matter aside. I forget what he said, but he acted as if our killing three Japanese soldiers right above his command post was no big deal. He tried to sound nonchalant, but he was furious. He had been shown up by a lowly second lieutenant, and a *Marine* second lieutenant at that!

Flash forward forty years to 1982 and a reunion for Guadalcanal veterans held at a hotel in Honiara, the island's capital. There I met a former Army officer who had witnessed my exchange with the colonel while he was also a second lieutenant. He told me he was disgusted by the colonel's behavior, so much so that after my men and I left, he admonished his commanding officer: "Sir, we're both on the same side!"

What had possessed him to speak so boldly in my defense? Turns out he had been a Marine before the war, serving with the 4th Marines in China. After his discharge he joined the Massachusetts National Guard to make a little extra money. One thing led to another—a national emergency was declared, his National Guard unit was activated and federalized, Pearl Harbor was attacked—and in due course he had come to Guadalcanal as a second lieutenant on the headquarters staff of the 182d Infantry Regiment. But he had remained a Marine at heart. Once a Marine, always a Marine.

We laughed about the incident and the circumstances that had brought us together on a Pacific island battlefield. Even after forty years I was gratified to know that I had had an ally in that Army command post.

★   ★   ★

Thus far the greater part of two Army regiments had been committed to battle on the ridges and in the coastal flat west of the Matanikau and had made little headway. As usual, the Japanese were defending tenaciously. Time to send in the Marines.

Morning, 23 November, the situation was as follows: the 1/164 and 2/164 occupied a north–south ridgeline connecting Hills 80 and 81. In front of the ridgeline, to the west, lay a jungled ravine about two hundred feet deep and between fifty and one hundred yards wide. Beyond the ravine lay another ridge dominated by Hill 83 and occupied by the Japanese in positions of considerable strength. The 8th Marines, 1st and 2d battalions, were to advance side by side in columns into the ravine and then attack and capture the Hill 83 ridgeline. The 1st Battalion was to move forward on the right, B Company would lead the battalion's advance, and my platoon would lead the company's advance.

Following an artillery bombardment, 2d Platoon, with the rest of the battalion behind it, passed through the Army lines and advanced into the ravine. Enemy machine guns and riflemen fired down on us from concealed positions on the ridge some seventy-five yards ahead and above us. Machine guns chattered relentlessly, ripping through the jungle, rustling the foliage, clipping branches and leaves. Cpl. Orson DeMoss and his squad led the way, moving up out of the ravine and onto the ridge. Suddenly a voice shouted: "Baker Company, get off the ridge!"

Huh? I looked around at my men. *Who gave that order?*

Most of my men had gone to ground, hiding in the brush, and were as invisible as the Japanese. That's the nature of jungle warfare: everyone tries to stay hidden. You hardly see anyone, either enemy or friendly. The battlefield seems empty, and you can feel very alone and isolated on it. Especially when you're in command. Especially when you're in the middle of a firefight and somebody else starts giving orders to your men.

I looked around, and the few men I could see stared back at me, their blank expressions a firm denial: *It wasn't me.*

A few minutes later DeMoss and his squad returned to the ravine, having relinquished their brief hold on the ridge top. "Somebody yelled at us to get off," DeMoss explained. He thought one of our guys had given the order.

Then we both realized what had happened. Those clever Japanese. One of them, someone fluent in American English, had given the order. Very clever. He must be pleased with himself. He must be laughing at us just about now—him and his men, laughing.

And how did he know that we were Baker Company?

We resumed our uphill attack and again were met with devastating machine-gun and rifle fire. We kept going forward, firing on the move, leaning slightly into the incline, shooting from shoulder and hip, firing blindly at the top of the ridge. We couldn't see the enemy but we knew he was up there. DeMoss, on my left, banged away with his Springfield just as fast as he could work the bolt. And then his rifle seized up. DeMoss looked at me and I looked at him, and the spell was broken. Just that fast I came out of my battle trance.

I felt very exposed and insecure. Judging by the wide-eyed look he gave me, DeMoss felt the same.

DeMoss inspected his rifle and discovered that a bullet had pierced the magazine, barely missing his nose in the process. He never cursed, never uttered profanities; and now, true to form, his eyes still as big as saucers, he exclaimed, "Well, I'll be a dirty name!" Then he discarded his rifle and starting throwing grenades at the top of the ridge.

The reality of our sudden harrowing plight then struck me. This was my first major combat test as a platoon leader, and I realized that I had to take immediate and firm control of myself. I could not show fear in front of my men.

A couple of feet to my right Pvt. McCoy Reynolds had also been hurling grenades, one after the other, each time courageously standing and exposing himself to the enemy's fire. He crouched down next to me and scanned the top of the ridge. Then he exclaimed, "I see them!" and stood and threw another grenade. In the next instant he was shot through the neck; killed instantly, he fell at my feet. For a moment I just looked at him. His eyes, wide open but lifeless, stared back at me. Then I realized that now more than ever I had to get a grip on things and seize control of what was becoming an increasingly chaotic situation.**

I decided at once that we needed support from our mortars and backed a little way down the ridge, out of the field of fire, to further assess the situation. I could see that my guys were all very much in the fight, putting out a lot of fire and throwing grenades. But the volume of enemy fire remained undiminished. We were also running low on ammunition. "Hold your fire," I shouted, and the shooting from our side soon ceased. I called for mortar fire and requested more ammo.

A few minutes later, shortly after our mortars began pounding the ridge top, several men came running up the ravine lugging ammo cans and festooned with bandoleers of ammunition, carrying them draped over their shoulders or wearing them across their chests like Mexican bandits. It was a stirring sight. I think it gave us all a lift to see them coming. Our fellow Marines, our brothers-in-arms, were running into battle to help us. It was as if they were telling us

---

** Shortly after this battle I spoke with Captain LeBlanc about McCoy's heroism under fire. LeBlanc, a former New Orleans newspaper journalist, wrote an eloquent commendation based on my input. Reynolds was posthumously awarded the Silver Star, and a destroyer escort, DE 440, was named in his honor. Commissioned on 2 May 1944, the USS *McCoy Reynolds* sank two Japanese submarines: *I-175* near Guam on 26 September 1944 and *I-177* near Kossel Island in the Palaus on 19 November 1944.

by their actions, and by the speed of their actions, that we weren't alone in this fight. As if they were encouraging us, saying, "Go get 'em, guys!"

The ammunition was quickly distributed and once again we moved uphill, shooting as we went. Another of my men, Pvt. Walter Kuss, was fatally hit while scouting up the ridge from a different direction. At the moment of his death, as he exhaled his last breath, he let out a long rising howl of pain and anguish like a dying animal. Several attempts were made to reach him and drag him back, all unsuccessful. Pfc. James Bell said, "I'm going up there; I'll bring him down." He was off and running before anyone could stop him and was shot through the chest well before reaching Kuss' body.

We were able to retrieve Bell, and he was still alive as we carried him down and out of the line of fire. But he was just about gone: he had a sucking chest wound that made it increasingly difficult to breathe. This was the first time I had seen such a wound, and it was a terrible sight. Our corpsman tried to patch him up, but there was little he could do. A sucking chest wound needs to be sealed internally as well as externally, and the corpsman could only treat the outside. Finally, Bell said, "It looks like this is good-bye." And then he very calmly died. *Just like in the movies,* I thought, *with last words and everything.*

Soon after that we quit attacking and withdrew. We couldn't dislodge the enemy from the ridge. We had been defeated.

Our losses were heavy. My platoon alone suffered seven casualties: four killed (Reynolds, Bell, Kuss, as well as Pvt. Robert Kessinger) and three wounded (Pfc. James Harris, Pvt. E. J. Mc Burnie, and a private named Manderville). Total casualties for 1st Battalion were nine killed and twenty-three wounded. Overall in the period spanning 18–23 November the 8th Marines lost forty-two men killed and many more wounded. The Army units also suffered heavy casualties. Our high command, convinced that further fighting would only produce more losses for little if any gain, called a halt to the offensive. American forces subsequently withdrew to the line of ridges connecting Hills 66, 80, and 81 with Point Cruz, which would constitute the front line until mid-January. Elements of the 8th Marines, including B Company, went immediately to the rear for two weeks of rest. We badly needed it.

Just before we pulled back, Pfc. Elias Kuykendall spoke with me about Kuss, who had been his foxhole buddy and best friend. They had joined the Marines together and had gone through boot camp together. Kuss had turned seventeen just a few days ago, which meant that he had been only sixteen when he enlisted. "How old are you?" I asked Kuykendall. "Same age as Kuss," he replied: just turned seventeen.

This conversation made a lasting impression on me. To this day I find myself thinking how fortunate I am to have lived to a ripe old age. Fortunate and blessed.

★　★　★

The next day, 24 November, Captain LeBlanc sent me on a "special mission" to a nearby Army command post. The Army unit had moved into the vicinity of the previous day's fighting as our relief, and its commander had requested information about the terrain and the enemy's dispositions. Since I was familiar with the area, having led my platoon in our regiment's failed attempt to capture Hill 83, LeBlanc decided that I was just the man to tell the Army commander, in person, everything he wanted to know.

I wasn't happy about the assignment. I had no desire to go anywhere near the place where we had met with defeat and death. I wanted to go to the rest area in the rear with my unit. I thought we should let the Army guys find out for themselves what it was like up there. Find out the hard way, as we did.

But something else was troubling me too: LeBlanc.

We called him "Little Napoleon." He was notoriously eager to make a name for himself and just as notoriously averse to taking risks. His men took the risks, and he took the credit for their successes. He would say, "C'mon, we've got a tough job to do," and then he'd assign someone else to do it. Sometimes he'd announce that we were going out on a reconnaissance patrol, and then he'd turn to Murdock or me or one of the other junior officers and say, "Hey, how about you leading it."

But orders were orders. "Go on up and tell 'em all you know," LeBlanc said to me. And I replied: "Well, okay, sir." And off I went.

I cut low across the ridge's east-facing slope, walking in the grass at the edge of the jungle. I was beneath the crest and felt reasonably safe. The area was deserted, a true No man's land. I found this very disconcerting. It was eerie. Then I came upon the body of an American soldier. He lay slightly above me and to my right, astride a narrow trail leading to the ridge top. His abdomen had been torn open, and his intestines had spilled out and were spread across the ground: a grisly and heartrending sight. I hurried on past him thinking, *I wonder what his dreams were? Will that happen to me?* In print these thoughts might come across as banal. But they were not banal at the time. Not then, not now, not ever.

I arrived at the Army CP to find it in turmoil. An anxious captain and his visibly agitated staff stood around a field radio listening to a report from the front line. Emanating from the speaker were the sounds of battle mixed with the crackle of static. And a frightened voice crying out: "We're taking a lot of fire . . . platoon leader hit . . . leg blown off . . . get us out of here."

I could hear the actual sounds of the battle outside, not too far away. Machine guns, rifle fire, grenades, mortars. The usual mayhem.

I reported to the commanding officer and told him what I knew. He listened distractedly, and I realized that he was just then in the process of learning everything I was saying. That his unit was reenacting our experience of the day before, getting clobbered as we had been clobbered. Finding out the hard way. At his request I pointed out the Japanese positions on a map. Then he turned back to the radio to attend to more urgent matters—namely, trying to figure out a way to rescue his beleaguered men. In doing so, he effectively dismissed me from his presence.

I left the CP. Laid out close by were as many as a dozen bodies covered with ponchos. I hurried on. Instead of staying low on the slope I headed toward the top of the ridge. I don't know why I did this. Maybe I was curious to see what was up there. Maybe I was trying to see where I was in relation to our lines. Probably, though, I did it because I was so tired and burned out that I was no longer thinking clearly. Whatever the reason, it was a foolish and reckless act, and I nearly paid for it with my life. When I reached the top of the ridge, I stuck my head above the crest. In the next instant a Japanese machine gun cut loose at me with a long burst, sending a stream of bullets snapping just inches above my head. That brought me to my senses, and I ran down the slope and into the jungle. I stood there for a minute gasping for breath, shaking, and thinking, *Holy smokes. Almost bought the farm on that one. Holy smokes.*

I returned to B Company in a foul mood and reported to LeBlanc. I told him what had happened to me and what had transpired at the Army CP. I was boiling mad at him and I let him know it. Without raising my voice I demanded to know why he had sent me on the mission in the first place. I told him it was all a waste of time and that I had almost gotten killed, twice, for nothing. And why, I fumed, had he sent me out there alone?

LeBlanc just looked at me and didn't say a word. He let me rant, and when I was all talked out he nodded, thanked me for my efforts, and walked away. Maybe he was shocked by my behavior. It was unlike me: I had a reputation for keeping my emotions in check. I wasn't the demonstrative type. But maybe, too, LeBlanc cut me some slack, because he thought I was as angry with myself as I was with him. And he was right.

CHAPTER FOUR

To the Bitter End

ON 25 NOVEMBER WE WERE PULLED OFF THE LINE and sent to positions in the rear near Henderson Field. For the next fifteen days we slept in open-sided tents in a grove of coconut palms on ground that was sodden from frequent heavy rain showers. Sometimes after a particularly intense downpour the ground refused to accept any more water, and the entire encampment was flooded to a depth of several inches. Afterward the skies cleared and the sun came out and the soil baked and steamed in the rising heat. The tall limbless shafts of the palm trees were chopped and splintered, their broad leaves torn and frayed and holed by bomb and shell fragments, their condition serving as a reminder that on Guadalcanal not even the rear area within the Lunga Perimeter was wholly safe and secure. Nightly visits by Washing Machine Charlie and the regular midday air raids plus artillery bombardments by the Pistol Pete guns and artillery pieces located in the hills west of the Matanikau kept us on our toes and ensured a certain level of hazard at all times. And there was always the possibility that Japanese warships would foray into Sealark Channel during the night and throw a few hundred large-caliber shells into our soggy environs. But these dangers were negligible compared with what we had recently been through on the front line, and we did not worry about them.

Actually we did not worry about much of anything. We were emotionally and physically drained and lacked both the energy and the inclination to worry. We mostly sat around doing nothing, partly because we had nothing much to do but also because we were in a sort of daze. You might say we were numb. It was not an unpleasant state. We were purely glad to be alive, and the fact that no one was shooting at us, at least not directly or intentionally, made us feel downright euphoric. We were living in the moment, and for the moment everything was fine and we were content.

The daily noontime air battles provided our chief form of entertainment. The long flight from the enemy airfields on Rabaul required precise timing for the Japanese to have enough fuel to conduct the raid and complete the round-trip journey. Their bombers took off early and flew to Guadalcanal on a straight and steady course down the Slot. As a result, they were easy to track—first by coast watchers and then by radar as they came closer. Their arrival over Guadalcanal could be calculated to the minute, and as they came in on their final approach, our fighters would be waiting at a higher altitude to jump them from above. Their primary targets were Henderson Field and our ships anchored off Lunga Point, and they went for one or both as their mission plans dictated or as opportunity afforded.

At the outset of the air battles the bombers were usually configured in a V-of-Vs formation whose geometric perfection was a marvel to behold, really a thing of beauty—formations so tight that they seemed a single entity and not the sum of their many machines. They came on with a dumb, plodding docility that actually bespoke the skill, determination, and courage of their pilots and crews. These men had to be very brave, because their aircraft, usually twin-engine Bettys, were unarmored and thus incapable of withstanding much punishment of the sort dealt by the big .50-caliber machine guns that armed our fighters. A single .50-caliber slug penetrating the fuselage or hitting anywhere near a Betty's gas tanks or fuel lines often produced an explosion that instantly erased plane and crew from the sky.

On their first diving pass, our fighters, mostly stubby blue-gray Grumman F4F Wildcats, ripped into the formations like hunting hawks. Maybe a couple of Bettys would blow up, while others began trailing plumes of smoke and wobbling as though trying to decide whether to stay the course or give up and plunge into the sea. But the formations themselves, although staggered, rarely broke, and the bombers droned fatalistically on toward Henderson Field or our ships riding at anchor in the Lunga roads.

As the F4Fs dove below the bombers and swooped up to regain altitude and make another pass, they were jumped in turn by escorting Japanese fighters. Then the two combatant packs of fighter aircraft scattered and the planes began dogfighting, and the air battle became a wild, swirling free-for-all. Round and round the planes went, trailing mist from their wingtips, machine guns firing in short jackhammer bursts. Meanwhile the bombers commenced their attacks. If their objective was to hit our ships, they descended almost to the water, which put them below those of us who were watching from high ground.

"God, it was fantastic," John Murdock recalled.

They'd be right out over the water in the bay and we'd all be cheering, thousands of guys would be shouting, "Get 'em! Get 'em!" You'd see a fighter coming up behind a Jap bomber, getting closer and closer, and we're yelling at our pilots, "Shoot, shoot! He's gonna get away!" You could see that the pilot was waiting to open fire because he had to get to within a certain distance. They were close enough to where you could hear the rattle of their machine guns. You could see the Jap planes going down. It was like a show; the bombers were right in front of us, like on a movie screen. And the whole island, you'd hear the guys yelling.

During this period a number of Marines took steps to upgrade their personal armament. The main object of their desire was the superb M1 Garand semi-automatic rifle that had been issued to the Army. The Model 1903 Springfield we carried was a fine weapon, but it was obsolete. The Old Salts loved the '03 like a Viking loves his broadsword, but the kids were unsentimental about the rifle because they had no history with it. The Old Salts might wax nostalgic about shooting perfect scores on prewar rifle ranges with their '03s and almost get teary-eyed as they recounted how its sturdy construction and reliable performance had saved their lives in Haitian and Nicaraguan jungles; the kids just shrugged. The M1 was easier and faster to operate, and it carried more cartridges in its internal magazine—eight to the '03's five—and that's really all that mattered to them.

Firepower also mattered to them, even at the expense of accuracy. Although the '03 was very accurate on the rifle range, it was less so on the battlefield. The herky-jerky motion of working the bolt tended to move your rifle slightly off target so that each time you jacked in a fresh round you had to take aim again. On the rifle range this was not a problem: you could take aim with care and at some leisure, because no one was shooting at you. On the battlefield, however, where the action was fast and furious, care and leisure went by the boards, and you worked that bolt frantically and repeatedly and accuracy was much diminished as a result—especially if, as was often the case, you were firing on the move.

With the M1 you kept the rifle on target and swiftly pulled the trigger eight times, and just like that eight rounds would be in the air simultaneously, one behind the other in split-second succession. And so what if your aim was a little off and some of those rounds didn't hit a vital part? So what if your hits wouldn't have scored well on the range? The combined effect of eight rounds impacting a man's body, no matter where, was almost always enough to knock him down at the very least if it didn't knock the life out of him. Marksmanship is a fine thing, but in battle firepower trumps it almost every time.

While some Marines acquired their M1s through honest scrounging and battlefield scavenging, others resorted to outright theft. One story has it that they'd drop by an Army mess hall, usually a big open-sided tent with long tables and benches. The Army guys would stand their M1s up against a nearby palm tree, then go inside and get in line for chow. The Marines would do likewise, standing their '03s against the same tree among the M1s. Nobody minded their presence. The Army cooks were generous and served all comers. But the Marines weren't really interested in eating. They'd wolf down their food and go outside, and as they passed by the tree where the rifles were stacked, they'd casually lift an M1 and walk off nonchalantly, leaving their '03s behind. It was a good deal for the Marines: they got a brand new semiautomatic rifle plus a decent meal, with food that was usually better than the swill their own field kitchens served.

This is an oft-told story with many versions that have appeared in both fictional and historical accounts of the Guadalcanal campaign. Its veracity is suspect if only because it strains credulity to think that the Marines could run this scam more than a few times before the dogfaces got wise to it. No one can be that clueless, not even soldiers of the U.S. Army. And yet from time to time guys from our company would return from a visit to the rear carrying M1s instead of the '03s they had left with. I never asked anyone in my platoon where and how he had gotten his new rifle, and, of course, no one ever volunteered to tell me.

Some of the guys, usually platoon sergeants, carried the Thompson submachine gun. These were older models for the most part with big, round drum magazines instead of clips and a knobbed pistol grip under the barrel. The drum-fed "Tommy gun" was notorious as the firearm of choice for bank robbers and bootlegging gangsters, "the gun that made the Roaring Twenties roar." It proved far less suited for military field use. Weighing more than fourteen pounds fully loaded, it was heavy and cumbersome. The drum and projecting pistol grip got caught in foliage and hindered movement, especially when you were crawling in dense underbrush. Firing from the prone position was difficult: you had to kneel or stand to use it effectively, which meant that you were that much more exposed to enemy fire. Reloading the drum took too much time, and the spring mechanism inside the drum had to be manually wound after each reloading. There was always the danger that you would wind it too tight or not tight enough, causing it to jam in either case. Extra drums did not carry well because of their shape and size, which also limited the number you could take into the field. Also because of their shape and size they were somewhat hard to handle, particularly in the thick of combat when you were trying to exchange a spent drum for a fresh one.

Later models were markedly improved by replacing the drum with a twenty-round box magazine. But this did not solve the problem that was fundamental to all Thompson models: short range and lack of penetrating power. The Thompson fired a .45-caliber slug originally designed for use in the Colt automatic pistol. Maximum effective range of the bullet was about fifty yards, if by "effective" you mean that it was still airborne and moving. As long as it was moving it was capable of killing someone, but at distances much past fifty yards, you were pressing your luck—a belt buckle or even a hard button could deflect it.

Many veterans of the Pacific War swore by the Thompson (the clip-fed model, at any rate), contending that it was ideal for the jungle, where its short range and lack of accuracy were not a liability and were, in fact, irrelevant. I thought that its weight and weak punch at all but very close range could not compensate for its one virtue, the ability to spray a lot of bullets at a relatively high rate of fire.

And then there was the Reising gun.

If the drum-fed Thompson wasn't good for much, it's fair to say that the Reising submachine gun was good for nothing. It was a piece of junk, badly designed and poorly made of soft, nonordnance steel. Its manufacturer, Harrington & Richardson of Worcester, Massachusetts, was able to foist it off on the Marine Corps, because we were in desperate need of submachine guns and the Army had first claim on the Thompson, which was then in short supply. We took what we could get, and we got the Reising.

It didn't last long in Marine service. Its inferior-grade metal was no match for the humid Pacific climate, which caused it to rust literally overnight. The Marines dubbed it the "Rusting gun."

Frequent cleaning didn't help. You could swab and oil the Reising vigorously, twice a day if you had the time and inclination, and the next morning you would find brown rust eating away at the barrel. Between cleanings, the Reising was only marginally operable, and less so with every passing day. Rust damage to the rifling inside the barrel and to the breech and trigger mechanisms was permanent and progressive; cleaning merely slowed the process of deterioration. The Reising tended to jam or break down outright whenever it was fired, a problem exacerbated by a design flaw in the clip attachment. Actually, to say that it "tended" to jam is to be generous. The Reising could be counted on to jam; sooner or later, usually sooner, it *always* jammed.

A Marine with a weapon that can't shoot isn't a Marine: he's a target. The Marines quickly became aware of the Reising's wretchedness and just as quickly acted to rectify the situation; they "tended" to "lose" them. I would venture to say that nearly every Reising carried by Marines who served on Guadalcanal was "lost" at some point. Since the Reisings on Guadalcanal constituted almost the entire inventory of that weapon in the military's arsenal, their disappearance pretty much ended its service career. As far as I know, few replacements were requisitioned, and fewer still provided. Those that did make it to the front lines soon suffered the same fate as their predecessors, getting "lost" in the jungle. Eventually the people back home in charge of weapons procurement got the message the Marines were obliquely but emphatically sending and stopped issuing Reising guns altogether. It was an important if unheralded victory for the Corps.

Just about everyone who used the Reising hated it, but John Murdock was more exercised than most. He regarded the Reising as an offense and an affront to every Marine, a matter to be taken personally—the more so when he learned that the government had given Harrington & Richardson an "E for Excellence in Manufacturing" award. Shortly after returning to his home in Massachusetts at the end of the war, he decided to pay a visit to the Harrington & Richardson plant in Worcester to express his displeasure. Showing up out of the blue at the plant's main gate, he demanded to speak with the company's top executives. Amazingly, he was granted an audience with one of the company's higher-ups, a man in a suit.

I don't know exactly what was said in that meeting, but I do know John, an Irishman with a rapier wit and great verbal dexterity. He's always smart and very funny when he wants to be, even when he's angry—perhaps especially when he's angry. According to John, he merely informed the executive that the Reising gun was a disgrace: "The worst goddamned weapon I ever had." I can just see and hear Murdock, eyes twinkling, talking in his dry, flat Bostonian accent, deftly combining charm, controlled outrage, and sarcasm to state his case. The executive heard him out, probably thinking all the while that Murdock was just another section-eight nut job produced by the war. Nevertheless, John was satisfied. He had gotten his feelings about the despised Reising off his chest and, in so doing, had upheld the honor of the Marine Corps. Overall, not a bad day's work.

★　　★　　★

On the night of 30–31 November a Japanese task force steamed into Sealark Channel bringing food to the beleaguered Japanese forces on Guadalcanal. Our warships sallied forth to intercept it, meeting the enemy fleet in that oft-disputed gap between Savo Island and Guadalcanal just off Tassafaronga Point. Because our bivouac was situated inland on low ground, I heard the battle but did not see it. But for the Marines positioned on the high ground, the Battle of Tassafaronga, as it came to be known, was a virtual replay of the Friday the Thirteenth Battle: big guns thundering and flashing, fireballs and tracers streaking across the sky, sweeping searchlight beams, ships blasted and burning in the brilliant spectral light of star shells and flares.

Our fleet took an awful beating. One of our heavy cruisers, *Northampton,* was struck by two torpedoes within a matter of seconds. Consumed by fire, she sank a few hours later. The heavy cruisers *Minneapolis, New Orleans,* and *Pensacola* were severely damaged. All three ships made it to Tulagi, *New Orleans* with her bow entirely shot off. All three would be out of action for some time to come to undergo repairs. The battle had been a clear tactical victory for the Japanese.

But a strategic defeat. The task force had failed in its primary mission: to deliver food to the Japanese army on Guadalcanal. This was a calamitous development for the Japanese. Even before the battle their food stocks were desperately low. Now they began falling below subsistence levels. The entire enemy army was growing physically weaker, because the soldiers simply didn't have enough to eat.

★　　★　　★

We were in better shape than the Japanese overall, but only in a relative sense. The 1st Marine Division in particular was greatly reduced by illness and sheer exhaustion, as well as by the battle casualties it had suffered in four months of fighting. A large number of its men were unfit for duty, and many more were only marginally capable of rendering effective frontline service. The high command, recognizing that the entire division had just about reached the end of its operational utility, pulled it off the front lines and began sending its units to Australia starting on 9 December. On 8 December Maj. Gen. Archer Vandegrift, USMC, handed over command on Guadalcanal to Maj. Gen. Alexander M. Patch, USA. Henceforth the battle for Guadalcanal would be fought and decided by the 2d Marine Division and the Army, which now had the larger force on the island.

On 11 December the 8th Marines returned to the ridges across the Matanikau, relieving the Army units that had replaced us after our abortive November offensive. Immediately to the west ran the parallel line of ridges we had assaulted, which remained firmly in Japanese hands. B Company was positioned in typical fashion, with the rifle platoons deployed just a few yards below the crest in foxholes that formed the main line of resistance (MLR). Machine guns and 37-mm antitank guns, with canister rounds supplanting their armor-piercing ammunition, were also posted along the line. Barbed wire had been strung a few yards below the MLR on the forward slope (i.e., the west slope, facing the Japanese), and outposts had been established farther forward where the terrain allowed. The company's base area was centrally located in the jungled draw at the bottom of the reverse (east-facing) slope.

The Japanese were similarly ensconced on their ridges. In most places the crests of their ridges were between one hundred and two hundred yards from our ridge tops—we were that close to each other. No man's land encompassed all the ground between the two ridgelines, including the forward slopes and the jungled draws at the bottom.

These dispositions, both ours and those of the enemy, remained substantially unchanged for the next thirty-four days. The brass, anxious to avoid a repeat performance of the November battles, had ordered a temporary halt to large-scale offensive operations. Instead we were to hold the line and harass the enemy with aggressive patrols and raids. In the meantime our air and naval forces would strive to interdict the Tokyo Express and thereby block the flow of enemy reinforcements and supplies to Guadalcanal. The combat effectiveness of Japanese land forces would thus progressively erode even as our strength was building. Eventually the Japanese would be weakened beyond their ability to stop us, and we would launch what was meant to be our final, decisive offensive.

During this period our most violent encounters with the Japanese took place at night. During the daylight hours we pretty much left each other alone, if you discounted occasional sniping and periodic shelling by mortars and artillery. We got very bored, and some Marines relieved their boredom by engaging in shouting matches with the enemy. The Japanese were happy to play along. Evidently we weren't the only ones who were bored. "Fuck Babe Ruth!" they'd yell, and you'd hear them laughing. "Fuck Tojo!" our guys would retort, also laughing.

Every now and then one of the guys would take a peek at the enemy. If you got out of your hole and stood up, you could look over the crest and see the Japanese on their ridge moving about, and maybe one of them would be looking right back at you. You didn't do this for long—a couple of seconds at most. Any longer and you risked getting your head shot off by a sniper. But the risk was slight, because generally the Japanese refrained from taking potshots. Nobody can fight all the time, not even the Japanese. We exercised the same restraint, for the same reason. Thus the policy became one of live and let live during the day.

A much different policy ruled the night.

After nightfall, if you didn't go out on a foray into No man's land you kept to your hole and waited to see whether a Japanese foray came to you. Two men occupied each hole; one would sleep while the other stayed awake (and presumably alert), trading off at regular intervals until dawn. Because we were spread so thin along the line there were wide gaps between the holes. These gaps seemed to grow wider in the night, and the Japanese continually probed them, looking for a way through to our rear. Now and again they tried creeping up on one of the holes. If both occupants were caught sleeping, they likely never awoke, being quickly dispatched by the knives and bayonets of their assailants.

It should go without saying that we kept to our holes during the hours of darkness and treated any movement without as hostile. We had passwords and countersigns, but we didn't use them because no one was supposed to be outside his hole anyway. The rule of thumb if movement was detected was to throw a grenade first and ask questions later, or, more precisely, to ask questions never.

But the Japanese were masters of stealth, and all too frequently we didn't know they were coming until they were right on top of us. Even the most vigilant and experienced Marines fell prey to their nocturnal predations. For example, a machine-gun crew from D Company was nearly wiped out—and the gunners were no novices to combat. They had set up shop about one hundred yards to my platoon's right on the point of a spur that jutted like a grassy promontory from our ridge straight at the Japanese-held heights to the west. A narrow jungle-choked declivity at the base of their position where the spur's two flanking ravines came together was all that separated them from the Japanese. By day, that high bastion's excellent fields of fire compelled the Japanese to maintain a very low profile on their ridge. At night, however, the jungles below became inky chasms in which the enemy could move about freely and invisibly.

Well aware of the threat this entailed, the gunners usually evacuated the position at dusk, lugging their weapon and its appurtenances back to the MLR. The Japanese would come up out of the jungle at night to slash and topple the post's sandbag parapet, just to aggravate us. They were gone by first light, when the gunners returned to the position and rebuilt the parapet before settling in for the day.

But sometimes the machine gun crew stayed out all night. One night during a heavy downpour the Japanese crept up from the ravines, the sound of their movement masked by the falling rain, and jumped the crew. A ferocious hand-to-hand struggle ensued. I heard our men yelling, "Help! Oh, God, they're in our hole. Help! Help!" Their blood-curdling cries and thrashing sounds were plainly audible to everyone in the vicinity. We listened, horrified, but stayed in our holes. The Japanese might have attacked the machine-gun post precisely to draw us out of our positions, either to ambush the would-be rescuers or to get us out of our defensive posture preparatory to launching a big attack. The machine-gunners were on their own.

Suddenly the yelling and sounds of fighting ceased. We anxiously waited and listened, peering through the rain into the darkness. Then the Japanese began probing our positions all up and down the line, running up to the crest and chucking a few grenades over the top at our holes and then running back downhill. After the grenades exploded, usually harmlessly, our guys would leap from their holes, dash up to the crest, and throw grenades at the fleeing enemy. Then they'd scamper back to their holes, and the Japanese would return and hurl their grenades. Back and forth it went through the night: intervals of silence and then the flash-bang of grenades exploding and men hollering and cursing in English and Japanese.

The next morning we discovered that one of the men in the machine-gun post had been killed, bayoneted to death. The others had been wounded but had somehow beaten back their attackers.

Usually the Japanese raids were in-and-out affairs: they came during the night and left before dawn. But not always. Sometimes one or two of them would stay in what was for them a kind of safe zone, down the forward slope a little way but too close for us to hit them with our mortars. We tried rolling grenades at the places we suspected they might be, but without much success. More often than not the grenades rolled behind them before exploding.

★   ★   ★

The reader should not infer from the preceding that we just sat on our hands for thirty-four days and waited for the Japanese to attack us. We also conducted aggressive patrols and probed their lines at night, giving as good as we got, or better. If more frontline Japanese soldiers had survived the war, maybe you'd be reading memoirs by those veterans of the Guadalcanal campaign recounting how the U.S. Marines terrorized them at night on the Matanikau front.

And terrorize them we most certainly did. Some of the guys really enjoyed this part of the job—teenagers who found their true nature in the jungle, who discovered that they were born for the warrior life. There were a few in every unit; more than a few, actually, more than you might expect—more than I expected. They went after the Japanese with a competence and enthusiasm that made them almost as frightening to their officers as they must have been to their enemies. "It was just amazing," observed Murdock, "how you could take kids like this and put them out into the jungle, and in just a few weeks they'd be great at jungle warfare. For them it was like playing cowboys and Indians. They'd come back from a patrol and you'd hear them talk. 'How many teeth did you get?' or 'How many did you kill?' And they'd brag, 'Well, I killed two, I killed four.'"

In keeping with the Wild West motif, we called No man's land "Indian Country." Naturally, we saw ourselves as the cowboys and the Japanese as the Indians. The Japanese played their part well. "They used to act like Indians," Harold Park recalled. "They'd run around at night making all kinds of noises, trying to get you to shoot: they'd make bird noises and take pieces of bamboo and whack 'em together." And as during the day, so too at night: "They had some English-speaking guys, and these would listen to our guys who were bullshittin' in their holes. Then pretty soon they'd say something like, 'Hey, Park, why don't you pull down off the ridge?' And sometimes they'd just swear at us and tell us that we were sons-of-bitches for taking souvenirs from the dead bodies of their buddies we'd killed. They were trying to provoke us to shoot our rifles and give ourselves away."

The little set-piece battles that ensued could be frenzied affairs, with the adversaries filling the air with grenades, pitching them at each other with wild abandon. They never lasted long—a minute at most, usually less. You couldn't see the Japanese and they couldn't see you. You threw your grenades at sounds, at where you thought the enemy might be, at muzzle flashes if somebody made the mistake of firing his weapon. If you happened to be looking at an exploding grenade you could be temporarily blinded by the bright explosion or permanently blinded by the eyeful of shrapnel you received. The battle was over when you ran out of grenades or men to throw them. Whoever ran out first left the battlefield first.

These grenade battles were participatory events, and the more the merrier—which is to say, the more men you had on your side, the more likely that your side would prevail. A few guys preferred a more individualistic approach to fighting the war. Such men were rare birds, and maybe not altogether sane. Sgt. T. S. Jones from A Company, positioned on our immediate left, was one of them. One night Jones armed himself with a Thompson submachine gun and strolled casually along the wire seeking action. Our mortars were firing on the enemy positions at the same time—also on our positions, as it turned out. A round dropped short on our side of the wire, and Jones was hit and both of his legs were blown off. His platoon leader, 2d Lt. Davies Wakefield, and several members of his unit rushed to his side and tied off the stumps. Then, as they lifted him on to a stretcher, his left arm fell off. Still conscious as they carried him from the field, he cheerfully remarked, "At least I have one good arm left to rap the bar with so I can order a drink!"

Almost instantly word of this incident and Jones' incredibly insouciant attitude spread all across the front. It made a big impression on everyone and was eventually written up in the *Saturday Evening Post*. Hardly a reunion of the 2d Marine Division goes by without the guys recounting Jones' story. Wakefield would always get very emotional when we talked about it.

Jones and those like him had a kind of crazy courage that set them apart from most Marines. But there were plenty of guys who were equally as brave if not quite so nonconformist. They came from all parts of the country, all backgrounds, urban and rural and everything in between. It was a tall order to command such men. As an officer you were supposed to set an example for them to follow; in practical terms that meant following *their* example and then bettering it. Some officers just weren't up to the job. Captain LeBlanc, B Company's commander, was a case in point. Eventually he was relieved and replaced by Murdock, who was ideal. A Boston Irishman, Murdock was very funny and very tough, a superb combat commander and a bit wild too—all traits that his younger charges greatly appreciated.

One manifestation of his toughness, apart from his courage and coolness under fire, was his disdain for medals and commendations. Very few men who had him as their CO (including me) received decorations. Murdock explained, "I didn't recommend many people; I didn't care if a machine-gunner killed fifty men; that's what he was supposed to do. That's what he's getting paid for. That was my attitude. Once in Hawaii we had a big formation with the division and they decorated all these guys. One company would give forty medals out; I'd give out one. My attitude was, "Hey, killing Japs is our job. We're not doing it for medals.'"

I understood this attitude, and it didn't bother me at all. Murdock will say that he didn't feel bad about it either, but he has also expressed regret that he wasn't more open-handed with his commendations. He's particularly concerned about Harold Park. Even as this book was being written Murdock was asking me how he could get Harold the medal he deserved for his actions on Guadalcanal—and, as we shall see, elsewhere.

As for Murdock: "Myself, I got a lot of publicity, but I never got any medals."

And, typically, he's quite content with that.

★   ★   ★

One of the themes running through the preceding anecdotes is the merciless nature of the Pacific War. The Marine Corps had tried to prepare us for this in our training. Bayonet drills were especially important. In reality, in combat, there were few instances when men used bayonets in the traditional manner, fixed to their rifles. Bayonet drills were performed for their psychological effect, so that men would learn the "psychology of the bayonet"—namely, to kill brutally, quickly, and unthinkingly, without compunction or moral qualms.

But our training merely paved the way for our transformation into hardened killers; exposure to actual combat accomplished and completed the process. You got hard or you died. It was that simple.

And the Japanese made it simple. They were notoriously unsparing. Their reputation for ruthlessness and savagery was widespread and well founded. We knew all the stories: the rape of Nanking, the Bataan Death March, atrocities committed far and wide and often against prisoners. We believed, correctly, that we could expect no pity if we fell into their hands. They neither asked for nor gave any quarter, and we responded in kind. If they had set the rules, as we believed, we were damn sure going to play by them. What other choice did we have? They simply would not surrender. They would not stop coming at us until we had killed them. Very quickly we learned that trying to take prisoners was a waste of time. And dangerous: even the wounded, if we went to treat them, would try to kill us, usually by blowing up everyone—themselves and the corpsmen who had stooped to help them—with a grenade. The "dead" had a nasty of habit of rising up from the ground and attacking us. So we made sure the dead were truly dead. No sense in taking chances.

This kill-or-be-killed approach to war was as brutalizing as it was brutal, and it affected everyone to some degree. Murdock recalled a corpsman who "came to me and said, 'Hey, Lieutenant, I got a live one, can I shoot him?' I said, 'Sure, go ahead.' Corpsmen weren't supposed to have weapons, and we shouldn't have shot a wounded guy. But I let him do it. We did it all the time. Because if we took a prisoner it would take two men at least to send him back to the rear. And we were so thin—our lines were really thin because a lot of guys were sick; our units were very much depleted."

Thus we became inured to the horrors of war, and, not surprisingly, we sometimes did horrible things. Not without reason: when your enemies behave in a bestial fashion it is only natural to look on them beasts, natural and to some extent justified. But we were not without sin in this regard. Far from it.

Murdock, for example, "never took any prisoners."

> I wasn't nice. I did bad things. Looking back over the years, I can say we probably committed as many atrocities against the dead bodies of the Japanese as they did to ours. For example, we'd heard the Japs wanted to die looking at the sun. So we'd roll them over and stick their faces in the dirt so they couldn't see the sun. Our guys would cut their fingers off. Make watch fobs, believe it or not—with the finger, the Jap fingers hanging down. And they'd go out there with knives and pliers, trying to pull out the gold teeth.

But if some of the men truly relished battle—embraced and enjoyed the killing, the brutality, the horror, all of it—it is important to establish that, on the continuum of brutal human behavior, the rest of us were not all that far removed from them, and we tended to move closer as the war went on. Some men are more capable than others when it comes to killing, but all men are capable. One way we "improved" on this capability—such improvement being vital to our effectiveness as Marines, not to mention our very survival—was to look on our enemies as hateful creatures, less than human. From a psychological standpoint, it became easy to kill them. We were killing animals, not men. And after killing them we could look upon their dead bodies and feel nothing—no remorse, guilt, horror, pity, whatever. From there it was really just a small step to a place in the geography of the mind where pulling the gold teeth out of corpses was not at all outrageous.

And the guys who couldn't hack it, who couldn't adopt that mentality? "We simply got rid of them," said Murdock.

> They'd have to go back. Because they were no good to us. They'd just disappear; they'd be sent back to the States. It was a self-weeding process. The guys who remained were the guys you could depend on. When I became company commander [in New Zealand], that was an awful thing I had to do. We could send 3 percent of our personnel home, every so often, so they could start new outfits back in the states. But you never sent the good guys home. You sent the shitheads and the screw-ups. I wanted the best men with me. I didn't want any of my good men to go.

In New Zealand, just before we sailed for Tarawa, Murdock told our company, "Now listen, I'm going to send some of you guys home. If you fuck up, you're going to go." But, he told me later, "these kids were so good, they just wouldn't do that. They wouldn't fuck up on purpose. They would do their job and do it well, and they didn't want to become known as a fuck-up. And a lot of those kids were killed on Tarawa, that I could have sent home before. But that's what happened. Because I wanted to keep the good guys with me."

The Marines who couldn't hack combat were, for the most part, just ordinary guys—not bad people. Murdock, more than most, understood this.

> I had one guy, a lieutenant platoon leader; we called him "Mac" [not his real name]. He was a Yale graduate, came from Connecticut, very well brought up, had money. Nice guy, too. And handsome—a rugged, good-looking Marine. But on Guadalcanal he'd go on a patrol, and he just could not handle it. Wally Godinius was his platoon sergeant, and he'd have to take over Mac's patrols all the time. Mac tried but he couldn't do it. I respected him for that, his trying. The kids were calling him yellow, and they'd say to me, "We don't want that guy, he's yellow." And I'd say, "Now, wait just a minute. The guy is *not* yellow. He *tried* to do the job. But he just

could *not* do it. It's not that he's saying, 'I won't do it, I'm not going there.' He tried. There's a difference."

And I told them, "A yellow man doesn't go out and try. He quits. And Mac won't quit."

This guy, physically, mentally, he just wasn't able to handle it. He would try, the poor bastard, and I felt for him. Then finally I just couldn't do it anymore. We made Wally Godinius a platoon leader and Mac never went out on a patrol after that.

Mac was married, too. And what happened was, in New Zealand, he was fooling around with all the broads in Wellington, like everybody else. But he was always talking about his wife, how much he loved her. He was always saying, "When I go home, I'll see my wife," and all that crap.

As I said, at that time we could send 3 percent of our personnel home to form the nucleus of a new outfit back in the States. Naturally, Mac was the first guy I picked to send back. And he had a pair of expensive Bass boots—not Marine issue. They were positively beautiful. They were high; they came up on your calf, almost to your knee. So I got him in the office and I said, "Listen, Mac. If you prove to me that you really want to go home and see your wife and you're not screwing around with every broad in Wellington, I'll send you home. But there's another catch. You won't go until you give me those boots! I want your boots!" I was a bastard. But he gave me those boots, and I sent him home. They were the most wonderful boots. They were waterproof; they were just great. I wore those boots the rest of the war. I wore 'em out.

The story has an amusing—one might say ironic—postscript. "I met him again at Pearl Harbor, after Tarawa," said Murdock. "It was just before we were going out to Saipan. And he's a *captain* now!"

I said, "Jesus, Mac, where did you get those captain's bars? How the hell did you make captain?" And he said, "Well, John, I'll tell you. You won't believe it, but when I went back, I was a big hero. Coming from Guadalcanal, they thought I was something special. Oh, they couldn't do enough for me. And I didn't disillusion them."

I had never put Mac's conduct on patrol in the report; and his running around in New Zealand—I didn't write that up, either. And now, here it is, I'm still a first lieutenant and he's a captain! The guy I sent home because he was no good was a captain.

★   ★   ★

By December our long sojourn on the front line had taken a big toll. We were wasted by illness, many by multiple illnesses, and we were malnourished and looked it. We went about shirtless, showing scrawny bodies with protruding ribs and vertebrae and sallow skin stretched tautly over them. Our faces were drawn and angular beneath scraggly beards, and our eyes were recessed in their orbits. We didn't receive a change of clothes during that period, and we became unimaginably filthy. We looked scary and menacing and pitiful all at once.

The constant threat of enemy attack punctuated by intermittent bouts of actual fighting was tremendously stressful. It seemed that much of the time we were either waiting to be attacked or being attacked or attacking the enemy ourselves. Or we were just sitting around, trying to get some rest, but feeling cruddy because we were sick, and always tensed up because we were thinking and worrying about our next combat action. Depending on how your day was going such concerns might be in the forefront of your thoughts, incessant and acute, making you all edgy and fretful, or they might be buried deep. Usually they were somewhere in between. But they were always present, in your head and on your mind. You could never fully let go or get rid of them.

The unrelenting mental strain, not to mention the physical dangers that caused it, made us twitchier with each passing day. Many men lost their appetite and didn't eat much even though food was available. At first and for a long time we subsisted mostly on C-rations, awful stuff. Around December, however, K-rations were issued, and these were an improvement. But we never had enough water. Never. We were always thirsty and sometimes dangerously dehydrated; every day men were felled by heatstroke brought on by too much exertion and not enough water. Getting sufficient quantities of water to the frontline troops on Guadalcanal remained a problem throughout our time there.

Murdock explained why Guadalcanal holds a special place in our memories, if not our affections: "Each campaign was different, with different problems. Tarawa was the worst in terms of fighting. But that battle lasted only three days. Right after it ended we were taken off Betio and sent back to Hawaii. But we were on Guadalcanal for three months. For the amount of time we were there, we didn't do all that much fighting. But there were other things. The sickness and the heat especially. The living conditions were the worst on Guadalcanal."

As bad as it was for us, it was worse for the Japanese—much worse. Their condition was no mystery to us. As December gave way to January there was a noticeable drop-off in enemy activity that we correctly ascribed to their deteriorating health. Their nocturnal probes dwindled and in time virtually ceased altogether. They simply lacked the energy to come at us in the night. After awhile they didn't even bother to yell at us.

They rarely achieved success when they did attack. In battle, we found, as we had been told on Samoa, that the Japanese made the same mistakes over and over. For instance, they would commit their units to battle as they became available instead of holding them back and massing them for a single powerful blow, and they would keep coming at us until most were killed, primarily by our artillery. The carnage was sickening, even to us, and we couldn't understand why they never seemed to learn from their experiences and make the necessary adjustments.

The Japanese thought their indomitable will would provide them with the margin for victory. It did not occur to them—or they could not acknowledge—that the Marines and soldiers they were battling were equally indomitable and, in the end, victorious.

★   ★   ★

On 10 January the final offensive began with Army units on our extreme left driving west into a group of hills known as the "Galloping Horse." Shotguns were also issued, two or three per squad. A lot of close-quarters combat was expected, and shotguns were thought to be ideal for the job.

On 13 January we went on the attack, with the 2d Marines on our immediate left jumping off at 0500 and the 8th Marines moving out a few hours later, after the 2d had reached its objective. The 6th Marines were in reserve. The "Pogey Bait Sixth" had arrived on the island on 4 January. For the first time, all the units of the 2d Marine Division were together overseas—the 2d, 6th, 8th, and 10th regiments with other supporting units.

The battalions of the 8th were deployed with the 1/8 farthest inland, the 2/8 on its right, and the 3/8 by the shore. We would initially be fighting on familiar ground, the scene of our abortive November offensive, attacking downhill into the draw cut by Mbokona Creek between the ridge connecting Hills 80 and 81 to the east and the Hill 83–84 complex to the west. Our mission orders, issued by General Patch, were to "attack and destroy the Japanese forces remaining on Guadalcanal"; our ultimate objective was Cape Esperance on the island's western tip, where we were to meet up with the 25th Division in a pincers movement aimed at trapping and annihilating the enemy. As it happened, the Japanese, recognizing the inevitable, had already started evacuating their troops from Cape Esperance and were in the process of withdrawing units to the embarkation point.

The Guadalcanal campaign was almost unique in the Pacific War in that the Japanese chose escape over total annihilation of their defending force. Evacuation was a concession of defeat, something the enemy rarely did, at least in large numbers and in an organized fashion—unless their willingness to be exterminated en masse itself constituted an admission that they could not and would not prevail. When our final offensive got under way, our high command had no inkling that the enemy intended to abandon the island, much less that they had commenced doing so. They weren't alone in their ignorance. Our experience on the ground gave no indication that the Japanese were giving up.

But we knew that they were on their last legs. I thought they wouldn't put up much of a fight, that they would just give way before us. I was wrong. Pfc. Paul Kennedy (a.k.a. "the Greek"—his real name, Apostalous Kinackas, was "Americanized" by an Irish immigration officer at Ellis Island), explained:

We got the word we were going to make a push, and Ladd says, "Oh, don't worry, we're gonna get a barrage, we're gonna have planes come there and bomb, they're gonna shell. . . . We're just gonna walk in there." Hah! I think our artillery must have shot one 155 round. And then Ladd said, "All right, we're moving out." So we started moving down into this draw. The Japs were in a cave and we're coming down toward them. And this guy in B Company was setting up a machine gun, and I was standing right next to him. A Jap came out of the cave and shot the guy. Boy. Didn't kill him, but it must have hit a bone, because he was moanin' and groanin' like crazy. So then we knew the Japs were in the caves.

The Jap who shot the guy, he went back into the cave. Then Ladd says, "All right, Greek, go down in the draw there, and throw some grenades into that cave." I looked at him, and I said, "Oh, man!" I was scared! And Ladd said, "Don't worry, we'll cover you." I thought, *Yeah, you're gonna cover me—with a blanket.* Anyway, I went down there and threw grenades into the cave. Maybe there were about ten, thirteen Japs in there.

According to Kennedy, Captain LeBlanc immediately radioed a report of this encounter to battalion HQ that reflected very well on him, informing his superiors that "*we* just wiped out *twenty-six* Japs." Translation: the enemy position had been reduced by B Company acting under LeBlanc's inestimable command. Technically this was true. But the real truth was that the Greek had done it all single-handed.

LeBlanc had exaggerated the toll of enemy dead. Not only that, he had spoken too soon.

Kennedy added:

> Then the Japs were trying to crawl out of the cave, and they were all wounded.
>
> One guy was almost helpless; he was crawling toward me and moaning. I went over to him and started talking to him. I said, "Hey, man, where you from? San Francisco?" Don't ask me why, it was the first thing that came to mind. Then this corpsman come up behind me with a .45, he was standing behind me, pointing the .45 at the Jap. He's got the pistol in back of my ear, and, man, he shot the Jap right in the forehead. You know, with a .45! The bullet went right out the back of the Jap's head. And I turned to the corpsman and said, "What the hell you doin'?" And he said, "I wanna get a Jap too."

The Greek allowed himself a moment to feel a little pity for the dead enemy soldier. Then he proceeded to do what most Marines would have done in the same situation: he searched the dead man's body for souvenirs. He got the man's wallet, packed with photographs, and he got the battle flag the soldier had wrapped around his body. It was a good haul.

★ ★ ★

We pushed on. We moved up and over Hill 82. The hill and the jungled draws below were infested with Japanese. My men saw a single Japanese soldier and opened fire, killing him instantly. I collected some personal effects from his body: a diary, a lock of hair, a first-aid kit, a photograph of a group of soldiers, and a "thousand-stitch belt"—a piece of cloth embroidered with a thousand stitches by well-wishers—that he carried for good luck.

Like all Marines I wanted souvenirs of battle. Maybe taking them was a way of connecting with the enemy, with the men we had killed. It led eventually to a connection I could never have anticipated, one that was very gratifying—even redemptive.

We continued our advance. Pfc. Boyd "Red" Nelson was scouting to our front when a Japanese soldier armed with a captured Tommy gun and hidden from view loosed a short burst at him. He spun around and dropped. We all hit the dirt.

"I'm hit!" Nelson cried.

"We can't get to you," we called back. We couldn't see his attacker, but we knew that if we moved forward to help Nelson, the enemy soldier would get us with that Tommy gun. "Can you crawl back?"

"I'll try."

He did, and he made it. We found that a .45-caliber slug from the Tommy gun had entered his left shoulder just under the skin, crossed *over* his spinal column—miraculously without damaging it—and lodged in his right shoulder. Taken to the rear by a corpsman, he would come back to us just two weeks later. His wound was superficial. Incredible. At the time I couldn't believe that a bullet of that caliber could travel under the skin like that. I still find it hard to believe.

We moved on. Shots were fired, grenades exploded. Privates, First Class Isabelle and Kuykendall were wounded. They were quickly patched up and sent to the rear. We moved on. A Japanese soldier broke cover just a few yards from a shotgun-armed Marine and tried to run away. The Marine fired and hit a grenade on the man's belt; the grenade exploded, blowing him to bits. The shotgunner was unharmed. We moved on.

The Japanese began lobbing "knee mortar" grenades at us. Down in the dirt again. One of the grenades landed a few yards uphill, rolled down, and stopped next to my feet and those of a man lying at my side. I frantically kicked the grenade away. It hit a rock and bounced back. But it didn't explode. It was a dud. My lucky day—so far. But there were still a lot of days to go. We got up. We moved on.

The fighting was constant but not everywhere at the same time: one squad might be resting while nearby another was engaged in a sharp fight with a sniper or a machine-gun nest. All up and down the line automatic weapons rattled, rifles cracked, grenades popped. The air carried the astringent smell of cordite. In places where there had been a lot of firing the atmosphere was hazy with gun smoke and the smoke of burning foliage. There was a lot of shouting, some screaming, and the frequent cry: "Corpsman! Corpsman!" Stretcher bearers, many of them musicians in the division's band, ran around the battle-field picking up the wounded and carrying them back to the battalion aid station, where they would be treated before being taken by jeep farther back to a hospital.

Occasional but heavy artillery fire dropped in on us without warning. We would throw ourselves down and try to push ourselves into the dirt, and the shells would slam in very close. You just knew that some guys had to be getting torn up by shrapnel. But the shellfire was surprisingly ineffective. After a barrage, most men would rise again, hastily checking themselves and each other to see whether they had been wounded. The advance then resumed, with scouts in the forefront cautiously probing to draw fire so that enemy positions could be located.

Some positions were too strong and too stoutly defended to take by infantry firepower alone; the difficulties and potential for casualties were too great. We might call in mortar and artillery support fire to reduce them, bringing it down as close as possible without hitting our own positions. Sometimes too close: one of own 60-mm mortar rounds impacted no more than fifteen yards from where I was hugging the ground. The shrapnel flew upward, and I was as low and flat as a human can possibly be, pushing so hard into the dirt that I was practically eating it—and I didn't receive so much as a scratch.

Or we might simply bypass such strongpoints. "The hell with them," the guys would say. "Leave 'em for the Army!"

We tried to keep moving, to keep our momentum going. We moved through jungle, dense foliage, towering trees. Our company clerk, Pfc. Emory Swaney, passed beneath a tree where a sniper was hidden. The sniper fired right down on Swaney, hitting and piercing his helmet, knocking him down. While some of the guys took out the sniper—BARs and rifles roaring in unison, blasting him to bits—several of us rushed over to help Swaney. We thought he must be mortally wounded with a bullet in his head. But after removing his helmet, we were surprised to find that the bullet had merely spun around inside it, grazing his scalp and right shoulder. Swaney was okay, somewhat dazed but grinning. Being that he was half Irish and half Flathead/Nez Perce Indian, born and raised on a reservation in Montana (where he lives to this day), we joked with him about how he would someday tell his grandchildren how close he came to getting scalped by a wild bullet.

Swaney got to his feet, and we moved on. We advanced a few yards, fought some more Japanese, and then halted for the night.

Dusk. We're dug in, tired but alert, ready for anything. Well, not quite. Suddenly the ground began to shake violently. I thought: *We're being shelled.* But no shells were falling, none exploding. *What the—?* And then we realized: earthquake!

Later and throughout the night, many of the Japanese we had bypassed attempted to infiltrate through our positions to their own lines. They were all around us, small groups and individuals creeping through the brush, running across open ground, shadowy figures darting this way and that. They tried to avoid us but couldn't always, since they couldn't see us. Now and then they blundered on one of our foxholes and a brief, sharp fight ensued, rifles shooting and grenades exploding, men shouting and cursing.

On and on it went, all night long, these sporadic clashes. It was all very exciting, and we took it in stride. Apprised of the situation, our battalion commander, Joseph McCaffery (affectionately known as "Little Joe"), said, "Well, I'm not too concerned. Wake me up if it gets serious." And with that he lay down in his foxhole and went to sleep.

★ ★ ★

14 January. We continued to advance. The action was much the same as the day before, intermittent clashes with Japanese diehards. Some of the Japanese we came upon blew themselves up in their holes or just sat there and let us kill them with grenades. My platoon made good progress. We moved beyond Hill 82, descending into a draw and then climbing the next hill to the west, Hill 86. This was our objective, and we reached it before any of the other units reached theirs; we were maybe a hundred yards ahead of everyone else. George Stein (a high school classmate who enlisted when I did) and his mortar section joined us, and we took a break. In fact, we were done for the day.

A little while later, as George and I were chatting, a grim-faced Captain LeBlanc walked over to us. "Gunner Lund is no more," he said solemnly.

LeBlanc went on to tell us that he had received a report that Marine Gunner Otto Lund, commanding 3d Platoon, had been shot and killed. George and I got up and went over to the side of the hilltop that provided a view north into the part of the draw where 3d Platoon was fighting. We couldn't see Lund's body because it was beneath the jungle canopy—but we did see Joseph Washvillo's body sprawled in a patch of open ground near the ravine. A recipient of the Silver Star for his role in the action in which Barney Ross won fame, Washvillo had also been shot and killed.

I would later learn from his buddies that Washvillo had gotten careless while scouting ahead of his platoon. In those circumstances "careless" probably means that he was too tired to think straight and had reached a state of emotional exhaustion, very common, where he figured, *To hell with it,* and barged into the draw without taking any of the usual precautions—and was killed.

Shortly thereafter it fell to me to break the news of Lund's death to Cpl. Herschel Wilski. "Ski," as he was known, was a BAR man and a squad leader in Lund's platoon. He took Lund's death very hard. Gunner Lund was a popular figure in B Company, an Old Salt who was trusted and respected for his courage, competence, and commonsense battle wisdom, and loved for his rough humor and for the obvious and genuine affection and concern he felt for his young charges. Before the war he had been a seagoing Marine, serving on the beloved aircraft carrier *Lexington* (sunk in the Battle of the Coral Sea). He always seemed to be smoking a cigar. How he was able to keep himself stocked with stogies on Guadalcanal is anyone's guess; such are the talents of an Old Salt. He used to say that after the war he was going to buy himself a big, shiny Cadillac convertible and ride around in it smoking his cigars—a simple dream for a simple and very good man. A dream never realized.

All the kids looked up to Lund, Wilski in particular. Ski idolized Lund. The gunner was everything to him: hero, mentor, father figure, older brother, best friend. At first he refused to believe that Lund had been killed. "I was just talking to him a few minutes ago," he said. But then the truth sank in and he became distraught and threw his weapon to the ground. "This damn war!" he exclaimed. Ski then announced that he was quitting the Marine Corps, quitting the war.

Ski meant what he said. He was about to head back to the rear when Murdock arrived on the scene. Murdock calmed Ski down and told him that he couldn't just up and quit; that would be desertion in the face of the enemy, and he would get in a lot of trouble for it. Murdock spoke softly with him for several minutes in this vein until Ski came to his senses.

Ski picked up his weapon and rejoined 3d Platoon, and Murdock assumed command of that unit. But Ski was a changed man. Exchanging one madness for another, he went from being a Marine who did his job and did it well to being a Marine who did his job with a singular passion. From that day forward he hated the Japanese with a savage intensity and took it on himself to personally avenge Lund's death, often going off by himself to hunt the enemy. If you were a compassionate man, you might say a prayer for any Japanese soldiers who crossed his path. He always returned, eventually, but with little to say about his exploits. He was the quiet type. Guys like him usually are.

Ski came back from one of his solitary forays carrying a samurai sword with blood on the blade. He told us that he had encountered a Japanese officer who was foraging for food, and he had taken the sword from the officer and killed him with it. That was all he said. We could only imagine the ferocity of their struggle, however brief. We believed him. Guys like Ski don't lie.

"Much later," Paul Kennedy said, "they sent Wilski back to the States with me; we were on the same ship. These sailors were asking, 'Hey, you guys got any souvenirs?' Wilski says, 'Yeah, I got a Jap sword here.' I don't know whether he was going to sell it. A sailor took the sword, and he came back with it and he said, 'Hey, there's blood on the end of the sword, there.' Wilski says, 'Ah, that's just ketchup.'"

Guys like Ski never brag, either.

With Ski back on the team, George Stein and I sat down again on the hilltop and talked about Lund. Our conversation abruptly terminated when a bullet hit the ground between us, kicking up dirt. We threw ourselves aside and scrambled for cover. The Japanese just wouldn't let up. Overall it was a bad day for the 8th Marines: too many men were killed and wounded, and very little ground was gained.

★　★　★

And so, to the end. My memory of the final days of the January offensive is blurry, and I find it difficult to remember the details. At reunions we reminisce about our very limited personal perspective of the offensive and the countless little battles that were fought as we went forward. At that perilous time we focused primarily on our own concerns about adequate cover from incoming artillery and other life-threatening events in our immediate area.

We advanced on a broad front but never in an even line. Some units always moved faster than the others, depending on the terrain and the resistance they encountered. We went up and down more hills and ridges, up and down, up and down: sometimes fighting and killing the Japanese, sometimes just killing them.

Starting on 16 January the 6th Marines began passing through our lines. The 8th and some of the 2d Marines were pulled from the line (finally!) and sent back to bivouacs in the vicinity of Henderson Field. Meanwhile, the 6th Marines joined up with elements of the Americal Division to form the Combined Army-Marine Division, or CAMDIV. This formation would continue to drive along the coast toward Cape Esperance and its eventual meeting with the 25th Division.

End of January, our last week on Guadalcanal: B Company was bivouacked by Henderson Field, awaiting transport off the island. While there, I came down with jaundice and lost a lot of weight. I would be getting off the island just in time.

In the meantime, there were still duties to perform, some of them very unpleasant. One of Murdock's responsibilities was to record the location of battle-site graves on an overlay. It troubled him that the locations couldn't always be specifically pinpointed, so there could be no assurance that the bodies would later be found for relocation to permanent cemeteries. He had to write letters to many families, telling them that their loved ones might have to remain in an unmarked, unidentified grave on the battlefield.

Guadalcanal had yet one more scare to throw at Murdock. Hot-water showers had been set up in the base area, and Murdock decided to avail himself of what was truly a luxury at this stage in our lives. He had hung up his clothes and was enjoying his shower when three naked Japanese entered the stall. To say that Murdock was alarmed would vastly understate what he was then feeling. Murdock said he "almost had a heart attack," and I can well believe it. The three men, seeing the panic in his eyes, hastened to assure him, in English, that they were our very own nisei interpreters. Relieved, Murdock went back to enjoying his shower. As for the three nisei interpreters, though they probably didn't know it, they were lucky to be alive. Had Murdock been armed he would have shot them on sight.

★   ★   ★

On 31 January the 1/8 and the entire 2d Regiment boarded the troop transport *Crescent City*. The next morning the ship weighed anchor and steamed away from Guadalcanal, New Zealand bound. While the 1/8 boarded ship, the Japanese landed a battalion of new troops at Cape Esperance. They made a suicide stand at the Bonegi River on 31 January and 1 February, delaying the American advance for two days.

The Army's 147th Infantry Regiment took the Bonegi River position on 2 February and on 6 February was in turn relieved by the 161st National Guard Regiment from my home state of Washington. My father had served with this regiment on the Mexican border in 1916 and during the First World War as a first sergeant. The 161st Regiment continued the drive toward Doma Cove, about eight miles south of Cape Esperance.

During the first week of February the Japanese managed to evacuate more than 11,000 troops from Cape Esperance, a minor triumph that did little to offset the magnitude of their defeat. They lost upward of 25,000 men in the Guadalcanal campaign; of these, maybe 1,000 were taken prisoner. Our losses were comparatively small. According to Army historians, about 1,600 were killed and 4,245 were wounded.

On 9 February the rest of the 8th Marines left Guadalcanal aboard the troopships *Hunter Liggett* and *American Legion*. That same day Guadalcanal was declared secure.

I would eventually return to Guadalcanal, but not until forty years had passed. Most of the men who served on that island, lacking any desire to revisit hell, never returned. Too many never left. But one way or another, for the living and the dead, the fighting on Guadalcanal was over forever.

CHAPTER FIVE

Heaven

WE DIDN'T KNOW OUR DESTINATION when we boarded the troop transports at Guadalcanal, but we were pretty sure it would be either New Zealand or Australia. We had no preference: one was as good as the other. We just wanted to get away from Guadalcanal. We couldn't climb aboard our ships fast enough, but more than a few men could barely climb aboard them at all. Just about everyone was ill to some degree, and a number were almost too weakened by their maladies to pull themselves up the cargo nets.

When we learned that we were going to New Zealand, we were very happy. Most of us knew little or nothing about the country except that it was populated mostly by white people who spoke English, and the climate would be cool and there were no jungles. Those were reasons enough to like the place and to look forward to it. But there would be many others.

Our ship docked at Wellington, New Zealand's capital, situated on the lower end of North Island—a beautiful little city, red-roofed buildings on steep hills, reminding us of San Francisco. We could see tall trees with branches with leaves on them just like the trees in America; not a palm tree in sight. There were pine trees too, and the air was cool and soft, easy to breathe.

After the ship docked, we went ashore with orders to return by midnight. We fanned out through Wellington's central waterfront district, packs of thirsty Marines clothed in tatters, walking on pavement and dodging traffic for the first time in more than a year, looking for pubs, craving beer. The pubs were closed for the day, but we found something just as good: ice cream parlors and milk bars. We gorged on ice cream and milkshakes and frappes, a heavenly bounty of dairy products, sweet and cold and thick. We didn't have New

Zealand money and we didn't know the rate of exchange, so we just handed the Kiwi shopkeepers American dollars and hoped they would do right by us, which they did.

There were girls. Holy smokes, were there ever girls! Young girls, pretty girls, smiling girls—they were everywhere, lots of them. They stared at us and smiled and we stared at them and smiled, and in many instances we greeted each other and exchanged pleasantries and actually conversed with them. Even the Casanovas among us had a hard go of it at first. It had been a long time since we had seen and spoken with girls, and we were out of practice.

We were also "gazy"—staring inward, a thousand yards back into our heads, flashing on thoughts and visions Guadalcanal had put in there. Our faces were sun darkened and tinted yellow (a side effect of quinine, a symptom of jaundice, or both): the Kiwis told us we looked like the Japanese. They were joking. It was their way of telling us, amiably, that we were kind of scary looking. Guadalcanal and New Zealand were two different worlds: one was hell and the other, heaven. The contrast was immediately apparent and profoundly jarring. We had learned how to handle hell, but heaven would take some getting used to. Aboard ship we hadn't been aware of our gazy condition. We had seemed normal to each other. But here in this beautiful city, among these wonderful civilized people, among all those pretty girls, it was possible to see how far from normal we were. What would they think of us?

They loved us. And we loved them right back. It didn't take long for that love to blossom. It started that first night ashore. The start of a beautiful relationship—one that endures to this day.

They were unbelievably friendly and hospitable. A Marine might be walking down the street in any town, and a Kiwi would just come right up to him and start a conversation. More often than not, the Kiwi would invite the Marine to his home for dinner or even for an extended stay. The Marine might respond, "You're kidding!" The reply would then be, "No, I'm not. I'll drive you to your camp to get your things and then show you some trout fishing like you've never seen. You can stay as long as your leave lasts."

The Kiwi girls, as one might expect, were instrumental in forming this unique and lasting bond between the U.S. Marines and the New Zealanders. It turned out that the girls were as glad to see us as we were to see them. There was a shortage of young men in their country. Most had long since been sent to the other side of the world as soldiers in the British army, fighting Germans and Italians in the North African and Mediterranean theaters. They had been gone, many of them, for well over two years. Many had been killed in the Western Desert, fighting the Afrika Korps; many had been captured in

Greece and Crete. Efforts were under way to bring the rest home and get them involved in the war against Japan, defending their homeland. In the meantime, we had the field pretty much to ourselves.

It was, as they say in the Corps, a target-rich environment, Wellington in particular. A labor shortage in the nation's capital was another consequence of the call-up and departure of so many of New Zealand's young men for military service. Single girls from all over New Zealand had flocked to the city to take the jobs vacated by the young men. Most were on their own for the first time in their lives, earning their first paychecks. It was all very thrilling for them. The absence of single young men had been the only major drawback. Then the Marines arrived. Problem solved.

Our arrival solved another problem too. Previously the country had been virtually defenseless against a Japanese invasion or aggression of any sort. This was especially worrisome in the early months of the war, when the Japanese seemed unstoppable and their aims for conquest limitless. If the Japanese came, older men and boys would be thrown against them, a dismaying prospect. Some New Zealand regular army troops remained in-country, but not enough to mount a viable defense. The Battle of the Coral Sea did much to ease invasion concerns, as did the Battle of Midway and Australian successes on New Guinea's Kokoda Trail. Then the 1st Marine Division arrived, staging for Guadalcanal, but its stay was brief. Now the 2d Marine Division was on the scene: diminished, to be sure, by its travails on Guadalcanal, but with men who were battle-hardened and capable, with a decisive victory under their belts, and still with plenty of fight in them if fighting were needed. The Japanese threat receded over the horizon and disappeared forever. Instead of the Japanese, New Zealand had been invaded by a horde of American Marines—and more were on the way, replacements from the States to fill our depleted ranks. There would be problematic aspects to this invasion, but there would also be lots of fun. Good times would be had by many, if not all. Very, *very* good times.

★   ★   ★

Before the good times, however, there was work to be done. The day after our arrival in Wellington the 2d Division regiments dispersed to separate camps outside the city. The 8th Marines boarded a train at the Wellington train station and rode to a campsite near Paikakariki ("Perch of the Parakeet" in Maori), a small town about thirty miles north of Wellington. The train took about an hour to reach the campsite, a pleasantly slow journey through a peaceful bucolic countryside, soothed by the rhythmic clack of carriage wheels on the tracks.

The 1st Battalion was to be quartered in the part of the camp closest to Wellington, in a mostly empty pasture on the south side next to the railway. A few huts had already been constructed on the site, but for the time being most of us would have to sleep on the ground beneath our shelter halves, just as we had on Guadalcanal. But this was not Guadalcanal: there was no mud, no rain, no bombardments and air raids, and, most important, no Japanese.

We spent the first week or so at "Pai-Kock" building the camp, a task that mainly entailed erecting the big pyramidal tents that would be our homes for the duration of our stay in New Zealand. The tents sat about three feet off the ground on plywood decks and were furnished with bunks and small coal-burning potbellied stoves with aluminum flues that poked out of the peaked canvas tops. We needed those stoves even in February when we arrived. This was midsummer in New Zealand, but the nights were cool just the same—and would get cooler as the seasons changed and winter came on.

Just after our arrival we were given ten days of leave. I was in a group of B-Company officers that went up north to a sheep station, or ranch, owned by a family named Bousfield. The station was near a small community called Waipukarau, south of Napier on the east coast.

The Bousfields organized events and activities to entertain us. There were turkey shoots, rabbit-hunting expeditions, and sightseeing excursions in their car. They took us to a sheep auction and a sheep dip, where the animals were bathed in a solution to rid them of fleas and where the Kiwis demonstrated sheep-shearing techniques. One night a dance was held in Waipukarau, and Mrs. Bousfield arranged for a number of local girls to attend. The girls were all from prominent ranching families and as such represented the district's social elite. Since we were officers, we were considered suitable company for them, and they for us. During the party, however, one of our guys, Bill Hagan, sneaked outside to smooch with a Maori girl who had caught his eye. Mrs. Bousfield later found out about his dalliance and quietly but sternly reprimanded him for what was, in polite New Zealand society, a severe breach of conduct: "You must remember that you're an officer and that you should not be consorting with *those* people," she said. "They're the wrong class of people for you."

The Bousfields had sons off in the war, but they didn't speak much about them. Mrs. Bousfield once mused about how much the New Zealanders missed their young men: "We wish they were back, even the wild ones," she said, and spoke wistfully about how one of her sons had gotten drunk and wrecked the family car.

John Murdock took his ten-day leave on a sheep station owned by a family named Foster on South Island, below Christchurch. There was a mother and father and two daughters in their late teens; a son was serving overseas in the British army. The first day there, John watched in amazement and delight as the family's two young daughters whistled up the dogs to transfer the sheep from one pasture to another. He admired their skill—"It was just remarkable; I'd never seen anything like that before"—but, of course, he also did not fail to notice that the girls were very comely as well. Later that evening, after dinner, John and his hosts were sitting in the living room, chatting and getting to know each other, when the mother asked, "Would you like Kitten to go to bed with you tonight?"

John was momentarily dumbfounded. *Geez,* he thought, *which one of the sisters do they call "Kitten"?* Then, recovering, he said, "Oh, I think that would be very nice."

They continued talking for another hour or so, and all the while John was looking at the sisters, appraising them, wondering with growing anticipation which one would share his bed that night. At last the Fosters announced that bedtime had arrived and the mother said to John, "Go into the bedroom and get in bed; I'll see you in a minute."

And John thought: *Oh, Jesus, is she* [the mother] *Kitten?*

He got into bed as instructed and waited, blankets pulled to his chin. A few minutes later Mrs. Foster came into the room with a hot water bottle encased in a crocheted coverlet. Placing the hot water bottle against John's feet she said, "There now, 'Kitten' should keep you warm tonight." Then, bidding him a cheery "sleep well," she left the room, closing the door behind her.

So, John thought, *a hot water bottle is a "kitten" here.* He didn't know whether to be relieved or disappointed.

Maybe a little of both.

★   ★   ★

We also went into Wellington on liberty, swarming into the city's restaurants to consume huge meals with portions enormous even by American standards. The steak-and-eggs platter, costing a mere twenty-five cents, became everyone's favorite. The Kiwis pronounced it "styke-'n-aygs," and pretty soon we did too. There was mutton, vegetables, milk, and cheese, also in huge quantities. And there was beer, lots of beer, served in pint glasses at room temperature and considerably stronger than American beer.

There were five Red Cross clubs in Wellington, and all five were jam-packed every night with Marines and Kiwi girls. There were other venues—the Allied Services Club, for example—but they were all more or less the same: thick with cigarette smoke and gloriously noisy, filled with the din of music, raucous laughter, and shouted conversations, dancing feet stomping on wood floors. The Kiwi girls taught us line dancing; we taught them how to jitterbug. We were smitten by their good looks, their gaiety, their accents. We loved their slang, even when we didn't understand it. Murdock recalled:

> One night I was dancing with this girl, and after awhile she says to me, "I'm knocked up." And I says, "You are?!" My heart sank. She had to explain that she meant she was tired. I also learned that "getting screwed" meant you had gotten paid. The girls would say, "I got screwed today," and we'd say, "Well, did you like it?" One time I was with George Stein and another guy, we were up in Napier, and I held a chair for a gal to sit down at the table, and I said, "Park your fanny here." And, oh, there were giggles and giggles. "What'd I say now?" I asked. They wouldn't tell me. So when I got back to the hotel, I asked the desk clerk, "What the hell does 'fanny' mean in your country?" And he said that it was the "front end" of a girl, not the rear.

Everyone, the Marines and the Kiwi girls, were living life to the limit; there was an inclination to let go completely, to have as much fun as possible while fun could be had. Older New Zealanders, the mothers and fathers of the girls we were chatting up and romancing, understood what was going on and showed remarkable tolerance when one thing led to another, as it often did. One of Murdock's (many!) experiences in this regard was fairly typical:

> I went home with this gal; it was the weekend, and her parents invited me to stay over. I'm being very coy, you know? Separate rooms. And eventually after I felt the parents were asleep I snuck in with the little gal, and I was there in the morning, and when I woke up the mother's standing at the foot of the bed. And I'm thinking, *Oh, God, what's gonna happen?* I'm looking for windows to jump out, and I'm thinking, *Where the hell are my clothes?* And all the mother said was, "What would you like for breakfast,

John?" And she's right there and I'm in bed with her daughter! And this was a nice middle-class family. And the father, he later said to me, joking: "I don't care. You can have my wife; you can have my daughters; but don't touch my beer!"

John was a man with a mission: "I was a virgin when I went into the Marine Corps. I was making up for it. I figured I could be killed at any time. My attitude was eat, drink, and be merry, for tomorrow we may die. I took that attitude to its logical conclusion."

So did a lot of Marines. Just about the entire 2d Marine Division, actually.

★　★　★

Liberty was so enjoyable in that country that many men couldn't bring themselves to return to duty after it was over and went AWOL. The typical punishment when they finally returned was to be reduced one grade in rank and confined in the brig for thirty days on bread and water, with a full ration of food every third day. The brig warden was a strict disciplinarian who made their stay as unpleasant as possible: he had them run laps around the compound and put them to work polishing a rusted sewer pipe, over and again, for hours on end. But most of the Marines who did time in the brig thought that all the fun they had had with their girlfriends and buddies was worth the price.

In B Company, the first sergeant was the first to deal with the Marines who went AWOL or who had otherwise gotten themselves in trouble. Then they would be referred to the company commander, in our case John Murdock, who had replaced LeBlanc when the latter was reassigned shortly after our arrival in New Zealand. John would talk to the miscreant and decide whether to give him a warning or send him to the brig. It was ironic that Murdock would be meting out punishment to B Company's troublemakers, since you could make a pretty good case for Murdock being the biggest miscreant of the lot.

"I had a good time in New Zealand," Murdock told me in this regard—a masterpiece of understatement. "We didn't have a Catholic chaplain in our regiment for a while, when we were in New Zealand, so I used to hold Sunday services. I had my missal with me, being a good Catholic boy. I would read the gospel of the day, say a Hail Mary and Our Father with them, something like that. And I'd be hung over, with a splitting headache. And they knew it! So I'd tell them, 'Do as I say, not as I do.'"

One of Murdock's forays into Wellington became legendary in the company and is still fondly remembered at division reunions. I'll let Murdock tell the story:

I was in this hotel; a woman owned it. And this woman, I got friendly with her that night at the bar; she was buying me drinks and stuff. She was older than me, about forty, but really a good-looking woman. When the bar closed we all said goodnight and everything, and I went up to my room. And I said to myself, "I'm going to find that woman." I knew that she lived in the hotel, in a suite on the top floor. So I climbed out the window on to the ledge. I was naked, but I didn't care, because I was drunk. Very, very drunk. So I got out on the ledge, buck naked, and I'm walking down this ledge, I dunno, two or three feet wide, looking for her, I'm looking in each window. Then I saw her and climbed in because the window was open. That's the last thing I remember. So, honest to God, I woke up in the morning, I don't have any clothes on and I'm in bed with this gal. And I said, "Oh, God," and, "How did I get here?" I was stiff as a hooty owl! I never could have done that otherwise!

She was very nice about the whole thing. She gave me a bathrobe and told me where my room was. Before leaving, I just had to ask: "Did I have a good time?" She said, "Yes." I said, "I did?!" I had no idea.

I never went back there again. I was embarrassed, I suppose. And she used to tell the guys, "Tell Lieutenant Murdock I want to see him. Tell him to come down and say hello." But I just couldn't.

After a few weeks in New Zealand we started training in earnest. We needed a lot of training both to get ourselves back into shape and to incorporate the replacements who were streaming in from the States. Our experiences on Guadalcanal provided the template for our training. We built positions on the Japanese model and practiced attacking them. We advanced through wooded areas against simulated sniper attacks. We worked on the use of supporting fires and we worked with tanks. One of the most important changes overall was to give the squad leaders more freedom of action to make decisions in combat, let them decide on their own how to maneuver their men and move around to envelop an enemy position or turn a flank.

In a related move, squads were reorganized to comprise three and sometimes four BAR teams instead of two. This plus the adoption of the semiautomatic M1 Garand, which replaced the venerable bolt-action Springfield, greatly increased squad firepower and for that reason may have been one of the most important changes we made in New Zealand, at least at the tactical level.

We were issued the new bucket helmets, discarding the old World War I helmets forever, and new clothing—jackets and trousers with camouflage mottling. The officers were issued M1 carbines, and many armored units replaced their M2 and M3 Stuart light tanks with the M4 Sherman medium.

We conducted amphibious landing exercises, usually at the beach near our camp. We went on long hikes over hilly terrain. American boots arrived, and the day after they were issued the brass in all its wisdom had us go on a fifty-mile hike with full combat loads. We were marching on a paved road, and those stiff new shoes were very hard on our feet. After only five miles men began dropping out left and right. Trucks picked up those whose feet had given out on them, but the march continued, and men continued to drop out. At about the forty-mile mark so many men had fallen by the wayside that the march was called off, and the remainder of men who were still on their feet were trucked to our destination. Of course, Tokyo Rose found out about the march and mocked us unmercifully, telling us she was "soooo sorry" that we Marines had to wear those boots and had had such a difficult time because of them.

★   ★   ★

Most Marines, myself included, had Kiwi girlfriends. Even John Murdock eventually got himself a steady girlfriend. Her name was Daphne Thompson, and they fell deeply in love. Toward the end of our sojourn in New Zealand, Murdock was hospitalized in Silver Stream Hospital outside Wellington with a bad case of rheumatoid arthritis that caused painful swelling in his knees. Daphne visited him a few times, but otherwise they did not see each other during this period. While we were at Hawke's Bay loading *Sheridan* for what we thought would be another amphibious exercise but turned out to be the real thing—the operation at Tarawa—John was told, "Hey, there's a woman out on the dock who wants to see you." John knew that the woman was Daphne. "I can't see her," he said. "I'm too busy." But the real reason he declined to see her: "I didn't want one of those sad farewells."

He never saw her again. But much later, after the war, he learned that she was pregnant when she came to the dock. He had no idea. She had not told him.

In 1981 a number of 2d Division veterans returned to New Zealand for a reunion. Daphne found out where they were staying and went to see Bill Crumpacker, one of the replacements from the States who joined my platoon in New Zealand. She asked Bill about John, and Crumpacker gave her Murdock's address and phone number.

Shortly thereafter she called John from her home in New Zealand. John was married and living in Massachusetts. He hadn't spoken with Daphne since he last saw her before shipping out for Tarawa, and he hadn't communicated with her in any way, even by letter, since before the invasion of Saipan. One day when John came home from work, his wife greeted him at the door. "You'll never guess who called today."

Uh-oh, John thought; *this can't be good*. He said, "You're right, I can't guess."

John's wife just looked at him for a moment. Then she said in a level voice: "Daphne."

John was thunderstruck. "Holy shit!" he said. "What did she want?" It should be noted that his wife knew all about John's love affair with Daphne; he had spoken of it when telling her stories about his time in New Zealand.

"Oh, I had a long talk with her," his wife replied. "She wanted to know all about you. What you looked like, how many children we had, what you had been doing all these years. She said she heard you lost an arm on Saipan and that you fell in love with a Navy nurse and married her. I told her that I hadn't been a nurse—that you and I met through a cousin of mine who knew you from college."

John at once recognized the story of him losing an arm and marrying a nurse as Bill Crumpacker's handiwork. It was the standard story that Marines told former Kiwi girlfriends who contacted them after the war.

John didn't call her back. He didn't have to: Daphne began calling him. "I'd get the calls about ten o'clock Sunday morning, after I came home from church. I figured out it was Monday night down there—probably she had had a few highballs and had gotten nostalgic and called me. Of course, my wife didn't like the idea. But I said, 'She's ten thousand miles away. Don't you worry about anything. I love you, not her.'"

It was during one of these conversations that Daphne told him, without elaboration, that she had given birth to a son in 1944. Shortly after that conversation she sent John a tie clip he had left with her way back in 1943. She also sent a photo of a boy and wrote on it: "My favorite child."

She never said directly that the boy was their son. But John did the math and realized that he was.

John learned that Daphne had married twice and was then living in a nursing home in Auckland. Eventually she stopped calling, and John lost touch with her forever. "After she called the first time I was gonna send her a Christmas card that year, or write her a little note," he told me. "But I thought it over, and I said to myself, *maybe I better not*—might open up a Pandora's box, you know?"

Some twenty years after the war ended, John (as well as other 2d Division Marines) would occasionally get letters from young men and women in New Zealand looking for the Marine veterans who were their fathers—Marines who had fallen in love with Kiwi girls and had fathered children during their short time together. John helped them with their searches and corresponded with many of them over the years. Sometimes he was able to put them in touch with their fathers. But all too often he had only bad news to give them: the men they were looking for had been killed in the war, leaving their young girlfriends or wives with a child they would never see. A significant number of these men were killed at Tarawa, a prolific widow-maker for Kiwi girls who had loved men from the 2d Marine Division.

The number of letters began trailing off in the 1980s and stopped altogether over the next ten years or so. I know of no one who has received such letters in the years since.

Most of the men and women involved in these wartime relationships were eventually able to put the past behind them and move on with their lives. They would look back on their brief but intense liaisons and smile with the affection that the maturity of adulthood bestows on the fondest memories of youth. But, as John discovered, this was not always the case, especially for the women—especially where children were involved. Consequently, every now and then in the years following the war's end the long-lost lover of one of these Marines would show up at the division's annual reunion, seeking the man who had fathered her child, or at least some information about him. Such appearances, usually made without any warning, were generally not welcome. Most of the Marine veterans were by then married men with children conventionally begotten, and many were completely unaware that these offspring were not the first of their seed to grace the world.

The mere possibility of this happening became the stimulus for many practical jokes. A note, perhaps slipped under the veteran's hotel room door, would inform him that a certain Miss So-and-So from New Zealand was also attending and that she wished to arrange a meeting with him, because she believed him to be the father of her child. The recipient's subsequent distress must be seen to be appreciated. Only the uproarious laughter of his buddies, revealing that he was the victim of a prank, could dispel it; and even then, and although he would be laughing along with them, his unease over what might have been would linger.

Sometimes, at one of the reunion's functions, an announcement in the same vein was read from the emcee's podium, to the general and raucously expressed amusement of all assembled. Everyone knew it was just a joke. Well, almost everyone. John recalled how one such announcement caused "this guy to jump up from his table, all white-faced and scared, and beat a hasty retreat from the room."

* * *

A few months after the Marines arrived in New Zealand there was strife between the Marines and New Zealand soldiers returning from the war in Europe. The Kiwi soldiers discovered the Americans courting their wives and girlfriends in a grand manner, and they didn't appreciate it. You couldn't blame them, really. They had returned home expecting to find faithful girlfriends and wives, and instead they found Americans romancing their women and lavishing them with expensive gifts.

There were barroom brawls and fistfights in the streets. Some of the confrontations developed into full-blown riots. The largest and most violent incident took place on 3 April and became known as the "Battle of Manners Street." It started in the Allied Services Club in Manners Street and quickly spilled outside and spread to Willis Street and Cuba Street. Upward of fifteen hundred Americans and New Zealanders, including civilians, are said to have been involved. Leather belts and knives came into play, and when it was all over, two Americans were dead and many were injured.

As for me: I steered clear of this and related incidents (there were many—barroom brawls, fistfights, and the like). I'd done enough fighting on Guadalcanal. And anyway, I was more interested in courting Kiwi girls than fighting with Kiwi men.

* * *

In October the entire division conducted an amphibious exercise at Hawke's Bay in the north. We no sooner returned to our camps than our division commander, Maj. Gen. Julian Smith, announced that he was not satisfied with our performance and ordered us back to Hawke's Bay.

I'm not going to say that we knew we were leaving for good, but many sensed this might be the case. So did everyone in Wellington—the girls especially. Just before our ships cast off again for Hawke's Bay, a number of girls, some hugely pregnant, came down to the docks to find out what was going on. Nobody could or would tell them anything, but many had dire premonitions that they would never see us again.

Our ships steamed north past Hawke's Bay and continued on a northerly heading. After a few days at sea it was announced that we were going to invade Tarawa Atoll in the Gilbert Islands. Maps and sand tables were brought out, and we learned about the forthcoming operation. Our sudden and permanent disappearance from New Zealand was very hard on our Kiwi girlfriends and wives. One day they woke up to find us gone and knew we were headed into battle. Then, toward the end of November, they started hearing rumors that a lot of us had been killed.

The rumors proved to be true.

CHAPTER SIX

Hell

AT BETIO THERE WERE MARINES whose entire combat careers lasted only a few seconds. These were the kids who joined the 2d Division in New Zealand, fresh out of boot camp. The landing craft ramps went down, they charged out, and they were shot dead. Just that fast they were gone, lifeless bodies floating in the water.

Some never made it off the ramp. Pfc. Elias Kuykendall was just behind me when the ramp dropped. In the next instant he took a bullet in the head, fell, and rolled off the ramp into the water.

Kuykendall was sixteen years old when he joined the Marine Corps, seventeen when he became a seasoned veteran of the Guadalcanal campaign, eighteen when he stepped onto that ramp: eighteen forever.

I didn't see Kuykendall get killed; I was told about it afterward. At the time, I was in the water, standing by the ramp, looking at the island while waving the guys forward and shouting, "Let's go, let's go!"

Then I started for the beach.

★   ★   ★

During the long hours of circling in our boat, Dick Stein, a green seventeen-year-old private, first class who had joined my platoon in New Zealand, had grown increasingly impatient: *Let's get the show on the road,* he thought. *Let's get to the beach.* He figured it would be a piece of cake once he got ashore. After the fury of the preliminary bombardment and the previous day's fighting most

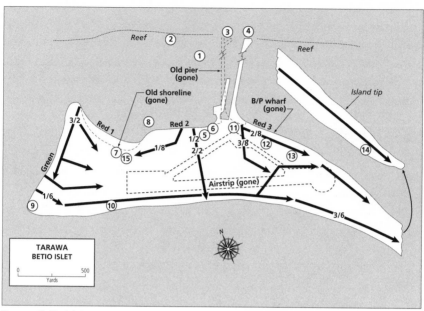

Tarawa, Betio Islet.

Notes:

1. Author wounded.
2. Beached freighter *Niminoa.*
3. Long Pier and seaplane ramp.
4. Present mole, site of British memorial dedicated on 25th anniversary November 1968.
5. New memorial dedicated on 45th anniversary November 1988.
6. Colonel Shoup's command post.
7. Final Japanese strongpoint in 1/8's AO. Wiped out by 1/8 and elements of the 3/2 Marines.

of the defenders would either be either dead or just about beaten and ready to pack it in. Many of the guys in the boat, even the veterans of Guadalcanal—myself included—shared this view. Some, especially the newcomers, worried that the Japanese would *all* be dead, depriving them of the chance to fight and prove themselves worthy as Marines.

"Then we reached the reef and they dropped the ramp," said Dick, "and when that ramp went down—my God, all hell broke loose."

From where he stood near the back of the boat, Dick saw Kuykendall fall and thought, *Boy, this is going to be a hell of a mess.* He saw me standing in the water at the front of the boat, calling the platoon into action. "Let's go!" he heard me shout. "Come on!"

And on they came. "Everybody rushed out," said Dick. "I never saw anybody hesitate. They went right forward just like you're supposed to. Nobody flinched or held back. And then it was my turn and I just ran like heck forward."

Dick lumbered down the ramp, jumped into the water, and began the six-hundred-yard trek to the shore. Curtains of machine-gun fire swept the lagoon. "Guys were getting hit; guys were dropping everywhere. I looked back and they were all over the place, floating." Before him lay the island, a dark blot on the water, burning from end to end, explosions everywhere, black smoke billowing. Dick accepted the situation in his own quiet way, telling himself: *I guess this is how it's supposed to be.*

He realized that he had better "go like the dickens" to get ashore or he wasn't going to make it. But he couldn't run in the waist-high water. It seemed to him that he was moving in slow motion. The water did offer a measure of protection, though, and he was not slow in taking advantage of it, plunging beneath the surface after pushing a few steps forward and staying under for as long he could hold his breath.

He did this continuously: a few steps forward, then down, then up; then a few steps forward and down again. At Betio, this was what it meant to be "going like the dickens."

He had gone about a hundred yards and had popped up for air when a bullet clipped his chin. The wound burned and bled a little but was other-wise inconsequential. He was lucky: had the bullet struck a fraction of an inch higher it would have torn off his chin. He was truly surprised to have been shot. "I figured that everybody else would get it, but I wouldn't."

He kept moving: ducking under, coming up, taking a few steps, ducking under again. Another bullet struck his rifle, splintering the stock and severing the sling. Then another bullet grazed three of the knuckles on his right hand, peeling them clear to the bone. His reaction?

"I thought, *Wow.*"

He discarded his broken rifle, knowing that he would find another on the beach. And he kept moving. A few yards to his front he saw his buddy Bill Crumpacker "making like an alligator": ducking under when the bullet splashes swept toward them, then coming up after the bullets had passed with just his eyes and nose above the surface.

He noticed that Bill was angling to their left, toward the pier. *Good idea,* Dick thought. The pier would provide some protection from the hurricane of enemy fire. And so he too headed for the pier.

Let us pause here to consider Dick's situation. He was unarmed, twice wounded, on his chin and right hand, and though the wounds weren't serious, they were certainly painful, and debilitating for just that reason. It is no small thing, however minor the wounds, to get shot in the face and then in the hand, and to see the knuckle bones on that hand exposed. It is no small thing to bear witness to your own mutilation and to know that you still have far to go and that the consequences of pressing on are highly likely to entail further (and more serious) mutilations or even death itself.

The prospects might have been, and perhaps by all logic should have been, unnerving. Dick might have acted accordingly by sitting in the water and "making like an alligator" and going nowhere until nightfall could cover his approach. Or, since he had been hit twice, he might legitimately have made his way back to the reef to board one of several LCVPs that were cruising around out there picking up the wounded. But Dick did not lose his nerve. He did not avail himself of the aforementioned opportunities to exit the battle. He pressed on.

To this day Dick Stein will deny that he was or did anything different from all the other Marines who took part in the Tarawa operation. He's right: the vast majority of Marines at Betio pressed on, just as he did. They did not falter, they did not fall back, they never gave up. They were faithful to each other, to the Marine Corps, and to themselves: faithful warriors, they pressed on, they fought on. Many died, many more were wounded—and they won the battle. Dick was no different from all the other Marines in the sense that all rose to unimaginable heights of bravery.

Nearly sixty years later, Larry Wade, a coxswain commanding one of the LCVPs that were picking up the wounded, told me, "Everybody at Tarawa who was there in any capacity was a hero whether he wanted to be or not." Dick will also deny that he was a hero or that he was particularly brave. Most Marine veterans of the Pacific War will say the same with regard to their actions at Betio and on all the other islands where Marines fought and bled and died. Let the reader be the judge.

★   ★   ★

When at last, after eighteen hours of circling, our LCVP started for the beach, Bill Crumpacker was also relieved. Crammed in the back of my boat with the other two men of his fire team, Henry "Hank" Farrell and Israel Rodriguez, he was fed up and itching to get ashore. Conditions in the boat had steadily worsened with the lengthening hours. Diesel fumes from the engine fouled the air with their oily stench, and even though the water was fairly calm, the craft pitched and rolled. This combination of movement and exhaust and nervous tension made several men sick.

"We had Van Camp's beans and ketchup sloshing all over the bottom," Bill recalled, refuting the popularly held notion that all Marines at Tarawa were served a hearty "steak-'n-eggs" breakfast before going into battle. I remember getting steak and eggs, but I was an officer. Bill and the other lowly privates ate in a different mess, and I would not be surprised to learn that they received more lowly fare. Or maybe they just came late to the chow line, after the good stuff had all been taken. In any case it was probably just as well, since their food didn't stay with them for long.

Bill didn't get sick, the fumes didn't bother him, and he wasn't especially nervous: "I was too damn dumb to get sick." He still thought the operation was going to be a cakewalk. Back on *Sheridan* in the predawn darkness he had stood at the rail watching the naval bombardment and had felt real pity for "all those poor sons-of-bitches on that island." He watched as the big shells from our battleships and cruisers soared across the sky, red-hot and whirring as they passed overhead, exploding on Betio and turning the island into a maelstrom of fire and smoke. "We all thought it was going to be pretty soft, even the guys who had been on Guadalcanal. We thought the battalions going in ahead of us would have it all cleaned up in an hour or two. All they had to do was hit the Japs in their heads with their rifle butts and then it would be over."

When the LCVP crunched up on the reef, it seemed to Bill that a strange otherworldly silence descended on the boat and the men in it. They stood there tensed and ready to go, like racehorses at the starting gate waiting for the bell. No one moved; no one spoke. The sounds of battle distant and muted. Time standing still. As if the whole world were holding its breath.

Then the ramp dropped.

Bill realized they were going to have wade in to shore. "And I thought, *Well, that's okay, so we're gonna get wet; let's go in and see how many dead Japs are lying around.* I thought it was gonna be interesting. I thought, *Well, hell, there's no problem here.* And about the time that thought went through my mind, here it came: all the firing."

Bill heard me shout, "Let's go," and watched as I crossed the ramp and jumped into the water. He saw Kuykendall take a bullet in the head and fall and tumble off the ramp. In New Zealand Crumpacker had shared a tent with Kuykendall. His other tent mates were Anthony O'Boyle and John Duffy. All three would be killed in the battle for Betio.

Even as Kuykendall fell, the other men were rushing past him. The boat emptied in seconds, with Bill and his fire team among the last to leave. Once in the water he was stunned, momentarily but profoundly, by the ferocity of the battle. *My God,* he thought, *what's going on here?* Unable to fully comprehend what was happening—it was all so unreal, so bizarre—he was still unable to feel properly afraid. Instead of worrying about himself, he worried about the pack of Camel cigarettes in his breast pocket. *If these damn Camels get wet,* he told himself, *I'm gonna be really pissed off.*

But the pack was in a little waterproof bag made of oilskin and tightly knotted, and he had secured his pocket with a safety pin. He remembered this and was comforted. "Then I looked around, and I'm seeing bodies in the water, and the water's turning red around them."

Before him he saw a line of men wading toward the beach holding their rifles up over their heads. He saw many of them cut down one after the other as though a scythe had swept across the surface of the water. Columns of water whooshed up where bigger shells exploded, and the surface was pitted and roiled where smaller bullets struck it. He watched as those swaths of disturbed water approached him in long curves, and as they came closer he could hear bullets ricocheting off the water—*zing! zing! zing!* He waited until one of the moving arcs of death, one of those curtains of fire, was just a few yards away and then took a deep breath and went under.

The curtain swept by, and overhead he could hear bullets skipping off the surface. When they had passed, he came up with just his eyes and nose above water in the manner that Dick Stein had likened to an alligator. He looked around to see where the bullets were hitting, and when he saw that they had moved off, he pushed on toward the island, half-wading and half-swimming, still with only his eyes and nose above the water.

He had gone maybe ten yards when he spotted another curtain of bullets arcing toward him, and he took a deep breath and ducked under as before. While submerged he took a few steps forward and found that he was able to walk underwater because the weight of his gear kept him down. When he could hold his breath no longer he "made like an alligator" for a few yards more before another curtain of bullets forced him under. And again while submerged he kept going, walking underwater, making for the beach.

To hear him tell it, you'd think nothing could be easier. But he's downplaying the difficulties, because he's modest and also because words do not exist that can adequately describe the situation. But consider this: there were multiple bullet curtains crossing and crisscrossing the lagoon, and their movements varied in speed and direction, making their paths hard to plot. In one moment nothing would be happening in your immediate vicinity, and in the next moment two or more bullet curtains would intersect right where you were standing, and you'd see the water boiling around you with impact circles dotting the water like raindrops on every side. And if your time was up, that was the last thing you saw. As well and in addition to all that heavy machine-gun fire that was sweeping the lagoon, the Japanese were shooting at us with rifles and automatic cannons and artillery. Which is to say that the absence in your area of a moving curtain of bullets was by no means a guarantor of safety. The air was at all times and everywhere thick with bullets and projectiles of various types and sizes.

And just when Bill thought things couldn't get any worse ... they did. Navy dive-bombers swooping in to attack Japanese machine-gunners aboard the wrecked *Niminoa*, about 150 yards to Bill's right, inadvertently attacked the Marines as well. Dive-bombing is an art, and some pilots were better at it than others. Those others who weren't as good dropped their bombs on or near the Marines. *Unbelievable,* Bill said to himself as a bomb exploded among several Marines. *This is just nuts.*

The force generated by the exploding bombs traveled through the water and slammed hard against him, and he began to worry that one of those punishing blows would injure his internal organs or knock him out. The planes dove in one after the other. He watched as each attacking plane released its bomb and then raised himself up out of the water just before it burst. He escaped concussion to his body in this fashion but also exposed himself to those ubiquitous bullet curtains. The trick, therefore, was to rise up before a bomb exploded and go back down before a bullet curtain enveloped him. Of course, it often happened that a plane dropped its bomb just as a bullet curtain came sweeping up or several curtains converged on his position. In which case he had a choice to make that was really no choice at all, an instance of being damned if you do and damned if you don't. All he could do was trust to luck and hope to God that he would be spared and then make his move, whatever it might be—rising up or going under.

He made those moves reflexively, operating on automatic pilot, acting consciously but without deliberation—as though the circuitry in that part of his brain in which sentience resided had overloaded and gone haywire, giving itself over to useless and irrational thoughts, much in keeping with his earlier concern for the welfare of his cigarettes. Early on in his trek he had discarded nonessential items of equipment such as his gas mask and rations—he didn't think he'd be eating or would need food anytime soon—and now amid the dangers and din of battle he found himself wondering, quietly and calmly and yet with real anxiety, whether he would be reprimanded for this misdeed. He thought that when they all got ashore our platoon sergeant, Sappington, would have them fall in and check to see whether they had all their equipment, and give them a tongue-lashing if they didn't.

Rising up, dropping down, walking underwater, pushing forward, half-wading and half-swimming: Bill kept moving, and so far so good—at least from a personal standpoint. But overall things were going very badly for the 8th Marines. The regiment was being systematically butchered in the open water. Men were dropping at every hand. Bodies were floating all around. The Japanese machine-gunners on *Niminoa* kept up their murderous fire despite the best efforts of Navy dive-bombers to silence them. And errant bombs from the warplanes continued to fall among the Marines even as they were being raked by *Niminoa*'s machine-gunners and by machine-gunners on the island. Bill decided he had had enough of this nonsense and began moving away from the hulk, to his left, toward the pier.

In doing so he made sure to steer clear of the groups that coalesced here and there, the Marines driven by instinct to find safety and confidence in numbers and finding death instead when, inevitably, their groupings attracted Japanese fire. He thought he was alone, but he wasn't: Dick Stein was a few yards behind him, following his lead.

★   ★   ★

Off to Bill's right, toward the middle of our assault wave, was B Company's headquarters boat carrying company commander John Murdock as well as George Stein, now his exec, and Headquarters Platoon. Aboard *Sheridan*, Murdock had watched with a certain detachment as the Catholic boys in B Company lined up to take communion. Although himself a Catholic, Murdock had refused to join them. They were just asking for it, he thought—taking communion was an admission that you were going to get killed, and this admission would become a self-fulfilling prophecy. On Guadalcanal it had seemed to him that the religious ones were the first to get killed. *Screw it*, he told himself, and turned away from the communion line. *I'm not going to be in a state of grace; I don't it need it because I'm not going to die.*

Murdock's confidence was attributable in part to his innate optimism coupled with the natural inability to conceive of his own death. But also he didn't think he would die, because like so many others he didn't think there would be any Japanese left alive on the island to kill him. The devastation wrought by the air and naval bombardment would see to that. "Everyone should have been dead on that island, the bombardment was so ferocious. The palm trees were all shattered. There was lots of smoke. The feeling among us was, what are we waiting for, there's nobody alive in that place."

He watched as the dive-bombers went to work, bombing and strafing. He noted the differences between pilots: some dove below the shattered treetops, going right down on the deck to press home their attacks; others, more timid or prudent, pulled out of their dives well above the trees.

Through the long night in his boat Murdock had remained awake and alert, unable to sleep because he had too much to think about. Having dismissed the possibility that he would be killed, fear did not enter into his thoughts. Rather, he pondered the task ahead. He figured that they would meet with at least some resistance from the few Japanese who were sure to survive the preliminary bombardment and the first day's fighting. So he went over in his mind, again and again, all the things he would or might have to do as the commander of a Marine rifle company in combat.

With dawn approaching, Maj. Larry Hays, the 1st Battalion commander, came by in his boat carrying the battalion headquarters section. "Whaddaya think we should do?" he asked Murdock. Hays and Murdock were by then good friends, but Murdock was nonetheless somewhat taken aback that his battalion commander was asking him for advice. He replied, "I think we oughta get the hell out of here. All of my guys are getting sick on this boat, and I bet the others are too, on the other boats. Nothing could be worse than this."

Hays' boat puttered off but returned a few minutes later. "Let's go. We're gonna go," he told Murdock.

The coxswains gunned their engines, and the boats charged toward the island. "We were happy as hell to start moving," said Murdock. And then— they hit the reef. "It was the biggest surprise in the world. I just couldn't believe it. There was just a big crunch. *Bang!* The boat hitting the coral. The impact jerking us around."

The ramp dropped, slamming into the water with a big splash. And for an instant he saw nothing but the water in front of it. At this point in recounting his experiences to me, Murdock laughed self-disparagingly. He admitted, "I never said, 'Follow me, men.' My motto was, 'I'll be right behind you!'" However, in fairness to Murdock, it should be noted that he was, in fact, standing at the back of his boat.

The dropping of the ramp provoked a controlled stampede.

The guys piled out, and they're shouting: "C'mon, let's go! Move it, move it, MOVE IT!" You don't let anybody slow down. And when I got near the front of the boat I could see that the water was just red with blood, and the bodies, the guys were floating in it, dead and dying. I was one of the last ones out. Bullets were coming into the boat; they were hitting all around. The guys were screaming, yelling. The bow of that boat was zeroed in. All I could see was the bullets splashing in the water. At least six guys were floating when I jumped out into the water.

He did not stop to help them—orders were orders. And despite the carnage, "I never thought I was going to get hit. I was too busy. Actually, once it started, I didn't think of anything but what I was doing. And my thought was, just get to that goddamned beach and reorganize, regroup."

But it would take time to get ashore, and even more to pull the company together. The water was more than waist-high and the noise of battle was deafening, the tumult confusing: "It was horribly loud. Everything was going on at once. The shooting, the machine guns, everyone screaming, yelling, calling for help."

He tried to rally his men.

And at that point I did actually say, "Follow me!" And, "Let's go! C'mon! We gotta get to that beach." And then I began wading through the spray of bullets coming at me. I'd go underwater—I kept ducking under. At first I was trying to hold my weapon out of the water. But forget that. I just hung on to it and dove under. I could see the water splashing as the bullets were coming across and I'd go under. The bullets were coming from all directions, different ways, you really couldn't keep track of anything. But you saw when you should go down.

His objective, *his only objective,* was to get to that beach quickly, just as fast as he could. "That's all I could think of."

★   ★   ★

BM3 Larry Wade, the coxswain of LCVP 13 off USS *Heywood* (APA 6), was involved in the battle for Betio from the very start. During much of the battle he operated under the command of Lt. (jg) Edward Albert Heimberger, a thirty-four-year-old movie actor known to the American public by his stage name, Eddie Albert. Eddie was the salvage boat officer aboard *Sheridan,* responsible for controlling the ship's landing craft. The job of salvage and control would be broadly interpreted at Betio. Larry's duties in that capacity would cause his path and mine to cross, and my life would be saved because of that meeting. It would be accurate to say that his job entailed salvation as well as salvage and that I was one of the many beneficiaries of his good work in that regard.

It was on one of Larry's rescue trips that I was plucked out of the water. Since the boat's ramp couldn't go down all the way, I had to be hauled up over the top. Larry recalled the wounded Marine who pulled me in: "His face was nearly shot off. Part of his ear and his face on that side. He was very strong, very powerful, and burly—maybe 240 or 50 pounds. It was a self-sacrificing thing he did, helping other wounded guys in his condition."

I was not the last Marine Larry rescued. That distinction fell to Ken Desirelli, a nineteen-year-old private, first class from C Company who had gone through boot camp with Bill Crumpacker and, along with Crumpacker and many others, had joined 1st Battalion in New Zealand. Like most of the unblooded replacements, he was not at all apprehensive when the order came to descend the cargo nets and board the LCVPs. "I wasn't nervous because I was dumb," he said, echoing Crumpacker's self-assessment. "I didn't have any fear because I didn't know any better."

In time he would learn more than he ever wanted to know about fear, but first there was the eighteen-plus hours of circling in the staging area beyond the reef to be endured. Ken and his buddies kept themselves occupied as best they could, which is to say almost not at all.

The boat went around and around and we sat on the bottom with our backs to the bulkhead, we gabbed and smoked cigarettes, we walked around as much as we could in the boat's narrow confines, stepping over the outstretched legs of our buddies. If you had to piss, you stood up so you were above the gunwhale and just let go, rocking with the motion of the boat, trying not to get any on you or inside the boat and making sure that you weren't pissing into the wind. We drank from our canteens but I don't recall any of the guys eating. Several guys got sick from the motion of the boat combined with the diesel fumes from the engines. To this day, if I get around a diesel truck it brings back memories of being in that boat.

Finally the boats formed up in line abreast and his coxswain called out, "We're going in." They all got to their feet, standing in a crouch to stay below the gunwales, and readied their weapons and got their gear squared away. As their boat closed on the reef they could hear the bullets zipping past, "making a loud buzzing that sounded like bees swarming around us." Ken wanted to look over the side to scope out the island but didn't dare because the "bees" were getting louder and more numerous; he stayed below the gunwales. "Then— *BANG!*—we hit the reef. We stopped as abruptly as if we had run into a wall, and we all lurched forward. Then the ramp dropped."

Everybody froze. Then somebody told Ken to get going and he stepped onto the ramp. "I wasn't running but I was moving fast; everybody was pushing to get off, and you could only go as fast as the guy in front of you. I jumped into the water, and everywhere around me I could see the little splashes where bullets were striking the water. I could hear shells passing over me, *swisssssh*—it was all very noisy."

He looked off to the right, and about a hundred yards away he saw an LCVP cocked at an angle on the reef, burning furiously. But he didn't see anyone nearby, "because I was focused on the island. It was as if all the guys in my boat had just disappeared and I was alone in the water. I don't remember the pier and I don't remember the wrecked ship and I don't remember the dive-bombers coming in to get it. I had tunnel vision for that island. That was the only thing I saw, or remember seeing."

He headed toward the distant beach. The water was nearly chest-high, and he was hunched over trying to make himself a small target. But not small enough. He had gone about a hundred yards when he was hit. "I felt like somebody had walloped me in the right shoulder with a baseball bat. And I said to myself, *What the hell's that?!* Then I saw that I was bleeding and I knew I'd been hit."

But he pressed on—"because that's what I was supposed to do."

Then I began to think, *Jeeze, I wanna go to sleep. I wanna lie down.* But I didn't stop, and I still had my rifle because I knew I'd be charged fifty bucks if I lost it. That was the main thing that worried me at the time. Meanwhile I'm getting sleepier by the second and my gear is getting heavier. I slipped off my pack and dropped it in the water. I kept going. I wasn't feeling any pain. Now I'm thinking, *Jeez, it sure is a long way in there.* Then for no particular reason I began to wander off toward my right, toward the *Niminoa*. I was just wandering about, standing upright, and I saw bullets hitting the water all around me and I couldn't care less about them. They didn't seem to matter much because they weren't affecting me at all. Then I looked around and saw a Higgins boat with its ramp halfway down and I thought maybe I ought to go over to it.

But the boat seemed so far away and Ken wasn't sure he could make it—he wasn't sure he *wanted* to make it. He was becoming increasingly lethargic and indifferent to his fate: death was creeping over and through him.

It would have been easy for me to just give up and die at this point. I was bleeding a lot and in shock, and all I wanted to do was lie down and go to sleep. But I made my way over to the boat and as I got close to it I could see that they were getting ready to raise the ramp. And I hollered, "Hey, wait! Give me a ride!"

I went over to the ramp but I couldn't pull myself up because my arm wasn't working. So I put my rifle on the ramp and this big guy reached down and grabbed me and lifted me aboard. He was wounded in the face and head and he was all bandaged and bleeding a lot. But he just grabbed me with one arm and picked me up and pulled me in. With one arm! I rolled down the ramp and passed right out.

He probably ended up right beside me, since I had been taken in immediately before him. But I can't say for sure. I wasn't talking to anyone, and he wasn't talking either. We weren't in any condition to talk. We were both barely alive.

Having rescued Ken, and with a full load of wounded Marines in his care, Larry Wade took his boat back to *Sheridan*.

For Ken, me, and the other wounded men in Larry's boat, the battle for Betio was over. We were fighting a different battle, struggling to survive our wounds. More on that in the next chapter. But for those who had survived the long walk to the beach the "real" fighting was just getting started—real in the sense that they could now fight back. Some veterans of Tarawa will tell you that once they got ashore the worst was over, that the wading in was the worst part. Some will say the worst part was the battle on the island. Most will not—or, more accurately, cannot—choose between the two. For most Marines, every part of the battle for Betio was the worst part.

About the same time I was hauled aboard Larry Wade's boat, Dick Stein was still "making like an alligator," heading for the pier but also pushing ever closer to the beach and the relative safety of the seawall. He kept his eyes focused on the shoreline. He knew men were dropping all around him—he could see them out of the corners of his eyes—but he didn't look in their direction. When he was within a few yards of the beach, however, he happened to glance off to one side and saw two Marines, one standing and the other inert and floating on his back, the former with his arm hooked under the latter's chin, bent forward and straining to pull him through the shallow water. Dick thought at first that the inert Marine was wounded, but then he saw the awful gray pallor on the man's face and recognized that he was dead. The other Marine may not have known that his buddy was dead, but in any case he was clearly determined to bring him ashore—dead or alive, he was not going to leave him in the water.

A few seconds later Dick stepped ashore. Momentarily elated, he told himself, *Well, they ain't gonna get me now.* Then he looked around and his elation evaporated. Nearby lay a dead Marine with a Japanese bayonet protruding from his chest and three dead Japanese soldiers sprawled around him. Dead bodies were everywhere, floating in the water, piling up at the waterline, strewn about the beach: guys from the 2d Marines who had landed the day before, guys from the 8th Marines too, and many Japanese.

The beach was strewn with rifles as well as bodies, and he took one off a dead Marine and took the man's ammo clips as well. Now he could fight back.

Close to where Dick came ashore, in a machine-gun position next to the seawall, a lieutenant Dick didn't know, probably from C Company, rose up to look over that barrier with a pair of field glasses. Dick was wondering why the lieutenant needed field glasses—the enemy was so close—when the man suddenly slumped on top of the wall, shot dead. His men pulled him off, and another Marine in that position took his field glasses and got up to look and was instantly shot and killed. "That impressed me," said Dick. "I hadn't been on the island for but a few minutes and already I'd seen two guys get killed right in front of me."

Shortly thereafter Dick met up with Hank Farrell, from Bill Crumpacker's fire team. No sign of Crumpacker, though—Dick had lost track of him. Making their way down the beach, the two men hooked up with Cpl. Wayne Hester, a squad leader from 1st Platoon, and a few others from his unit and our boat—including John Duffy, who had recently saved my life.

The other men from 1st Platoon were either dead or wounded in the water, still struggling to get ashore, or strung along the beach wherever they had landed. Undaunted, Hester got his little group organized and led this ad-hoc squad over the seawall. His aim was to find Murdock, and to that end they began working their way around to the left toward a big bunker where Col. David M. Shoup, CO of the 2d Marines, had established his command post—and which the Japanese still occupied.

Shoup had landed the day before and was in command of American forces on the island, a job he would hold until the third day (D+2), when the division commander, Maj. Gen. Julian C. Smith, came ashore. Shoup's CP was hard up against the outside wall of the bunker. The Japanese inside couldn't get at him, and needless to say, Shoup and his Marines couldn't get at them, at least for the time being. Undeterred by their presence, Shoup, who had already sustained numerous minor but painful wounds, went about the task of directing the chaotic battle as best he could. The Japanese in the bunker would just have to wait their turn.

Dick and the others saw Shoup—but no Murdock. There was an aid station at the CP, and a corpsman came over to Dick, put some powder on his wounded hand, and dressed it. While the corpsman worked on his hand, Dick watched as another man from A Company named Crook was shot in the butt, the round hitting with such force that it knocked him down.

Hester collected his men and led them back to the seawall. They found Murdock near a wrecked amtrac. In the mad rush to reach the wall and jump over it, Duffy somehow got separated from the group; they never saw him again. Sitting with his back to the wall, taking a breather, Dick looked over toward the shore immediately behind Murdock. "The incoming waves had washed dead Marines onto the shore and pushed them into small piles. It looked like a little mound. And on the top of that mound, facing the sky, was Anthony O'Boyle. His helmet was off and the top of his head was shot away, but he wasn't dead yet: his whole body was twitching. Hester looked at him and said to me, 'There's old Anthony.' And I thought, *Boy, that's got to be a hard way to go.*"

Dick reckons that O'Boyle convulsed for up to twenty minutes before he finally stopped moving and died.

Only seconds before, O'Boyle had been standing next to Murdock, peering over the wall. Then a Japanese bullet took the top of his head off, and he fell back into John's arms. John cradled O'Boyle in his arms for a long moment before laying him gently aside. Someone else must have hauled him to the pile of bodies at the water's edge to get him away from the wall.

During this time, someone from the company passing by Dick's position informed them that Duffy had been killed. "Duffy was a very quiet person; never talked much, but a real nice guy," Dick remembered. "He was a little older than most of us, in his early or mid-twenties, which made him an old man in our outfit. He was O'Boyle's best buddy. Now they were both dead, killed within minutes of each other."

After resting up, Hester and his men got down to business. Operating pretty much on their own initiative, without an officer to tell them what to do (Murdock was elsewhere, stalking the beach, looking for his men) and with Hester leading them, Dick Stein, Hank Farrell, and the others followed Hester over the wall to hunt the enemy. The Japanese proved hard to find. Even though they were everywhere, and always very close, they were mostly invisible, ensconced in bunkers, pillboxes, foxholes, and other fortifications and entrenchments. They rarely showed themselves; they didn't have to. They were an unseen presence, firing at the Marines from slits and apertures and camouflaged holes. If you peered over the wall (and didn't get killed in the act), what you saw was a blasted landscape, blackened and cratered by shellfire but nearly deserted. Small parties of Marines would be scurrying this way and that across the chewed-up ground, bent low under the weight of their packs to reduce their exposure to enemy fire, but the Japanese were nowhere in sight. Dubbed the "phenomenon of the empty battlefield" by military thinkers, the conditions that obtained on Betio were a feature of modern warfare forced on armies by the lethality of their weapons. In the circumstances concealment was the best protection; soldiers went to ground and stayed there until compelled by the course of events (and their commanding officers) to move on.

"I never did see too many live Japs that first day," said Dick. "I didn't get off a clear shot at any. I didn't even shoot that much. It was just about impossible to even get a clear shot at them. They were hidden good; every once in awhile they'd run from bunker to bunker and you'd take a shot at 'em, and everybody else would shoot; but you never knew if you hit 'em or not."

For everyone involved, Americans and Japanese, it was a peculiarly nasty way to fight a war. The situation favored the defenders, but only to a point. Battles are not won by staying in fortifications; they are won by attacking, and on Betio the Marines were the attackers. They had to assault each and every Japanese position, making short rushes across open ground through murderous fire. Heavy casualties were the result. But, ultimately, Japanese casualties were heavier—in fact, almost total. The Japanese would not yield, because their military ethos forbade it. To beat them, you had to kill them. But the Marines would not quit, and they could not be stopped. Against a foe such as the Marines, with their absolute determination and capability to win, the initial advantages enjoyed by defenders fighting from concealment could have but one outcome: annihilation. The Japanese meant, as always, to fight to the death, and for the most part, they did. At times they would evacuate a position, displacing to another bunker to continue fighting, but Betio is a tiny island, and you can only displace so many times before you have nowhere else to go. This happened sooner for some Japanese, later for others, and eventually for all.

Before they died, though, they killed many Marines. It seemed to Dick that we were getting the worst of it: "They were picking us off like flies," is how he put it. But the Marines persevered. Dick and the others mainly attacked bunkers and pillboxes. Hester, Dick, and Hank Farrell would scramble over the seawall and throw grenades into a bunker and then go inside to clear it out, finishing off the wounded with their rifles. No mercy could be shown to the wounded Japanese, given their propensity for detonating grenades when the Marines stormed in.

After clearing a bunker the team would dash back to the seawall, throwing themselves over the top and flopping down in the sand, there to rest, drink some water (if it were available), and rearm for their next foray. Dick has no idea how many times they went over the wall that day: "We did it over and over again, out and back, out and back."

Man, I'll tell you, when Farrell and I were going through the pillboxes together, it was hairy as hell. We went down into this one U-shaped pillbox that was covered for a little ways but open to the sky at the end, at the bottom of the U. We went through the covered part all hunched over and then we came to the open part and there're Jap bodies all over the place. I was standing on a body, talking to Farrell, and this arm came snaking over the pillbox wall and its hand was holding a little black grenade. It was just about five feet from me; I could have reached over and shaken that hand, it was that close. Then the arm raised up and the hand dropped the grenade, and I thought, *Uh-oh.*

The grenade fell right at my feet and I thought it was gonna blow me up, or blow my whole crotch off, or my legs. But it rolled between my legs and rolled under the bodies I was standing on and then it exploded. The explosion was unbelievable, it was so loud—deafening. *Oh, my God*, I thought. I felt no pain or anything, but you never know, so I felt my crotch. Everything was okay, I hadn't been hurt, except the blast made my ears ring. Farrell and I backed outta there in a hurry.

But they kept at it, out and back, out and back. All the while the noise of battle was "unbelievably loud, and constant." It had been loud enough out in the water; it had increased by several orders of magnitude on land. "Machine guns, grenades, rifles and small arms, artillery—everyone was blasting away, the din was terrific; you could hardly communicate with each other. You hollered to make yourself heard, even when you were helmet-to-helmet with someone, hollered right in his face."

Finally, with evening coming on, Farrell and Stein joined two other Marines in a pillbox in front of the seawall. The pillbox was octagon shaped, with shoulder-high walls, open on top. Also in residence were two dead Japanese and one dead Marine. Their presence did not upset Dick. He scarcely noticed them, and he certainly didn't care about them. He just wanted to sleep.

★   ★   ★

Bill Crumpacker swam on toward the beach with only his nose and eyes above the surface. As he approached the shore his progress was increasingly hindered by floating bodies and debris. He swam on through that grisly flotsam, pushing bodies aside until the water was too shallow to continue in that manner. He was then a only a few yards from the beach and just a few yards to the right of the pier, and the waterline was thick with corpses that had built up into a low berm that extended all along the shore. He stood and, stepping quickly over the mound of dead Marines, hustled up across the beach and flopped down by the seawall. Sitting with his back against that barrier, he checked on the pack of cigarettes in his jacket pocket. They were dry, and in that moment nothing else mattered to him and he felt pretty good about it and actually told himself that the rest of the day was going to be okay.

Next to him was a Marine who had landed the day before. Bill turned to him and gestured toward *Niminoa* and allowed as how the Japs on "that goddamn ship" had surely killed a lot Marines in the water. The man agreed, saying that he and his buddies had watched as the Japs swam out to the ship during the night. Bill gave the man a hard look. "Well, why the hell didn't you shoot 'em?" said Bill. "I mean, you had a clear field of fire at 'em, right?"

"That's true," the man said. "But then, they had a clear field of fire at us, too."

Then the Marine gave Bill a hard look of his own, a challenge—and a warning. There were many things Bill wanted to say to him, but he held his tongue and decided that the better course of action was to simply move on.

He moved on. He made his way to the right along the beach and shortly came across 2d Lt. Augustus "Gus" Jauregui and several others from B Company crouched below the seawall. Among them was John Duffy.

Jauregui told Bill and Duffy to go over the seawall to take a look around. They jumped over the wall and dove into a crater on the other side. Bill looked over at Duffy, and Duffy wasn't moving. He had lost his helmet, and there was a little welt of blood coming out of a hole in the top of his head. He was dead. Bill had propped his rifle up on the sand piled around the lip of the crater. Now, after looking at Duffy, he moved the rifle just a little without sticking his head up, and just that fast a shot rang out, the incoming round kicking up sand next to the rifle. The enemy sniper was no more than fifteen or twenty feet from the crater, and Bill sensed that he was mocking him with that shot: *I'm here,* the sniper seemed to be saying. *I'm waiting, and when you show yourself I'll kill you too.* Bill pulled the pins on two grenades and hurled them both, one after the other, in the sniper's direction. The instant the second grenade exploded he leapt up and threw himself back over the seawall.

He sat there for a few minutes, breathing hard, trying to calm himself. He was scared and frazzled but also very angry. He wondered why Jauregui had sent them over the wall: "We didn't accomplish anything—couldn't accomplish anything—and Duffy had gotten himself killed."

After that, Bill began firing over the seawall, rising above the rim for just as long as it took to get off a few shots and then ducking down again. The Marines directed their fire at the slits and apertures of the enemy fortifications in hopes of making the defenders mad enough to come out and fight. Mad the Japanese might have been, and in every sense of that word, but they would not come out, at least not in groups. Individuals were constantly moving around, though, darting from one hole to another and popping up and down—"like prairie dogs," said Bill—to squeeze off shots at the Marines.

Bill's group began to take more aggressive action.

> We'd go over the seawall and attack a pillbox, a bunker, a dugout, whatever. We'd crawl up right next to the slits and poke our rifles into them and just pull the trigger again and again, firing an entire clip, never knowing whether or not we got anyone. Some of the dugouts had pretty big openings, and we'd creep up to these from one or both sides and pour fire into it and then throw in some grenades. In every one of these forays a few guys would get hit, some would get killed. But we kept going, over and over again, surging forward and surging back, forward and back.

★   ★   ★

John Murdock came ashore just a few yards to the left of amtrac LVT1-44, which had been knocked out the day before as it was grinding over the top of the seawall. Years later, he was able to pinpoint where he landed after seeing a photograph of the wrecked vehicle on the cover of Joseph Alexander's monograph *Across the Reef: The Marine Assault of Tarawa*. Taken in the immediate aftermath of the battle, the photo shows the amtrac canted with its front end up on the wall's coconut logs and its back end down in the water. The tide has come in, with the water reaching all the way to the wall, and at least one body—almost certainly that of a Marine—can be seen floating in the foreground. The Marine photographer snapped the picture from the vehicle's left as you face inland—the exact spot, more or less, where John first set foot on Betio.

The beach at this spot was about thirty feet wide from the waterline to the wall. The height of the wall varied but was probably about four or five feet, offering some protection to those who stayed down behind it. But John did not stay down, and he did not stay put either. Instead he moved up and down the beach to see what had happened to B Company and to get it assembled and organized for offensive action.

The casualty toll was nothing less than catastrophic. In New Zealand the company had been beefed up to a little over two hundred men to give it extra punch in the assault; ninety were lost, killed, or wounded in the Betio lagoon. In other words, nearly half of the company was out of action *before anyone stepped ashore.*

The men Murdock found on the beach "were all exhausted, with this terrible look on their faces." But their shock and exhaustion did not, could not, concern him. "What I was more interested in was who was alive and who have I got, what have I got." To make that assessment, he continued "rounding up the guys on the beach, getting them back to my area."

At the same time, he was taking inventory of the weapons they had brought ashore. This meant more than merely counting rifles. In addition to their own weapons his men carried parts of disassembled crew-served weapons—mortars and machine guns—and the ammunition that went with them. He recalls yelling at people above the din of the battle, asking them what they had, and he located most of B Company's officers who had made it ashore. I was conspicuous by my absence, and John figured I had been killed.

All the while, enemy fire was flailing the beach. John ignored it. And when Anthony O'Boyle was shot and fell into his arms he wasn't fazed. And once he had laid O'Boyle's twitching body aside he didn't think about him anymore. He didn't have the time, much less the inclination, to grieve for Boyle or to feel horror for the slow, hideous way O'Boyle died. Instead he did his job. He will tell you that he did so not out of bravery but because he was simply preoccupied. But take my word for it: he was brave.

At length he got a number of his men and officers assembled around him. He took stock of the situation, saying to himself: *Now, what we gotta do is, we gotta get over this seawall.*

And his men, as told, went over the seawall, again and again. They didn't go far, typically diving into a crater abutting the wall on the enemy side, and they quickly returned, forced back after a few minutes by the withering enemy fire. Circumstances being what they were, John ruled out a concerted effort by his unit to storm the No man's land beyond the wall, knowing that his group would be wiped out in the attempt.

Finally the sun went down. John and his men spent a harrowing night on the beach, "packed in like sardines" against the seawall. The expected Japanese counterattack did not materialize and the fighting slackened. During this comparative lull John's men generally did not fire their weapons, but neither were they wholly inactive. Some went over the wall again, and this time they stayed on the other side, establishing footholds in the pocked ground beyond.

John, overcome by the day's exertions, collapsed in the sand and fell sound asleep. He was awakened in the night by a marauding Japanese bomber. The aircraft came in very low, flying just above the wall and along its length, dropping small bombs and strafing with its machine guns. A second lieutenant who also happened to be the son of an admiral threw himself on top of John, covering John's head and shoulders and upper back. John lay perpendicular to the wall, his legs extending back toward the waterline; the second lieutenant lay parallel to the wall and against it. The machine-gun bullets from the strafing plane spattered the wall and the ground a few inches on either side of it, and if that second lieutenant had not been on top of John, it is likely that John would have been hit in the head. A bullet or a piece of shrapnel struck his shoe, taking a piece out of it but leaving him unharmed. The second lieutenant was not so fortunate: he was hit in both arms. John carried him to a corpsman, but to no avail: the admiral's son died of shock before morning.

★ ★ ★

And the evening and the morning were the third day of the battle for Betio.

For Dick Stein, that third day of the operation—the second day of fighting for him and the rest of the 8th Marines—started with more of the same—going over the seawall and coming back, again and again. Fighting and killing the Japanese, still mostly invisible. But not for long.

Later that morning Dick and Red Nelson and 1st Lt. Newell T. Berg were resting next to the sheltering bulk of the wrecked LVT1-44. A pillbox was situated some distance in front of their position, and Berg went over the wall, crawled through enemy fire to the top of the installation, and dropped a white phosphorous grenade down the air vent. A few seconds passed, then they heard an explosion inside. White smoke poured from the entrance and as many as fifteen Japanese burst forth in panic, pushing and shoving each other, desperate to get out. Dick and Red Nelson fired a few shots.

"Don't shoot!" Berg shouted. "Let 'em run!"

Wise decision: Berg didn't want bodies clogging the entrance. Stein and Nelson ceased firing. As many as two dozen Japanese emerged, and the Marines waited until they were about forty feet from the entrance and then opened fire. Other Marines in the immediate vicinity also opened fire, and a slaughter ensued, lasting about a minute. The Japanese were all bunched up, easy to hit, and Red Nelson was very excited, shouting, "Oh, boy! This is like shootin' rabbits!'"

This was the same Red Nelson who had been hit by a Tommy gun round on Guadalcanal, the slug hitting him in one shoulder and traveling around his spine and lodging in his other shoulder. He was later killed on Iwo Jima. He should have been sent home after Tarawa, maybe after Guadalcanal. Nelson had long since "gone Asiatic," Marine-speak for someone who had become unhinged from too much overseas service, too much combat, maybe even too much time as a Marine.

The signs of going Asiatic were usually subtle at first, taking the form of eccentric behavior that was customarily tolerated if it didn't interfere with job performance. Which made sense, in the prewar era especially. If every Old Salt who behaved eccentrically had been discharged, the Marine Corps really would have been reduced to a just "few good men," and very few at that. But going Asiatic meant going beyond mere eccentricity, far beyond: it meant going insane. Red Nelson had been going insane since Guadalcanal. According to Dick, when we were in New Zealand Red spent a lot of time just lying on his bunk muttering endlessly and unintelligibly to the wall of the tent. He became a casualty of war long before he was killed.

★   ★   ★

Dawn found Bill Crumpacker and four other Marines under the command of Gus Jauregui hunkered down next to a pillbox out in front of the seawall. In a virtual replay of the previous day's action when Duffy was killed, Jauregui decided to take his group back behind the wall. "Let's go!" he said, leaping to his feet. In the next instant he fell to his knees, blood gushing from a bullet wound in his neck. First Lt. Warren Keck ran over and tried to help, but Jauregi could not be saved and died within seconds of being shot. The other men took off running, scattering as they ran. "We had only twenty yards to go," said Bill, "but that was a long way on Tarawa. We didn't try to cover the whole distance all at once. I was with George Wasicek, and we got about ten yards and were taking fire so we jumped into a shell hole. We had been in that shell hole for twenty or twenty-five minutes when I told George, 'Well, hell, we can't lay here all day. We better take a shot at it.' So we jumped up and threw ourselves over the wall."

They landed unscathed. One other Marine in Jauregui's group made it back. Two did not: Pfc. Ray Cywinski was killed and Pfc. Harold Engen went missing. Engen, a star basketball player from my hometown, later turned up wounded and would recover with me at Pearl Harbor naval hospital.

Later that day several of them went over the wall again. They began taking fire almost immediately and threw themselves into a rifle pit among six or seven dead Japanese. A connecting tunnel led away from the pit, and a sergeant armed with a flamethrower jumped in among them and told them to follow him down the tunnel. The moment he entered the tunnel, however, a shot rang out and he took a bullet in his leg. The group backed hastily out of the tunnel and returned to the rifle pit. One of the Marines stood and cocked his arm to throw a grenade into the tunnel but was shot in the shoulder and dropped the live grenade to the floor of the pit. *Oh, for crissakes!* Crumpacker thought, pressing back against the pit's circular metal wall, *here we go.* The grenade went off with a huge bang. Bill looked around and saw that everyone was okay, the Japanese corpses having protected them from the blast. "And I thought, *Hey, those were good Japs!* Double good—they were dead and they had saved our lives!"

He wasn't always so lucky. During one of the men's surges over the wall a hand grenade went off nearby, and a fragment hit him in the thigh just above the knee. It didn't do any real damage—just a flesh wound, very shallow, a gash about an inch and a quarter long. It didn't inhibit his leg movement. He didn't even put a dressing on it, and he wasn't about to go looking for a corpsman to bandage a wound so minor. Shortly the wound got packed with coral and stopped bleeding on its own. He finally got it cleaned and dressed after the battle, when the battalion returned to *Sheridan.*

Toward the middle of the day Bill noticed that things seemed to be getting a little better for the Marines—they seemed to be making some progress. Bulldozers had landed by then, and they pushed sand up against the pillbox entrances, sealing them and entombing the Japanese inside. "But the flamethrowers really did the trick. A flamethrower operator would get up to one of the pillboxes while we poured fire on every opening to keep the Japs down. The flamethrower would douse the pillbox, just burn it out, and then the bulldozer would roll in and push sand over the opening, covering them up."

★   ★   ★

At first light John Murdock took his men over the wall, joining those who had gone over during the night. He quickly found a big, deep hole and established his command post in it. The hole was some twenty to thirty yards from the seawall; on Tarawa, as Bill Crumpacker observed, that was a long way.

The 1st Battalion had been ordered to wheel to the right and sweep west on a three-company front into a complex of fortifications and entrenchments along the north shore between Red Beach 1 and Red Beach 2. But B Company, which was to advance along the shoreline, wasn't moving fast enough. In fact, it was scarcely moving at all and was holding up the whole operation. Major Hays met with John to express his frustration: "Reading my ass off," is how John put it. John was desperate and despairing, "praying I'd get shot so I could get the hell out of there. Everything I had tried didn't work. And guys were getting killed all around. You couldn't move. You couldn't advance. The terrain was chewed up, flat, just a mess of everything. The emplacements were still up."

At length a halftrack with a 75-mm cannon mounted on it arrived. Murdock told 2d Lt. Mark Thomlinson to get in the vehicle and direct the gunners. But the gun couldn't penetrate the enemy bunkers. The shells would gouge a shallow hole in the concrete, but coral and sand would slide down and fill it. Then Thomlinson, standing at the back of the halftrack, was killed by a burst of machine-gun fire that cut him nearly in half.

John climbed into the vehicle over Thomlinson's shredded body to see what, if anything, he could do. He saw at once that the gun was useless and jumped back out. Calling his platoon leaders to his side, he commenced to read them off. "C'mon!" he shouted. "If your men can't do the job, goddamn it, do it yourself!"

"I was pissed off," he later explained.

Thus inspired, 1st Lt. Charles McNeil started off with a small group that constituted the remnant of his platoon. He hadn't gone but a few feet when a shot rang out. He grabbed his groin and fell to the ground, dead.

Where the hell did that come from? John said to himself.

The platoon leader's sergeant ran over to the spot where McNeil had fallen. Same thing happened: another shot, and the sergeant grabbed his groin and fell, dead before he hit the ground.

John couldn't see who was killing his men. The ground where McNeil and the sergeant now lay was flat and open. Then one of John's men yelled, "Hey, Lieutenant, c'mere, lookit this." The man pointed at a drainage ditch with metal covers, mostly covered over with coral but with slots between the covers. John realized that the Japanese were in the ditch, shooting up through the slots at any Marine who stepped over them. The bullet would enter the man's groin and travel up through his body, ripping apart his internal organs and killing him instantly.

John had his men insert a bangalore torpedo into one of the slots. When they detonated it, every Japanese soldier in the ditch was killed. John checked the bodies and found no wounds or marks on any of them. They had been killed by the concussive force of the explosion.

The way was now open for B Company to advance, at least for a few yards. They pushed on to their next objective, an emplacement near the seawall. John and George Stein climbed up on top of it. There was ditch on the other side with a Japanese soldier at the bottom, lying on his back and aiming an automatic pistol at George. He had a clear shot at George but for some reason didn't shoot. And he didn't see John, who was standing just eight to ten feet behind him, looking down at the back of his head. John motioned to his men to be quiet. Then he aimed his carbine at the enemy soldier and squeezed the trigger. Nothing. He squeezed the trigger again and again—nothing. Then he realized that the weapon's safety was engaged.

"Oh, shit!" John exclaimed.

The Japanese soldier, hearing this, looked up and back at John and pointed his pistol at him. John dove across the ditch, but still the man didn't shoot. He just turned his head, following John with his pistol. John pulled the pin on a grenade and threw it at the enemy soldier. The latter, swinging his pistol like a baseball bat, knocked the grenade away. It exploded harmlessly a few yards from the ditch. John scurried to get around behind the man and threw two more grenades at him. The Japanese soldier knocked both away with his pistol. John pulled the pin on a fourth grenade, released the lever, and counted: "One, two, three." Then he threw the grenade. This time it went off before the Japanese soldier could bat it away, and that was the end of him.

John believes that the man didn't fire his weapon, because he had run out of ammunition. He is probably right. John took this as a sign that things were finally starting to go their way. He was right about that too. It was now early afternoon and John detected a slight but perceptible shift in the battle's momentum. "All of a sudden," he said, "things began to move. We were moving, but very, very slowly. Like a snail. My guys would go out ahead of me, and they'd be moving, and I'd run up with my gang and get in behind them. We were all very close to the enemy, a matter of feet, not yards. It was very small, very slow progress."

But it was progress nonetheless. For the first time since they had landed the day before, the men of B Company were advancing and not falling back after each forward push. The Japanese meant to fight to the last man, and they were coming ever closer to realizing that goal. Marine assault teams, mostly ad-hoc assemblages, destroyed the enemy bunkers one after another, killing the Japanese while they were still inside or when they ran out. The Japanese were slain literally in heaps. As their numbers were reduced, so too was the volume and intensity of their fire.

B Company pushed on. Around mid-afternoon a major from the 6th Marines arrived on the scene. The 6th Marines had begun landing at Green Beach on the island's western end toward dusk on D+1. The regimental combat team was now ashore and advancing east on a front extending from 1st Battalion's sector and across the airstrip to the island's southern shore. The 1/8 was moving west along the northern shore at the same time. The major had somehow gotten separated from his battalion and now found himself among the Marines of B/1/8. He saw that he outranked John Murdock by two grades and immediately asserted his authority, telling John what he was doing wrong and how he should run his company. But B Company was doing just fine and John wasn't doing anything wrong, and he wasn't about to let anyone tell him what to do. "I had a lot of words with him then," John said. "Choice words. I told him to get the hell out of there. I said, 'I don't know who the hell you are, but go back to your own outfit. That's where you belong. Not with me. This is my company. Nobody tells me what to do with my company.'"

The major took the measure of John's mood and wisely backed off and departed. But this was not the last John would see of him.

Finally, when John and his men had advanced as far as they could go, the battle "just sort of petered out." The shooting stopped, bringing silence to their sector of the battlefield and leaving everyone stunned by the abrupt end to the fighting. They didn't know quite what to do, and so "we just kind of sat down there and did nothing."

Bill Crumpacker remembered that it was late in the afternoon, around 1530, when "the shooting died down real fast and ended." Bill and his group were then next to the cove in the area where Red Beach 2 and Red Beach 1 met. "Nobody said, 'Okay, boys, it's over.' Everybody just sort of hung around in a daze, looking at each other, looking at the terrain. I remember thinking, *I guess I handled it all right.* But I also couldn't quite get a grip on what had happened. It was still, *I can't believe this. I . . . just . . . cannot . . . believe it.*"

Dick Stein recalled that "the battle didn't die down gradually, it didn't drag on; it just seemed like it was over. Bang! Just like that. Suddenly there was no more shooting. It just quit."

At the east end of the island the fighting would continue into the next day, with the 2d and 3d battalions of the 8th Marines taking part. But it was all over for the men of the 1/8 by the end of D+2. They had accomplished their mission: all enemy positions and pockets of resistance in the Red 2–Red 1 sector had been eliminated, and the eastward advance of the 6th Marines from Green Beach had effectively pinched them out of the rest of the fighting. They thought all the Japanese in their sector were dead. They thought they could take it easy.

And they did. John and several of his men were sitting, leaning their backs against the berm of an emplacement, talking softly, smoking cigarettes, or simply staring off into space in stunned amazement at their survival, when John's first sergeant suddenly straightened and stared intensely at a clump of straw sticking up out of the ground a few feet away.

After a second or two he said, "I think there's beer over there."

This first sergeant was an Old Salt who had served in China and had there come to know a few things about Asians, including the Japanese. For instance, and crucially in the circumstances, he knew that Japanese soldiers wrapped their beer bottles in straw.

In a flash the sergeant, Murdock, and several other men were on their knees around the straw, clawing at the sand with their fingers. Within the space of a few seconds they had uncovered two or three bottles of beer. A few seconds after that they were drinking from them. The beer was warm and bitter, and it burned going down like cheap whiskey, but it was nectar of the gods as far as these Marines were concerned. The bottles were passed around and all hands got a taste—a few sips, perhaps—and that little bit was all they needed to become mildly and pleasantly intoxicated, seeing as how they had eaten little or nothing in the past three days.

Evening found them back to leaning against the berm, feeling relaxed, a little drunk, and pretty damn good about themselves and the world. A private sauntered by, and Murdock called out companionably to him, "Hey, you want a beer?" And he said, "Yeah, sure!" And Murdock, gesturing toward the hole where the beer was cached, said, "Well, start digging!"

Everything was beautiful; everyone was wonderful. Murdock closed his eyes and fell fast asleep.

He slept all through the night and did not awake until sunup the next morning. During the night, on the island's east end, the Japanese launched a number of counterattacks. All were beaten back with the usual uproar of gunfire and explosions. John never heard a thing. Very probably most of the Marines around him—which is to say, those who had imbibed Japanese beer the evening before—slept as soundly. And why not? They had nothing to fear. Or so they thought.

The morning was waxing fair, and John and his men were lolling about like young lords when two Marine interpreters approached the emplacement's entrance with a Korean laborer in tow. The Korean began shouting into the emplacement, and a few seconds later some ten Korean laborers emerged.

John looked at his first sergeant; his first sergeant looked at him. "Holy shit!" John exclaimed. The first sergeant nodded solemnly. Korean laborers were technically noncombatants. But they were with the Japanese and were therefore considered dangerous. Certainly it would have been easy for these Koreans to creep out of their emplacement during the night and kill John and his slumbering Marines. Fortunately for the Marines, the Koreans had no desire to die for the Japanese emperor.

Later that day 1st Battalion marched over to the pier, where LCVPs waited to take them back out to *Sheridan*. On their way they witnessed a dual flag-raising ceremony for the Stars and Stripes and the British Union Jack, with a representative from His Majesty's government presiding. The Stars and Stripes went up first, but the Union Jack was given pride of place, on a higher pole, an acknowledgment of British sovereignty over the Tarawa Atoll. There were some muttered complaints from the men of the 1/8, but not much. Most just smiled grimly and shook their heads. Great Britain may have held title to Betio, but the Marine Corps truly owned it, now and forever.

CHAPTER SEVEN

Hawaiian Interlude

THE BATTLE FOR BETIO LASTED SEVENTY-SIX HOURS. Some 4,690 Japanese troops—about 97 percent of the garrison—died. A mere 17 Japanese were taken prisoner, as were 129 Korean laborers.*

The 2d Marine Division suffered 3,407 casualties. Of these, 1,115 Marines and sailors were killed and another 2,292 were wounded. The assault units lost 41 percent of their men, dead and wounded. The 1st Battalion, 8th Marines, lost more than 30 percent of its men just getting to the beach. Overall, the battalion suffered 343 casualties—108 killed and 235 wounded. Casualties in my platoon were 12 killed and 15 wounded (including myself), 75 percent of its original strength. Most were hit while wading ashore.

The names of those killed are: Pfc. Robert Bemis, Pfc. John Creech, Pfc. Raymond Cywinski, Pfc. Victor Damen, Pfc. John Duffy, Pvt. John Jacob, Pfc. Elias Kuykendall, Pfc. Anthony O'Boyle, Pfc. Walter Reeves, Pfc. Perley Sargent, Pfc. Kenneth Welch, and Pvt. James Ross.

Those who were wounded, excluding myself: Pvt. H. L. Carmichael, Pfc. John Durst, Pfc. Harold Engen, Pfc. James Harris, Pfc. Elwood Ferguson, Pfc. James Gibson, Pvt. Charles Lambert, Corp. D. J. Laughrey, Pfc. John McGrew, Pvt. Edward Mc Burnie, Pfc. Israel Rodriguez, Pfc. Richard Stein, Pfc. Henry van Acker Jr., and Pfc. Kenneth S. Welch.

Several newspaper reporters took part in the operation and provided accurate accounts of the battle as they experienced it. What each journalist experienced, however, was not the battle in full but a microcosm of it, narrowly

---

* Figures are from *Across the Reef: The Marine Assault on Tarawa*, by Col. Joseph H. Alexander, USMC (Ret.), (1993).

perceived and understood. The newspapers published those accounts without providing much in the way of a broader context, nor were they in any way restrained in their presentations. They took the story as it was given to them and ran with it, playing up the carnage-and-mayhem angle to the fullest.

This was not hard to do. Carnage and mayhem were salient features of the battle for Betio, and as such demanded much attention if the battle was to be honestly and realistically portrayed. But an honest and realistic portrayal would also have gotten across the fact that the Marines had won a great and important victory. This should have been the emphasis. The carnage and mayhem should have been described and explained in the context of that victory, but by and large, the media failed to do that. Instead they conveyed the sense that Tarawa had been a debacle.

Time magazine's 6 December account, based chiefly on the reportage of the inimitable Robert Sherrod, struck a common journalistic chord: "Last week some 2,000 or 3,000 U.S. Marines, most of them now dead or wounded, gave the nation a new name to stand beside those of Concord Bridge, the Bon Homme Richard, the Alamo, Little Big Horn and Belleau Wood. The name was Tarawa." These words were meant to stir the magazine's readers, and the article that followed was intended to be no less affecting. And so it proved—although in ways that the editors had perhaps not intended.

Sherrod had been in the thick of the fighting from the first day to the last, having landed on Red Beach 2 with the 2/2 Marines in the fourth wave of the opening assault. A writer of keen insight with powers of observation unsurpassed in his profession as well as the literary skills to exploit them, his narrative of the battle as he experienced it was gripping and adhered scrupulously to the facts. Americans who read his and other accounts were stirred, all right: to outrage. They wanted answers and accountability. Nor were they alone in this sentiment. Harsh words of blame and recrimination were exchanged at the highest levels of government and military command. Maj. Gen. Julian C. Smith was called before Congress to testify about "Bloody Tarawa," and a few congressmen briefly mooted the idea of conducting a special investigation.

In the final pages of the book he wrote about the battle (*Tarawa*, first published in 1944, before the war's end), Sherrod professed amazement over the mostly negative attitude about the "finest victory that U.S. troops had won in this war." He attributed that attitude to the "great chasm that separates the pleasures of peace from the horrors of war." The American people still had a peacetime attitude and found it impossible to bridge that chasm, in part because they "had not thought of war in terms of men being killed—war seemed so far away."

Sherrod went on to discuss Operation Galvanic in terms of the challenges Betio presented, the unforeseen problems we had encountered, and how the lessons we had learned in overcoming them would serve us in good stead in future operations. But he was quick to emphasize that even if we had gone into Betio knowing exactly what we would be facing and fully prepared to meet all exigencies, the battle would nonetheless have produced heavy casualties. The facts were cruel but inescapable: "There is no easy way to win the war, there is no panacea which will prevent men from getting killed. To . . . deprecate the Tarawa victory was almost to defame the memory of the gallant men who lost their lives achieving it." Why, he asked, did the American public "not realize that there would be many other bigger and bloodier Tarawas in the three or four years of the Japanese war following the first Tarawa?"

Note that Sherrod was anticipating a war lasting into 1946 or 1947, a fair assessment at the time. This was assuming, of course, that Americans would have the will to prosecute the war to a decisive end: the total defeat and unconditional surrender of Japan. Sherrod was doubtful. Total defeat would necessarily entail the invasion and conquest of the Japanese home islands, vast operations that would result in equally vast losses. Sherrod did not think Americans were prepared to make the sacrifices that invasion would require. Their reaction to Tarawa, which, terrible as it was, merely presaged much worse to come, was evidence of that.

Sherrod blamed this situation on a media that was supposed to inform and educate Americans about the war—and had failed miserably at both tasks. Put simply, "many Americans were not prepared psychologically to accept the cruel facts of war." By contrast, the men on Tarawa knew those cruel facts full well—and accepted them. "On Tarawa," Sherrod wrote, "late in 1943, there was a more realistic approach to the war than there was in the United States."

He could not know when he wrote his book that the panacea that would prevent American men from getting killed, and whose existence he denied, was then under development. I'm referring, of course, to the atomic bombs, the use of which shortened a war that might otherwise have lasted at least as long as Sherrod predicted and almost certainly would have resulted in catastrophic American casualties and possibly the near annihilation of the Japanese as a people.

★   ★   ★

At Tarawa, for a little while, it seemed that I would become one of Sherrod's "cruel facts." The hours of crisis came immediately following my return to

Sheridan, when I was very close to death. I can't say whether I was psychologically prepared to die—that I had accepted the looming fact of my own demise.
It is true that I was calm and quiet when brought aboard the ship. But it is also
true that I was numb with shock and stupefied by all the morphine that had
been pumped into me. I wasn't thinking clearly; I was hardly thinking at all. My
mind was shutting down, perhaps in anticipation of my body doing the same,
and I simply lacked the ability to get upset. If that counts as acceptance, then
you can mark me down as one of the most accepting Marines at Tarawa.

No sooner had my stretcher touched down on *Sheridan's* deck than I was
whisked away to the operating room in the depths of the ship. I was one of
the first wounded Marines to be treated, and the medical team was fresh and
rested and ready to go to work on me. I guess that qualifies as a stroke of good
future. Even better fortune awaited me in the operating room in the form of
Lt. Cdr. Lloyd Sussex, formerly an abdominal specialist at the Mayo Clinic,
now the key member of a three-man team of (two doctors and a corpsman)
that would save my life.

I was placed on an operating table, and the corpsman cut off my uniform
and turned me on my side to administer a spinal anesthetic—and all the pain
went instantly away. Then they put me on my back and erected a small tent
over my lower abdomen and got down to the business at hand.

The operation lasted about an hour. I was conscious the whole time and
didn't feel any pain. The doctors spent most of that hour bent over my lower
body, and although I could not see what they were doing, I could hear the little
clicking and snipping sounds made by their instruments as they worked. They
went into me at the bullet's point of entry and all but ignored the tiny exit
wound in my lower back except to put a patch on it. They spoke only rarely
to me and tersely to each other in soft utterances that were muffled but still
intelligible behind their surgical masks. They were guarded and business-like
in what they said, and I heard nothing that might give me cause for worry.
But they repeatedly glanced up at me to see how I was doing and frequently
checked my eyes for dilation, their own eyes narrow with the concern they
otherwise concealed.

Meanwhile I felt myself getting weaker and weaker. All I wanted to do
was just go to sleep. I was slipping away, a sign that shock was overcoming
my system. But I fought the urge to sleep, because I thought that if I lost
consciousness the doctors would give up on me and move on to the next
wounded man even before I died. So I watched them as they watched me,
and I made sure that they knew that I was still with them. Somehow I stayed

awake, and somehow they arrested my descent into oblivion. They repaired my bladder and removed a portion of my large intestine and gave me a blood transfusion. Then they closed my wound and that was that. I had made it through surgery, but it had been a close call. Dr. Sussex later told me that I could not have survived another two hours because of the toxins that were building up inside me.

Afterward I was installed in a bunk in sickbay with a corpsman assigned to stay with me through the night. I had tubes in me, tubes everywhere: tubes feeding fluids into me, tubes draining fluids from me. A heat tent was erected over me on the theory that it would help ward off shock. It was the last thing I needed. The temperature in sickbay was over 100 degrees and the air was saturated with moisture. I protested to the corpsman: "How long is this going to be on me?" He said, "It stays on you all night. You gotta keep it on. You're in shock." I became delirious and was later told that I spent much of the night trying to pull down the heat tent, with the corpsman restraining me.

A few days later I was checked over by a younger doctor, a gloomy fellow with a bedside manner to match. He told me dolefully that my wound was very serious and that I wouldn't live much past my fifties. What sort of doctor says such things to his patients? I reported his words to Dr. Sussex, who was appalled. "He shouldn't have told you that," Sussex said. "And there's no truth to it anyway!"

By then the units that had fought on Betio had returned to *Sheridan*, their numbers greatly reduced. A movie was screened in the ship's makeshift theater, a piece of Hollywood fluff whose title I forget and which was utterly out of sync with the way everyone felt. Even so, I made a point of attending. I struggled out of my bunk and walked all stooped over into the theater. My buddies could hardly believe their eyes. "Oh, my God, here's Ladd!" they exclaimed. First they'd heard I was dead, then they were told that I was grievously wounded, all torn up, a basket case, and now here I was, walking into the movie theater. They were grinning and laughing, amazed and delighted. As was I. It was good to be alive.

Apart from that one instance, and not counting trips to the head (after the tubes had been removed), I remained in my bunk in sickbay during the rest of the voyage to Hawaii, our next destination after Tarawa. The guys visited me often, and Platoon Sergeant Sappington came by to give me his written casualty report, a short but shocking document.

I didn't mourn for the dead; I didn't feel much in the way of grief. I had survived Tarawa. I had survived getting shot in the gut, a usually fatal wound, and I had neither the energy nor the inclination to dwell on all those who didn't make it. Not yet, anyway. When my buddies visited me it was all happy talk and laughter. My wound made laughing painful, but what the heck, it was a small price to pay. The only thing that really bothered me was the way everyone smelled. No one had thought to provide the victors of Tarawa with a change of clothes. They were still wearing the same dungarees they had worn on Betio, and they stank of death and sweat and smoke. Mostly of death. I could practically smell them coming down the corridor, and when they entered sickbay they filled the whole place with that terrible stench.

★   ★   ★

While I was recovering from my surgery, John Murdock dropped by to give me a samurai sword he had "souvenired" on Betio. "Hold on to it for me until I return," he said. He assumed that I had gotten the million-dollar wound and would be sent home (I thought the same). Left unspoken but implicit in what he said was that he didn't think he would be coming home: the sword was probably mine to keep. His was the common sentiment. I would venture to say that after Tarawa most 2d Division Marines didn't believe they would make it through the war.

★   ★   ★

After leaving Tarawa Atoll on 24 November *Sheridan* steamed to Pearl Harbor, arriving at the naval base nine days later. The ship rode high in the water, rolling on the swells, considerably lighter than it had been before Tarawa, having left so much of its human ballast behind on Betio. Frequently held burials at sea further lightened the load. The men who returned to *Sheridan* looked like hell—no surprise there, since they had spent the past three days in what was, if not hell itself, then a place that closely resembled it. To a man they were filthy and exhausted, physically and emotionally. They looked both stunned and angry, as if they'd all been whacked in the back of the head with a two-by-four and were still trying to figure out what had hit them. Hollow eyes and thousand-yard stares. Their clothes in tatters, stinking of death.

For the first few days of the voyage they just sort of sat around and talked with each other, quiet conversations about what they'd experienced, what they'd seen, the buddies they'd lost. So many were gone—good friends, members of our family. They could hardly believe what they'd been through. They could hardly believe they were alive.

Murdock took a head count of B Company, using a prebattle roster for reference, checking off one name after another from the list. He had known that the toll would be large, but even so he was shocked by the final count. *My God*, he thought; *my God*.

An announcement was made over the ship's PA system instructing us to bring our dungarees to the ship's laundry. This was no act of charity on the Navy's part. The stench of death permeated the ship, and the swabbies didn't like it. The Marines were happy to oblige them but could do so only with difficulty, if at all. They were wearing all the clothes they had. Their sea bags with their extra clothing had been left in New Zealand and were gone forever.

Many men had boarded the ship with their dungarees literally in tatters. Most had used their KA-BARs to hack off the legs and the sleeves. Their ragged, cut-off clothing, beard stubble, and haunted faces gave them the look of semidemented beachcombers after a weekend of binge drinking. Some men turned their clothes over for laundering and went about in nothing but their skivvies until they got them back. Others took saltwater showers while fully clothed. Many did nothing at all. They simply did not care that they stank. They didn't want to go to the trouble of taking their clothes to the ship's laundry and then waiting for them to be washed. They were too tired for all that. They just wanted to sit down and rest and be left alone.

The generally somber mood improved dramatically when the Marines noticed after a couple of days that the ship was bearing steadily northeast. Since they had not yet been told that our destination was Hawaii, they assumed they were going home, back to the States. The prospect warmed their hearts and also aroused their pecuniary instincts. They knew there was a great demand in the States for Japanese souvenirs, and hence a great opportunity to make money—a lot of money. Many of them had collected and accumulated Japanese bric-a-brac of all sorts during the Guadalcanal campaign and the battle for Betio: rising sun flags, Japanese money, bayonets and swords, equipment, articles of clothing, and other personal effects. Others who had not bothered to collect souvenirs realized they could manufacture the aforesaid items aboard ship and later pass them off to unwitting customers as the real thing. And that is what they did.

In short order *Sheridan* became a floating workshop, the 8th Marines a crafts guild. The Marines fashioned Japanese dog tags out of wooden orange crates and made small Japanese flags—red meatball on a white background—on some sort of cotton fabric, probably sheets. The idea of printing Japanese currency was mooted but quickly discarded, because we didn't have a printing press. But no matter, the Marines already had stacks of Japanese paper money and lots of coins as well, mostly taken from corpses on Betio.

Every ambulatory Marine stood at the rails when *Sheridan* docked at Pearl Harbor on 2 December. The mood aboard ship was jubilant now, because everyone thought this was just a temporary stop to pick up supplies before continuing on to San Diego. The Marines also thought they would receive their back pay and be given liberty on Oahu before shoving off for the States.

Sheridan was the first troopship to return from Tarawa, and its arrival was heralded on the wharf by a band that belted out military airs amid a crowd of onlookers cheering and yelling for souvenirs. Two shore patrolmen were posted at the bottom of the gangway to prevent any impromptu departures by the passengers. The crowd below was growing by the minute and becoming noisier, even unruly. Bill Crumpacker recalled: "We began tossing Nip coins down on the docks and soon had about two hundred people scrambling after them—officers and enlisted men, civilians, soldiers, sailors, and Marines. Some coins would roll, of course, and there would be four or five men running after a particular coin." The Marines were vastly amused by this spectacle and threw coins in every direction, hooting and roaring with laughter as packs of would-be collectors descended on a coin and fought over it, snarling and thrashing like wild dogs fighting over carrion.

They threw pennies, too, an act of pure malice and high hilarity. When the victor of the ensuing scuffle emerged from the scrum to find he had acquired the least valuable of American coins, he hollered and swore at the Marines and whipped the penny back up at them. The Marines, wouldn't you know, just laughed all the harder.

"Then we located buckets and ropes and began selling our genuine Japanese souvenirs," said Crumpacker. "Someone on the dock would offer a set sum and we would lower the bucket and have them put their money in it. Then we would hoist the money aboard and lower their purchase. Many small flags, bayonets, dog tags, mess utensils, and articles of clothing changed hands at the shipside auction. I saw a sailor offer twenty dollars for a Japanese pistol. 'Somehow' the seller 'confused' a Colt .45 pistol with a Japanese weapon, leaving the sailor with a stolen government firearm."

At some point in these raucous proceedings a black sedan pulled up next to the gangway. The driver got out, a junior officer with the dark good looks of a movie actor, dressed in starched khaki and gleaming shoes, wearing a smartly cocked khaki barracks cap.

Guadalcanal, north coast, looking west over a maze of grassy ridges and jungled ravines. Lunga River at bottom, just beyond first lateral range of hills; Sealark Channel and Point Cruz top right. (NARA)

B Company officers, January 1943. Left to right: 2d Lt. George Stein, author, 1st Lt. John Murdock, 2d Lt. Gus Krieger (KIA on Saipan), and Capt. O. K. LeBlanc, company commander. (Author's collection)

2d Platoon, B/1/8, on Guadalcanal, January 1943. Author is seated front row, third from left. Cpl. Orson DeMoss is on author's right; Paul Kennedy, a.k.a. "the Greek," second row, extreme left. (Author's collection)

Patrol led by John Murdock (front right) returns from the bush on Guadalcanal. Note World War I helmets. Murdock has a much-despised Reising submachine gun slung over his shoulder. (Courtesy John Murdock)

Marines crossing pontoon bridge, much used by author, on Matanikau River. (U.S. Marine Corps)

Solomon Islanders who assisted the author in finding his foxhole on Guadalcanal forty-three years after he last occupied it. (Author's collection)

Akio Tani (middle) with author (right) and Ohno (left), who served under Tani, at Tani's home in Tokyo. Tani, a.k.a. "Pistol Pete," is wearing army shirt worn on Guadalcanal. (Author's collection)

Going on liberty in New Zealand. Left to right: George Stein, author, John Murdock, Gus Krieger. (Courtesy John Murdock)

Author's 2d Platoon on the eve of Tarawa. Author is seated front row, fifth from left. Also pictured: Pfc. Bill Crumpacker (top row, first from left); Pfc. Thomas Sullivan (top row, third from left); P.Sgt. E. O. Sappington, on author's left; Cpl. Orson DeMoss, on author's right. (Author's collection)

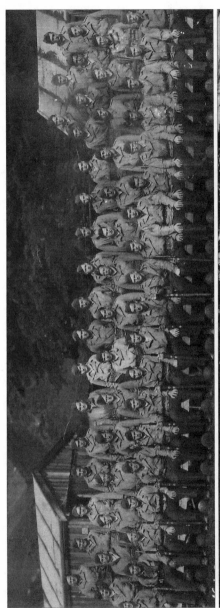

B Company, August 1943, at Camp Paikakariki, New Zealand. About half of the men in the photo were killed or wounded at Betio. Author seated front row, fifteenth from right. Immediately to his right are Krieger, Murdock, G. Stein, Wakefield, and Jauregui. Also in front row: Swaney (fourth from right), DeMoss (ninth from right), Sappington (twelfth from right), McNeil (fourteenth from right), and Sullivan (first on left). Middle: Engen (third from left) and Nelson (ninth from left). Top: Crumpacker (ninth from right) and Guarnett (twelfth from right).

Author with John Murdock's jeep in New Zealand. (Courtesy John Murdock)

LCVPs filled with 2d Division Marines approach Betio. (U.S. Marine Corps)

Red Beach 2 (top), Betio, where the 8th Marines landed on D+1. Note long pier to right. (U.S. Marine Corps)

The sea wall, Betio. (U.S. Marine Corps)

Marine dead on Betio's shoreline. (U.S. Marine Corps)

Wrecked LVT on Red Beach 2 marks the exact spot where John Murdock (commanding B/1/8) came ashore and Pfc. Anthony O'Boyle died. (U.S. Marine Corps

Photo taken by author in November 1983 of "landing" on Betio's Red Beach 2, forty years after the original landing. Dick Stein leads the way, hoisting a can of beer instead of a rifle. (Author's collection)

Two Marines are hit by enemy fire as their unit charges up the beach on Saipan. (U.S. Marine Corps)

Author (standing, center) with his 60-mm mortar section on Saipan. (Author's collection)

John Murdock, wounded on Saipan, "recuperates" in Hawaii with the help of two nurses. (Courtesy John Murdock)

Harold Park, half-Korean BAR gunner in 1st Platoon BAR, was mistaken by the Japanese for one of their own in a close encounter on Guadalcanal. (Courtesy Harold Park)

Japanese killed on Saipan in the war's largest banzai attack are buried in mass grave by bulldozer. (U.S. Marine Corps)

Marine infantry and tank advance through cane field on Tinian's southern tip. Note escarpment in background, where author fought his final battle. (U.S. Marine Corps)

Foxhole buddies Bill Crumpacker (left) and Dick Stein at 2d Marine Division reunion. (Courtesy John Murdock)

Old friends at 2d Marine Division reunion in Washington, D.C., September 2007. Standing, left to right: John Murdock, George Stein, author; Bill Crumpacker seated. (Courtesy John Murdock)

"Look!" one of the Marines shouted. "It's Tyrone Power!"

Tyrone Power was then one of Hollywood's brightest stars, a matinee idol of the first degree known for his athletic performances in swashbuckling movies, known for making women swoon. In fact, Power had recently been commissioned, with much publicity, as a second lieutenant in the Marine Corps. He would go on to become a pilot of transport planes, serving in the Pacific theater. The driver's resemblance to the actor proved an irresistible goad to the Marines on *Sheridan*, and they razzed him mercilessly.

"Yoo-hoo, Tyrone!" they cried. "We love you, Tyrone!"

"Hey, pretty boy, who does your khakis?"

"Can we borrow some of your Kiwi shoe polish?"

"Yoo-hoo, Tyrone, sell us a snapshot!"

Ignoring them, the driver opened the car's rear door and came stiffly to attention. Out stepped Adm. Chester W. Nimitz, Commander in Chief, Pacific Fleet and Pacific Ocean Areas. He began to ascend the gangway, accompanied by an aide.

His friends called him "Chet." So did the Marines. They figured their experiences had given them the right.

"Hey, Chet!" they shouted. "When are we goin' back to the States?"

"Chet, we can't wait for the Golden Gate. Does our skipper know the way to Dago [San Diego]?"

"How about some liberty, Chet? We gotta get off this tub to do our Christmas shopping!"

And perhaps most tellingly: "Hey, Admiral, get us someone who knows the reefs for our next landing!"

The Marines knew they would not be punished for their insubordination. What could Nimitz do, court-martial the entire regiment? Their own officers made no effort to restrain them. Instead, they backed away from the rails and otherwise made themselves scarce.

Nimitz and Commander Mockrish, *Sheridan*'s captain, disappeared into the latter's quarters, where they remained for an hour or so. The Marines kept themselves amused in the meantime by harassing the Tyrone Power lookalike. They also heaped abuse on the shore patrolmen standing guard at the foot of the gangway, calling them "Sneaky Pete" and cussing them out for preventing the Marines from leaving the ship, and simply for being who they were.

Murdock remembers the admiral speaking to them over the ship's PA, telling them that they were heroes and that everyone was very proud of them. *Yeah, sure,* said the Marines. *So what?* At length Nimitz emerged from the captain's quarters and descended the gangway. Once again the 8th Marines told their old pal Chet how they felt about the whole deal. According to Crumpacker, the admiral paused at the door of his sedan, looked up at the Marines, and nodded at them with "a very understanding look in his eye."

Shortly after Nimitz's departure the ship's PA announced that *Sheridan* would be proceeding directly to the Big Island. In other words: no liberty on Oahu. This didn't sit well with the Marines, and they went wild, hooting and yelling and whistling derisively, throwing all manner of junk down on the dock, pelting the band and the shore patrol. The bandsmen lowered their instruments and, accompanied by the SPs, fled into a nearby shed.

The 8th Marines achieved nothing with their show of angry emotion except perhaps to blow off a lot of steam and confirm to all concerned parties that they should not be given liberty. The brass was not about to turn these barbarians loose on the civilian populace of Oahu. The civilized world wasn't ready for us and, to be honest, we weren't ready for the civilized world. It was just as well. The brass had plans for us, for the 2d Marine Division as a whole, and these did not involve a return to the United States. First, we would go to the Big Island to rest, rebuild . . . and train for the next operation.

And so everyone resigned himself, at least for the time being, to staying aboard ship. Everyone, that is, except Murdock. John was determined to get off on Oahu, and to hell with what the brass had decided. To that end he suggested to Larry Hays that he be sent ashore to find and retrieve our mail, which was surely being held for us somewhere on the naval base.

"These guys need their mail," John explained to our battalion commander, speaking with urgency and conviction. "They need it badly, for their morale."

Hays fell for his gambit hook, line, and sinker. "John, that's a great idea!" he exclaimed. "Take one of the men with you and see if you can locate it!"

Our battalion commander was neither stupid nor gullible. But, like so many others, he could not resist John's charm and power to persuade, which were (are) at all times formidable—the more so in this instance because John's idea really did have merit.

Shortly thereafter—very shortly—John and P. Sgt. F. W. Dinsmore were descending the ship's gangway. On the dock and out of earshot of the shore patrol, John stopped and turned to Dinsmore and said, "You've got a job to do now. You're gonna find the mail . . . and I'm gonna find the officers' club!"

The two men went their separate ways, and John soon found what he was looking for. He entered the officers' club to find the place jam-packed with military personnel, most of them Navy, all of them neatly turned out. John, by contrast, wore his combat dungarees with a web belt around his waist and a knife on his hip—a rough customer, dangerous looking, dangerous in fact. The room rang with loud talk and laughter that was grating to his ears. Appraising the scene with eyes probably colder and harder than he knew, he scanned the bar where Navy officers stood in clean khaki uniforms and decided he didn't belong there.

At the end of the bar there was a little room with a sign over the doorway: "Flag Officers Only." John did not know what that meant. Somehow, he had served two years in the Corps without learning that "flag officer" means "admiral." He did know that the little room was (seemingly) empty and quiet, blessedly quiet.

John entered the room and marched up to its bar, the only customer. "Hey, Mac, how 'bout a drink?" John asked the bartender. "I don't have any money, but I can sign a chit."

"Gee, I can't serve you," said the bartender. "Sorry."

"What the hell you mean, you can't serve me?" said John.

"This room is for flag officers."

"Is that so?" said John. "Well, I'm a flag officer, see?"

The bartender, clearly a patient man—and maybe slightly fearful of the combat-outfitted, fiercely glaring Marine standing before him—shook his head and explained to John that a flag officer was an admiral. He nodded toward a man sitting alone at a table in the center of the room, a drink in his hand. "Like him."

John turned and looked at the admiral—a fierce look, no doubt. The admiral looked at John, taking in with a glance John's truculent demeanor, his hard, battle-haunted face. "What's the matter, son?" he asked. "Did you just get back from Tarawa?"

"Yes, sir."

The admiral smiled and waved John over to his table. "Sit down. I want to talk with you."

John sat and the admiral ordered a round of drinks. The bartender brought them, and John and the admiral raised their glasses to each other and each took a big gulp. John can't remember whether he had beer or whiskey, but he does remember that whatever he was drinking went down smoothly and tasted very good.

The admiral then began asking him about Tarawa, all kinds of questions. He was particularly interested to know whether it was true that the Marines at Tarawa had been drugged before the assault, inoculated with some sort of "happy juice" that would calm their nerves. Not true, said John. That was just scuttlebutt. "We wouldn't have been any good to anyone," John told the admiral. "Except, maybe, to the Japanese."

They continued drinking, talking companionably. The admiral ordered round after round, paying for every one. By and by, said John, they were both "totally smashed." He doesn't remember how the night ended. He woke up the following morning on the lawn in front of the club with a blinding hangover. His first thought: *Oh, God, where's Dinsmore?* He staggered back to the ship, arriving within minutes of its departure, and found that Dinsmore had already boarded with the mail. "Everybody was happy," said John, "except me. I had an awful headache."

★　★　★

Before *Sheridan* sailed for the Big Island I was carried off the ship on a stretcher and taken in an ambulance to Navy Hospital 10 (NH 10) at Aiea Heights. It was a brand-new facility that provided me with superb care as well as a panoramic view of Pearl Harbor and the verdant mountains of Oahu—a beautiful setting that certainly aided the healing process.

At the beginning of my stay at NH 10 I thought the severity of my wound had bought me a one-way ticket back to the States. Wrong. I made steady progress, and after a few weeks my doctors informed me that I would be able to return to duty. Six weeks later I was given a clean bill of health and received orders to report to the 8th Marines.

Toward the end of my stay at NH 10, several hundred patients, myself included, formed up in ranks in front of the hospital to be decorated with Purple Hearts by Admiral Nimitz himself. When the admiral came to me, he couldn't manage to stick the pin through my shirt's heavy fabric. "Ladd, you're going to have to finish this job yourself," he said. Then, handing me the medal, he moved on to the next man.

★　★　★

After stopping at Pearl Harbor to let off the wounded, *Sheridan* steamed two hundred miles to the island of Hawaii, "the Big Island," putting in at the port of Hilo. There the Marines of the 8th Regiment disembarked and were transported by truck and narrow-gauge railroad some sixty-five miles inland to what would become the 2d Division's home for the next five months, a

441-acre expanse of open country soon to be known as Camp Tarawa. The rest of the division arrived in the days and weeks that followed.

Located on the Parker Ranch, then the world's second-largest cattle ranch after the King Ranch in Texas, Camp Tarawa was situated at an elevation of five thousand feet in a saddle between two enormous volcanoes, Mauna Loa and Mauna Kea. The Parker Ranch had leased the site and forty thousand acres of land surrounding it to the U.S. government for use as a military installation, charging Uncle Sam a mere one dollar per year. It was a bargain for the military but a nightmare for its first tenants. The Marines arrived to find stacks of wooden tent decks and folded pyramidal tents beside them, and stakes driven into the ground to mark the camp's layout. Other than that, nothing: no shelter of any kind, no food preparation facilities, no running water, no latrines.

Somehow the U.S. Marine Corps had contrived to send an entire division destroyed from fighting the single most ferocious battle in its history to an empty pasture high in the remote mountains of a huge and mostly undeveloped island.

Well, hell, this is typical, the Marines said. *Another screw-up.* They were not surprised. After the screw-ups at Betio, nothing could surprise them.

Well, not quite: they were surprised, unpleasantly, by the weather. The climate in that area is temperate overall and downright cold in the winter months. The peaks of the volcanoes were even capped with snow. *Snow,* for crissakes! In Hawaii! The Marines had expected the sort of warm, breezy environment for which the Hawaiian Islands were famous and which indeed characterized the lowlands and coastal regions of Big Island itself. Instead of warm and breezy, they got cold and windy. And wet—there was bone-chilling rain and mist as well.

The camp had to be built from scratch, an undertaking that took the better part of three weeks and involved the entire division as well as units of Marine engineers, Seabees, and civilian laborers. In the meantime, everyone slept on the cold ground under blankets provided grudgingly by the Army. Army quartermasters had refused an initial request by the Marines for blankets, and issued them only after receiving a direct order from the commanding general of Army forces in the Territory of Hawaii. The Army also provided rations, which the Marines and Seabees roundly hated, finding them vastly inferior to the Navy fare that customarily stocked the larders of Marine encampments outside the war zone.

Clothing was also a problem. They had what they wore and little more, and in most cases that wasn't much. Then somebody got the bright idea to appeal to the Red Cross for disaster relief. The Red Cross came through by donating all the men's clothing it had stockpiled for emergencies. Murdock got a natty double-breasted pencil-stripe suit, which he wore at all times until the Marine utilities arrived. He looked ridiculous, but no more so than the men he commanded. "We were quite a sight," said John. "We were all going around in these civilian clothes of every color and style. What a bunch of raggedy-ass Marines we were!"

Also problematic, at least from the standpoint of the Marines, were the civilian laborers who helped build the camp. Many of them were either Japanese immigrants who had become American citizens or the children or grandchildren of those immigrants. They were loyal Americans, but the Marines regarded them, for reasons that should be obvious, with suspicion—and maybe some hatred too. By the same token, these Japanese Americans were wary of the Marines, believing that savage combat against their kinsmen in the western Pacific had transformed them into cold-blooded killers. Nor were they the only dwellers on the Big Island to hold this view; many civilians of every ethnic strain were fearful of the Marines, of what they had supposedly become.

The Marines shortly dispelled their fears, winning the hearts and minds of the populace through ceaseless efforts to improve the region's primitive infrastructure or to create infrastructure where none existed. They repaired roads, built housing, constructed reservoirs, established a modern hospital. They mixed with the locals on liberty and spent money in their villages. The locals discovered that the Marines were good kids and, equally important, a boon to the economy. They came to like having us around and would be sorry to see us go.

By the time I reported for duty at the end of January the hard work was over and Camp Tarawa was fully operational. Immediately on arrival I dropped by the B Company area and looked up my buddies. I especially wanted to find Murdock. I still had his sword and I meant to give it back to him—a gesture of friendship both real and symbolic, a way of showing him that I was alive and kicking; a way, too, of showing him how much I appreciated his friendship.

I found him in his tent, sitting at a small desk doing some paperwork. Sword in hand, I entered the tent. He glanced up at me and did a double take. For a moment he was dumbfounded, speechless. Just for that instant, he later told me, he thought he was looking at a ghost. Then he grinned.

"What the hell are you doing here?" he said. "I thought you'd died!"

"Well, I didn't," I said. "And now I'm back."

"You're back?" he exclaimed. "You can't be back. You got shot in the belly, for crissakes. At the very least they should have sent you home."

I had to agree with him on that one. But "they" had felt otherwise; "they" had judged me fit for duty—which I was, and which meant that I wouldn't be going home anytime soon.

"Unbelievable," was all John could say. "Really unbelievable."

I handed John his sword. "I thought you'd want this back."

John kept the sword and eventually brought it home with him. Many years later he gave it to one of his grandsons, who still has it.

★   ★   ★

I was still in Naval Hospital 10 when Murdock was notified that he had been promoted to captain. John promptly turned B Company over to George Stein, his executive officer, and went off with the commanders of A and C companies, Capt. Harry Philips and Capt. Howard Guenther, to celebrate. It was still early morning, but the three captains were eager to get the party started. They piled into a jeep and drove to a nearby village where, very much to their dismay, they discovered that the taverns thereabouts did not open until noon, several hours distant. They were standing in front of a shuttered drinking establishment, looking forlorn and wondering what to do, when one of the villagers approached them.

"Hey, you guys looking for a drink?" the man asked.

"We sure are!" chorused the three captains.

"Well, c'mon to my house, I got some Three-Island gin."

This was a bootleg potable made from sugarcane, harsh tasting but packing a powerful wallop—just what the occasion warranted. They went straightaway to the man's house and imbibed liberally through the morning with their newfound friend. At precisely the stroke of noon they decamped, going back into town and returning to the aforementioned establishment, which was now open for business. They had not yet eaten—in their eagerness to start the party they had skipped morning chow—and their recent host had been generous with his liquor, so they were fairly inebriated by the time they entered the tavern. They kept drinking and soon were very drunk indeed.

They were having a high old time and making a lot of noise, and they probably scared everyone else in the room. All were garbed in combat fatigues, all wore big KA-BARs strapped to their belts, and all had seen too much combat and too much death to get so drunk and stay happy. Perhaps inevitably John conceived an intense dislike for the bartender, who was Chinese but looked Japanese, at least to John and his companions. John had just about decided that he was going to go over the bar and kill him when, very fortunately for the bartender, a certain Marine major entered the room.

John recognized him as the major from the 6th Marines who had tried to tell John how to run his company on the third day of the battle for Betio. At the same moment, the major looked at John and recognized him as the insubordinate first lieutenant from Betio who had told him to buzz off, or words to that effect. The major marched over to the bar where John and his companions sat, looked them up and down, then looked at John and said, "You're disgraceful."

Whereupon John hauled off and punched him square in the face.

A brief fistfight ensued. Very brief—just two or three seconds in duration. John landed several punches; the major, none. He never had the chance. The major hit the floor and that was the end of it. Then a couple of shore patrolmen entered the bar. They were very quick on the scene, probably because they had been hanging around outside waiting for something like this to happen. They should have arrested both John and the major, or at least have taken them into custody to sort things out, but they didn't. They weren't sure how to handle the situation, officers fighting each other. Should they use force, maybe knock them around a little, then cuff them? They could do this to brawling men without repercussions. But roughing up an officer was an altogether different matter. That could get you in trouble . . . right? The shore patrolmen had to think about that one.

While the SPs were thinking, Philips and Guenther grabbed John and hustled him out of the bar. They dumped him in the back of their jeep, drove back to camp, and deposited him in his bunk. He awoke the next morning with a devastating hangover, a sore hand with bruised knuckles, and only a dim memory of what had transpired the day before. Broadly speaking, he remembered the altercation with the major and knew he had gotten the best of the man, but the details were sketchy.

Shrugging off what little memory he had of the incident, he went outside to hold the morning formation. While Murdock was standing before his men, the company's top sergeant stepped forward and pinned a pair of captain's bars, purchased that day at the camp post exchange, on John's collar. Everyone in the company was very happy for John, because his promotion was much deserved and long overdue. John, despite his hangover, was also happy—for about two minutes. Then a runner from battalion HQ arrived.

He had been sent by Larry Hays with orders to find *Lieutenant* Murdock of B Company and inform him that he was to report at once to the battalion commander. The runner approached John, saluted, and opened his mouth to speak to *Lieutenant* Murdock; then he saw the captain's bars on John's collar. The runner, a private, became visibly confused and incapable of speech. For a few seconds he silently worked his mouth as he tried to decide how to address John. Then he stammered, "Uh, Captain Murdock ... uh, Lieutenant Murdock ..." Murdock just looked at him, wondering why the private didn't address him as "captain." Finally, the private said, "Uh, Mr. Murdock, Colonel Hays wants to see you in his tent. He told me to tell you that you were to come right now. Sir."

Once again John turned the company over to George Stein and hastened to battalion HQ and there found Larry Hays in an agitated state.

"Holy smokes, John," Hays said. "Where were you last night?" He took a sheet of paper off his desk and held it up before John. "Did you do all this?"

"What does it say I did?" John asked.

Hays read from the sheet: "Assault and battery against a senior officer, drunk and disorderly, conduct unbecoming an officer ..." His voice trailed off.

John said, "Jeez, Colonel, it sounds like I must have done it. I dunno, I can't remember."

"Well, you know what I gotta do," said Hays. "I gotta put it through the chain of command."

John knew what that meant: a general court-martial. "Okay, you do what you gotta do," he said. He returned to B Company, which he still commanded, still as a captain, but very concerned about his future. *What the hell am I gonna do?* he wondered.

Then he remembered that one of his best friends, a captain and fellow Irishman from Chicago named Jack O'Hara, was the personal aide to Maj. Gen. Julian Smith, who was still the 2d Division commander (Maj. Gen. Thomas Watson would replace him in April). John phoned O'Hara at division HQ.

"Jack, I've got a little problem here," he said.

"What's a 'little' problem, John?"

"Well, I might be facing a general court."

"That's not a little problem, John."

"Tell me about it."

"No," said O'Hara. "*You* tell *me* about it."

John told him. He recounted what he remembered of the incident in the bar and recited the list of charges that had been filed against him. "Can you help me, Jack?"

Silence at the other end of the line; O'Hara pondering. Then O'Hara said, "Yeah, sure, I can help you." Sounding genuinely upbeat, optimistic. "Don't worry about it."

"Easy for you to say."

"Just listen," said O'Hara.

I want you to call me every morning, tell me where you're gonna be with your company that day. You know, at the rifle range, the jungle training area, wherever. 'Cuz the general, see, he comes in every morning and he says, "Where are we going today, O'Hara? What are we gonna do today, O'Hara?" I'm the one who decides; he leaves it all to me. So you'll tell me where you're gonna be and I'll tell him, "Let's try the rifle range, sir," or, "Let's go to the jungle training area." Then I'll take him there and you'll be there too. And then—do I have to tell you what to do after that?

"No, you do not," said John. "I read you loud and clear."

Their scheme was duly implemented. As yet General Smith knew nothing about John's "problem." But he saw John and B Company every day. He saw them at the rifle range, the jungle training center, etc., etc. What he saw in each locale was a picture of military perfection, a rifle company operating at peak efficiency under the firm guidance of its extremely proficient commanding officer. The commanding officer issued clear, succinct commands, and his men obeyed them with alacrity and did not make mistakes. They were all very gung ho, running through their exercises with vigor and enthusiasm, singing and counting cadence on road marches, double-timing from one training area to another.

General Smith was very, very impressed.

The men of B Company were co-conspirators in the scheme, of course. John had told them all about his problem, asked them for their help—and they gave it willingly. John was popular with his men because he was fair. He was a fighter, he was smart, and, not least, he was funny. Also, the guys did not have to try hard to look good, because they *were* good.

It took about two weeks for John's court-martial papers to work their way through channels, finally landing on the desk of Col. David Shoup, now the division chief of staff. O'Hara was present when Shoup handed the papers to General Smith. By then the general had seen a lot of John and B Company and held them in high regard. According to O'Hara, Smith reviewed the papers and then turned to Shoup and said, "That's Murdock, from B Company! We can't give *him* a general court. We don't want to lose him; he's one of our best company commanders!"

Shoup agreed but demurred when the general suggested that all the charges against John be dropped without prejudice. "We gotta give him *some* punishment," Shoup said. "Too many people know about the fight. Hell, *everybody* knows about it. We can't just let a captain beat up a major and get away scot-free."

Smith and Shoup decided between them that the best course was to tear up the acceptance papers for John's captaincy and confine him to his tent for ten days. The first night of John's confinement O'Hara dropped by John's tent and presented him with a bottle of Four Roses. "Courtesy of General Smith," O'Hara explained. "He wants you to know that he's very sorry he had to punish you. So he asked me to give you this bottle."

Needless to say, John and O'Hara drank the bottle empty that night.

Subsequently, and probably at the behest of either Smith or Shoup (or both), orders were cut transferring the major out of the division. John retained command of B Company, but as a first lieutenant. Around this time George Stein was promoted to captain—but remained B Company's executive officer. John described what had suddenly become a somewhat awkward situation: "For about a week I had a captain, George, coming into my tent asking, 'What do we do this morning?' And I was just a first lieutenant! He outranked me but I was still giving him orders!"

George wasn't uncomfortable with this arrangement—after all, John was a close friend—but John felt bad about it and repeatedly asked Larry Hays to give the company to "someone who deserved it," namely George. John didn't want to lose the company but felt that stepping down so that George could take command might be in everyone's best interest. Hays disagreed.

"Now, John," he would say. "Don't get so upset. I want you to stay. I need you to stay."

Thus, when ships carrying the 2d Marine Division put to sea for the voyage to Saipan, 1st Lt. John Murdock still commanded B/1/8, and Capt. George Stein still served as his executive officer.

★ ★ ★

I remained with the 1st Battalion of the 8th Marines but did not return to B Company; my days as a platoon leader were over. Although I had been judged fit for duty, I was in fact still in recovery, still weak from my wound, not capable of strenuous activity. For that reason I was given a number of limited-duty assignments that would keep me usefully occupied without overtaxing me. I was battalion mess officer, in charge of procuring special food items, often from Hilo; I was a court recorder, assisting the battalion adjutant in documenting proceedings for minor infractions; and I was the battalion chemical gas officer. In the spring, toward the end of our stay at Camp Tarawa, I received my most substantial assignment and became a combat loading officer.

In time, I was able to take part in the training the division was undergoing for its next operation. We conducted several exercises in the Hamakua sugar-cane fields. These were set on fire while we maneuvered through them, and we were taught how to set backfires to counter the threat of encroaching flames. *Hmm,* we thought, *this is something new*—and perhaps revealing. Would our next operation place us in sugarcane fields?

Our training stressed the combined-arms approach to warfare. Working with aircraft, armor, and artillery, and with our own machine guns and mortars providing suppressing fires (and everyone using live ammunition), we assaulted fortifications of the sort we had faced in the past and would likely face in the future. In these mock assaults we practiced newly acquired demolition skills, first blasting bunkers and pillboxes with flamethrowers and then blowing them up with explosives. Special emphasis was placed on improving infantry-tank coordination, an area of past difficulties due to the inability of the two to communicate in the midst of battle. The problem was solved by mounting a telephone on the back of each tank, an innovation that allowed infantry to talk to tank commanders and direct their actions from a protected position (behind the bulk of the tank itself) while the vehicle remained buttoned up.

We also conducted amphibious landing exercises on the beaches of the Kohala coast, some ten to fifteen miles west of Kamuela near the ruins of Kamehameha I's domain. There we used rubber rafts to get from ship to shore. However, in bigger amphibious exercises held at Maalaea Bay on Maui we used amtracs and LCVPs.

For the veterans of Betio and Guadalcanal, many aspects of this training were old hat. But the replacements the division was receiving almost daily needed all of it. Replacements were pouring in, arriving in numbers that underscored our losses at Tarawa, reminding of us of something that needed no reminder—the death of friends. Most were fresh-faced teenagers straight out of boot camp, eager kids who had no combat experience and no idea what they had gotten themselves into. The rest of us just looked at them and shook our heads. We *did* know what they had gotten themselves into, and we wondered how they would survive the battles to come, never forgetting that our own survival thus far was due in large measure to the vagaries of chance and circumstance, and maybe, just a little bit, to the grace of God as well.

Luck and God's grace were desperately slim reeds on which to hang our hopes; slimmer still for the replacements because of their inexperience. We expected that many would die. The odds were against them, because they had seen no action. But we also expected to die. The odds were against us because we had seen too much action. Either way you did the math, it came out bad. And if the war went on for another two or three years, as we expected it to do, culminating in the invasion of the Japanese home islands—well, forget about it; everyone who was here now would die. The war would have to be fought to a conclusion and won by kids who were now just freshmen in high school.

We were especially skeptical about the draftees, of which there were a significant number. These "selective service Marines" were something new for a heretofore all-volunteer force: new and unwanted—and a matter of grave concern for the rest of us. Would draftees measure up to Marine Corps standards? Would we be able to depend on them in battle? We had our doubts.

We were wrong to doubt them. In battle, when the chips were down, they proved that, like the volunteers, they were worthy to be called Marines.

In April I took over a 60-mm mortar section in C Company. I was just starting to get to know the men in my unit when the division began embarking for the invasion of Saipan. Equipment and supplies were trucked to the docks at Hilo and loaded into troop transports and freighters. The loading process took several days and was followed by the embarkation of the troops. We left Hilo in mid-May and proceeded to Maalaea Bay to rendezvous with ships carrying the 4th Marine Division, which had been training on Maui and was also slated to take part in the Saipan operation.

Rehearsal landings were conducted at Maalaea Bay and on the island of Kahoolawe. On the way to one of the landing sites we encountered heavy seas that severely battered several LSTs, swept three deck-loaded LCTs overboard, and inflicted twenty-nine casualties to the 2d Division. The damaged LSTs were sent to the West Loch area of Pearl Harbor for repairs. On 21 May, while one of the vessels was being unloaded, it was suddenly obliterated by an enormous explosion. The blast started a chain reaction of explosions that quickly destroyed five more LSTs anchored side-by-side in the harbor. As many as 163 sailors and Marines were killed, and another 396 were wounded. The cause of the initial explosion has never been determined, but it is thought that a welder making repairs to the first ship somehow set fire to a crate of mortar shells, igniting the contents. All the LSTs lost in the incident were crammed with munitions, which accounts for the massive and catastrophic nature of the explosions that destroyed them.

Ships carrying the 2d and 4th Marine divisions and their equipment began leaving Pearl Harbor at the end of the month. Another group carrying the U.S. Army's 27th Division, which had been allocated a support role in the operation, left Pearl Harbor around the same time. The ships with the Marine divisions rendezvoused at Eniwetok on 9 June. The ships with the Army units met up at Kwajalein. Two days later our ships weighed anchor and headed out for Saipan. D-day was set for dawn, 15 June.

CHAPTER EIGHT

Saipan

Morning, 15 June 1944. Shells rain down on our assault waves, kicking up tall columns of water around the plodding amtracs: a forest of water columns rising and falling, rising and falling. Shells burst above the amtracs spraying the passengers with shrapnel; tracers from antiboat guns dart and skip across the water. Every now and again a plunging shell scores a direct hit on an amtrac, exploding inside the troop compartment, momentarily lifting the vehicle out of the water and then blowing it apart, scattering fragments of metal and men over a wide radius. But the amtracs push on, stoic and determined, driving through the whooshing geysers, through the glancing tracers, crawling up and over the reef, flopping into the lagoon beyond, waddling to the shore.

The Marines of the 1/8 watch all this from amtracs loitering near the line of departure, waiting for the order to head for the beach. As shellfire engulfs the assault waves, the veterans of Tarawa, myself included, cannot help but think that once again we are going to get clobbered on our approach to the beaches. Earlier we had studied our naval and air bombardment of the enemy shore with practiced and appraising eyes and had noted with approval that it was far heavier and more intense than the bombardment that had preceded the Betio landings. I even managed to convince myself that this bombardment would surely destroy the Japanese positions and obliterate the defenders, and never mind that I had given myself the exact same assurances before the ramp fell on the reef at Betio. This time, I thought, the preinvasion bombardment really would accomplish its purpose and the Marines really would land without too

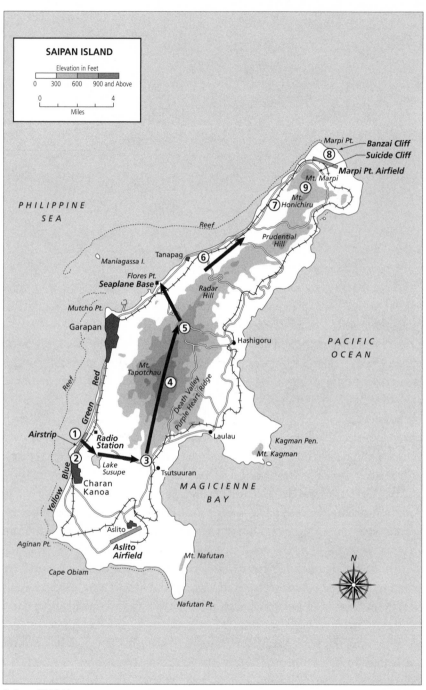

Notes:

1. The 1/8 made assault landing here 15 June 1944, dug in just before reaching Lake Susupe and endured very heavy enemy shelling all night. Author slightly wounded by own mortar fragment as unit resumed advance next morning.
2. Location of destroyed Japanese sugar refinery and smokestack used effectively by enemy artillery spotter. Murdock wounded in attempt to direct fire on smokestack.
3. The 2d Marine Division held ridge here several days waiting for front line to pivot toward north end of island. Lt. Gen. Holland Smith (USMC) relieved Maj. Gen. Ralph Smith (USA), commander of the U.S. Army 27th Division, for not being aggressive enough in this realignment.
4. Mt. Tapotchau taken by a surprise ascent on 28 June and held against a fierce counterattack.
5. Author wounded for second time on 2 July by tree burst from Army 155-mm artillery.
6. Largest banzai attack of war stopped here 7 July.
7. Banzai assembly area. Admiral Naguma, commander of Japanese garrison, committed hara-kiri here.
8. Island secured on 9 July. Hundreds of enemy military personnel committed suicide here, jumping off "Banzai Cliff." Japanese civilians killed themselves at "Suicide Cliff."
9. Present site of Far East Broadcasting Co. and Japanese-built golf course.

much difficulty. But as I watch all those geysers springing up around the assault wave amtracs and all those tracers streaking at them, I begin to have doubts.

We had started the day with high hopes for an easy landing. And with good reason. We came to Saipan with a mighty armada of eight hundred ships, including 110 troopships carrying more than seventy-one thousand troops from two Marine divisions (2d and 4th) and one Army division (27th). At 0815, following a massive bombardment by warships and Navy aircraft of the beaches around the town of Charan-Kanoa on the island's southwest coast, amtracs carrying eight battalions from the two Marine divisions started for the shore. At the same time, our warships shifted their shelling farther inland, and Navy aircraft swooped in low over the beaches to bomb and strafe enemy positions. Operation Forager, the invasion of the Marianas, was under way, and nothing could stop us.

Encompassing seventy-two square miles, Saipan is the largest island in the Marianas group, which includes Tinian and Guam, also slated for invasion. The Japanese home islands lay just twelve hundred miles to the west, not a great distance by Pacific Ocean reckoning—they were practically in the same neighborhood—and well within operational range of the new B-29 heavy bombers that would deploy to bases in the Marianas soon after the islands had been secured.

Intelligence estimates placed some fifteen thousand Japanese troops on Saipan. The estimates were wrong: the number was at least twice that. The combat effectiveness of Japanese forces varied from unit to unit. Several units comprised a mix of troops, including survivors of troopships sunk en route to the island by U.S. submarines. But even these ad-hoc formations had significant assets, namely the Japanese themselves. Whatever the state of their forces overall, the individual Japanese soldier could be counted on to fight fiercely and bravely. Unfortunately for us, the state of their forces overall was generally quite good. In particular, their artillery arm was large and proficient and that made things very rough for us, especially in the invasion's opening stages.

The 2d Division would conduct its initial assault with four battalions drawn from the 6th and 8th Marines landing side-by-side on beaches north of Charan-Kanoa. At the same time the 4th Division's assault battalions would go ashore on beaches south of the town, on the other side of Afetna Point. My battalion, the 1/8, would land shortly thereafter along with the 1st Battalion of the 29th Marines, temporarily attached to the 8th Marines to augment its combat power. The Army division would remain aboard its ships, to be committed when and where it was needed.

The Marines of the 1/8 first boarded LCVPs, then transferred to amtracs near the line of departure. We were not yet a primary target of Japanese artillerymen, but even so we were not beyond the range of their guns and they could not resist throwing a few shells our way. One of them burst above Dick Stein's squad as it was transferring from an LCVP to an amtrac. Dick's squad leader, Corporal Davies, was hit in the shoulder with shrapnel. Dick urged Davies to go back aboard the LCVP and return to their ship for treatment. Davies refused. "No," he told Dick. "I'm going in."

But most of the enemy shellfire was directed at the assault amtracs. As at Tarawa, a reef lay between the invasion fleet and the beaches. We were not overly concerned about it, though, since this time we would all be going in on amtracs. There would be no replay of LCVPs getting hung up on the coral barrier. A number of the amtracs had been fitted with turrets armed with 75-mm cannons. These craft would accompany the troop-carrying amtracs up onto the beaches to provide close-in fire support. They would prove effective against the few Japanese who remained on the beaches but were of no use whatsoever against the enemy's medium and heavy batteries, which were

dug in on the reverse slopes of the foothills in front of Mt. Tapotchau. Our
warships had targeted these batteries but failed to destroy them. The Japanese
opened fire on the incoming amtracs as they approached the reef and deluged
that barrier and the lagoon beyond with shellfire.

The first amtracs reached the beaches at 0843. Many of the 8th Marines'
amtracs had veered to the left as they made their way to the beaches and
landed most of the regiment's two assault battalions in the same place, where
they got mixed up with each other and with elements of the 6th Marines'
3d Battalion. The resultant crowding and confusion delayed movement inland
and presented Japanese gunners with the kind of target artillerymen dream of:
a mass of men and vehicles jammed together and halted on open ground. The
Japanese saturated the area with shellfire, and casualties among the Marines
quickly mounted.

Fortunately, most of the Japanese troops had withdrawn from the landing
zones, leaving only snipers and small rearguard units to contest our landing.
Thus, when the amtracs of the assault waves crawled up on the beaches, they
did not have to contend with much in the way of small-arms fire. But the artillery bombardment was bad enough.

The amtracs carrying the 1/8 and the 1/29 crossed the line of departure
about thirty minutes after the assault waves went ashore. Japanese artillery
continued to rain shells into the water even as it tore up the beaches. At Betio's
reef we had met with curtains of automatic weapons fire, mostly from machine
guns; at Saipan's reef we were enveloped by curtains of shellfire. Explosions
walked up and down the reef as our amtracs approached it, and from where I sat
in the front of my amtrac, the prospects of making it through those shell bursts
without getting hit seemed unpromising. John Murdock—still commanding
B Company, still a first lieutenant—recalled the experience:

> Our amtracs were in line abreast and we were taking artillery fire, the
> heaviest we had ever encountered. You could see the shells hitting the
> water, exploding and making the water splash way up. Just off to my right a
> shell scored a direct hit on one of my boats, and *Pow!* It just went to pieces.
> There was a flash and a big explosion and I could see pieces of men flying
> out of it. I thought, *Oh, shit.* But also I thought, *Thank God it wasn't my
> boat.* Mostly I was thinking, *Who was it who got hit, and how many guys am
> I gonna be without?*

★ ★ ★

When my amtrac reached the reef we were all crouched below the sides. There was too much metal flying through the air to risk popping up for a look around. The guys had their heads pulled down between their shoulders, and they stared at each other with big eyes and said nothing. The veterans of Tarawa had been through this before and were probably having a harder time of it precisely because of their prior experience—because they knew how bad things could get. The new kids were mostly better off, because they didn't have a clue. Certainly they were scared, but they were also fascinated and awestruck by all the noise and commotion, and these emotions blunted their fear. Nothing in their experience had prepared them for this—the live-fire exercises in Hawaii were puny by comparison—and so they did not realize that our situation was terrible and likely to get worse.

You can be sure that I was scared, but, fortunately, I had the concerns of an officer to distract me. My mind was racing, filled with thoughts about what I had to do to get my unit organized and into action once we reached the beach. Then our amtrac hit the reef and all I could think about was getting across that barrier. I'm betting everyone in my amtrac was thinking and feeling the same thing at that point. We felt the tracks grip the coral. The front end of the vehicle tilted up as it climbed onto the reef, and we urged it forward with our thoughts. *Don't stop, don't stop, don't get hung up on the reef.* But for just a second the amtrac did stop, or seemed to stop, and our hearts stopped beating too and we all gasped and held our breath. The amtrac teetered on the reef as if it were uncertain about whether to continue on, and then the front end tilted down and the vehicle belly-flopped into the lagoon. We could breathe again; our hearts were beating again. But we still had a long way to go.

Here and there an amtrac did hang up on the reef, its treads futilely grinding on the coral. A few seconds later the crew and the Marines inside would be seen jumping and throwing themselves over the sides and then scrambling along the reef to get as far from their crippled machines as they could before a shell struck it.

I went to the front of the LVT and looked through a gun port to see what was going on up ahead. Our entire assault wave was angling to the left, heading in the direction of a tall radio tower that rose above the enemy's radio station and communications center, located some distance inland from the beach. Between the reef and the shore, columns of water rose and fell. Enemy artillery plowed up the beach. A TBF Avenger torpedo-bomber was hit by antiaircraft fire as it strafed enemy positions on the beach. The plane bellied into the water just offshore and remained afloat just long enough for its three crewmen to escape. An F6F Hellcat was also hit. The plane nosed into the water and exploded a quarter mile off to our left.

Dick Stein also saw that F6F go down. Having cleared the reef safely, his amtrac was then waddling toward the beach through geysers of shellfire. He and Davies were seated on the left side of the vehicle, shoulder to shoulder, with their backs pressed against the bulkhead, about six feet from the front. Suddenly a mortar shell hit the opposite side of the amtrac, exploding with a tremendous roar. A big piece of shrapnel blew out Davies' back, killing him instantly. Others were hit: "There were bodies all over. Guys were lying on the deck and it was a mess in there, just a mess—blood was everywhere. It was terrible."

Dick was unscathed.

Dazed, he slid away from Davies and went up to the front of the craft, stepping cautiously over the wounded and the dead. Some of the wounded men were moaning softly, but otherwise everyone was silent and still, stunned by the blast—or dead. The deck was wet with blood and covered with gunpowder, brass shell casings, and slugs from the amtrac's .50-caliber machine guns. The explosion had destroyed the boxes holding ammo for those guns, and the force of it had separated the casings from the slugs and had scattered gunpowder everywhere. Dick spared a moment to ponder this phenomenon and wonder why the gunpowder hadn't exploded. Then he peered through the bow gun port and saw that his amtrac had crawled to within a few yards of the beach. Dick clutched his rifle, threw one leg over the side, and watched as the amtrac moved closer to the shoreline.

Suddenly a private named Jewitt leapt to his feet and started praying: "He was pleading with the Lord, out loud, real loud: 'Oh, God, oh God, oh God, help me! Please save us!'" Dick stared at the man. Jewitt was falling apart right before Dick's eyes, and his collapse was in its way as devastating to those around him as any shell burst. Terror itself is terrifying—and contagious. All the more so in this instance because Jewitt was no greenhorn but a veteran of Tarawa and Guadalcanal who had performed well and ably in both places. For the first time that day Dick began to feel really afraid. And he said to himself: *Boy, oh boy, this is bad; this is real bad.*

In the next instant it got worse. "I was getting ready to jump out and then, BAM! we took another round, on the right side again. My God, the noise was deafening! The front part of the amtrac was already on land. It just stopped—the driver had been killed—and I bailed right out right there into knee-deep water. I got to the beach and I didn't see anyone coming out of the amtrac."

In addition to the driver, Jewitt had also been killed. Dick doesn't know what happened to the other men. They belonged to a machine-gun platoon he had transferred to during the final days in Hawaii and he was only casually acquainted with them. Dick wasn't even nicked. At Betio and now on Saipan, the Japanese had tried and tried again to kill him, and had failed every time. That man had more lives than any ten cats.

Dick ran up on the beach, looking for the rest of his platoon. He couldn't find it. Instead he found—who else?—his good friend and foxhole buddy, Bill Crumpacker.

Bill still belonged to my old unit, 2d Platoon (B Company), now commanded by 1st Lt. Robert Sullivan. Bill's amtrac had driven to within a few feet of the shore, and he was getting ready to jump out, mightily pleased by the prospect of making a "dry landing" with only his boots getting wet, but when he went over the side he caught the lower part of his trousers on a cleat and flipped over. Suddenly he found himself hanging upside down. *Ah, for crissakes,* he told himself, *you are such a klutz.* Then he kicked his leg a couple of times and freed himself from the cleat—only to fall head-first into two feet of water. So much for a dry landing.

The beach was under heavy bombardment and Bill's water-soaked gear was slowing him down, so he shucked off his pack, threw away his gas mask, and took off running. "I went up on the beach with just my rifle and cartridge belt, and as I'm running along I'm thinking, *Jesus, good ol' Crumpacker, he really knows how to go ashore.*"

It was at this point that Bill met up with Dick Stein. The two men soon found Lieutenant Sullivan, who was forming up 2d Platoon. Dick attached himself to his old unit and would remain with it for the next few days.

★   ★   ★

My amtrac finally reached the shore and rumbled a few yards up the beach, then lurched to a stop. "Let's go, let's go," I shouted, and we vaulted over the sides and hit the beach running, my men straining and stumbling in the soft sand under the weight of their mortar tubes and base plates, moving around or stepping over dead and wounded Marines from the preceding assault waves. The wounded Marines were screaming and moaning and crying out for corpsmen. Some reached out to us as we ran by, but we did not stop to help them. Our orders were to keep moving, and we did.

But only for a short distance. A few yards from the waterline there was a brushy, sparsely wooded strip that ran parallel to the beach. When we reached it we threw ourselves to the ground, diving into shell holes and bomb craters. Enemy small-arms fire was almost nonexistent; apart from a few snipers and small, scattered groups of diehards the Japanese had withdrawn from our immediate area. But guns and mortars positioned farther inland pounded us relentlessly, and everywhere we looked the sand was erupting in explosions; everywhere we looked Marines were dropping to the sand, dead or wounded, wounded and dying, their bodies torn, dismembered, bleeding. Several nearby holes held the bodies of dead Japanese, but not a few contained dead Marines as well.

We stayed put for about twenty minutes, trying to get organized, trying to stay alive. The ground beneath us shook from the exploding shells, and the noise of the bombardment was painfully loud and punishing to the ears. I was able to locate my guys quickly. Our amtracs had pretty much kept together on the approach to the beach, and we quickly found each other once we had landed. But most units were disorganized to some degree and many were completely scattered. Marines looking for their units were running all over the place. Some were wandering about slowly with blank expressions, addled by the concessive blast of shells bursting too close to them.

Nor did my unit make it through the bombardment unscathed. Pfc. Donald Maines, a small, slightly built gunner in my section,* had just finished clawing a hole in the sand and was crouched below the rim when a mortar shell hit a few yards behind him. A hot wind sent shrapnel skimming overhead, and the next instant dirt and burning branches from the ground scrub were falling on him. His eardrums were nearly blown out by the blast, but he was otherwise unharmed. The other two men in his crew were still digging their holes when the shell landed just about on top of them. Ears ringing, Maines poked his head out of the hole and saw both men sprawled dead on the ground, their utilities dark with their own blood, their mortar broken into pieces.

So many good men were killed that day. One of them was 1st Lt. Newell T. Berg of B Company, a former schoolteacher who had performed valiantly on Betio, a man I counted among my best friends. Just seconds after he jumped out of his amtrac in B Company's landing zone (located just to the right of C Company), shell fragments sliced off one of his legs. No corpsman could be found to help him, nor were there any aid stations nearby, and though his men did what they could for him, they were unable to stanch the gushing blood

---

* I was surprised at the 1986 reunion of our division association in Orlando when Don introduced himself to me. He had grown from a skinny teenager to a tall, well-built man. Like many of the Marines, Don hadn't finished growing when he joined up. He was very proud to have been one of the Marines selected for the honor guard at President Roosevelt's funeral.

or treat him for the shock that was quickly killing him. As his femoral artery pumped the last of his blood onto the sand, he looked up at those gathered around him and whispered, "Get the men off the beach." And then he died.

Around the same time John Murdock, who was running up the beach after disembarking from his amtrac, came across Gus Krieger, one of B Company's veteran first lieutenants and a close friend. Krieger was lying on the sand with no one around him, his body perforated by shrapnel. He was alive, but just barely. John knelt beside his friend. "I looked at him to see what I could do for him," John recalled, "but he was bleeding in so many places, I knew I couldn't do anything. He wanted a cigarette, so I gave him a cigarette, lit that for him. And I said, 'Gus, you'll be okay. I gotta go.' I had to go—there was too much to do. I had to get the company organized. And I left him there. So he died there; he just bled to death."

Thus, within the span of a few minutes John had lost two of his seasoned platoon leaders. As events were to prove, this was not an unusual occurrence— casualties among officers in the 8th Marines were disproportionately high in the landing and consolidation stages. Larry Hays, our friend and 1st Battalion commander, was hit by shrapnel and evacuated off the beach; fortunately his wound was not serious and he shortly rejoined us in the field. Also wounded and put of action were the 2d and 3d battalion commanders, Lt. Col. Henry P. "Jim" Crowe (former commander of the scout-sniper I attended outside San Diego just before Pearl Harbor) and Lt. Col. John Miller.

The rally point for B Company was supposed to be a clump of trees in that brushy strip between the beach and the airfield. But what had shown up as trees on photographs taken from reconnaissance aircraft turned out to be knee-high shrubs. When John got to that point, only a few of his men were waiting. *Oh, shit!* he thought. *Where is everybody?* In fact, they were all spread out, looking for that clump of nonexistent trees. John and a couple of his men set off to find his company. They split up, and John moved around the beach shouting out the names of his platoon leaders and sergeants, yelling, "Hey, where the hell are you?!"

Meanwhile, I lay in the brush with my men and tried to free myself from the despair that suddenly gripped me. The situation seemed hopeless—it was Tarawa all over again. *How,* I wondered, *are we going to get out of this mess?*

The feeling soon passed. I just didn't have the time for it. At my command we moved out. Everyone rose from their shell holes and craters and went forward. No hesitation. Emerging from the brushy strip, we lumbered about ten feet to the airstrip.

"Keep going, keep going!" I heard myself shouting. "Don't stop!"

The runway was about sixty yards wide. We crossed it quickly but cautiously, dashing a few yards, dropping to the ground, jumping up and running again. A few rounds zinged by, but that was the extent of the small-arms fire we encountered. Japanese artillery continued to hammer us. After crossing the runway we halted in a wooded area about three hundred yards west of Lake Susupe and seven hundred yards from the shore. I went a few yards farther toward the lake to place myself between my mortar section and the company CP, so that I could easily communicate with both if and when a fire mission was ordered.

With shells swooshing in and exploding all around us we attacked the ground with our entrenching tools, hacking and shoveling furiously, almost dementedly, to dig foxholes and get down into them. Sometime either during or immediately after the completion of these frenzied excavations we discovered that we had established ourselves in the midst of the airstrip's fuel supply dump. Scattered around us in the brush were fifty-five-gallon fuel drums filled with highly flammable aviation gasoline. We tried not to think about what would happen to us if shellfire hit those drums. We were lucky: by some miracle, not one was hit.

While we were digging in, the rifle platoons kept going, advancing to the edge of the swamp just north of Lake Susupe. Some units pushed into the swamp, only to withdraw a few hours later when it became apparent that they could not make it all the way across before nightfall.

On our right, Murdock led the remnants of B Company across the airstrip and set up his CP on the other side. He spent the next several hours running back and forth across the strip, through heavy shellfire, trying to locate the rest of his men. Assisting him was one of the company barbers, an Old Salt named Beaver. "He was an older guy and very savvy," Murdock recalled.

And he always seemed to be smoking a cigar. We'd be standing on the airstrip and I'd hear those shells coming over and I'd hit the deck, just drop to the ground. And I'd look up and see Beaver standing there, puffing on his cigar, smiling a little smile at me. I could read his mind: *What's the matter with this son of a bitch?* He knew by the sound of the shells, a kind of whispering noise, that they weren't going to hit anywhere near us. But I wasn't going to take any chances; I hit the ground anyway. And then I looked at him and he's still standing there, smiling, and I said to myself, *Oh, Jesus, Murdock, pick it up and be brave.*

★ ★ ★

By late afternoon the 8th Marines had advanced about one thousand yards and were dug in along the western edge of the swamp north of Lake Susupe. The 6th Marines were on our left, occupying a line that curved back from the previously captured radio station/communications center to a point just north of Red Beach 1 on the coast road to Garapan; the 2d Marines were starting to land on the beaches behind them. The 1/8 anchored the regiment's (hence the division's) extreme right flank. My outfit, C Company, was the last unit on the right, positioned more or less where the swamp and Lake Susupe merged. Here the line bent back to the sea, leaving a wide gap between the 2d and 4th divisions that extended west from the lake all the way to the shore between Afetna Point and Charan-Kanoa. In other words, our right flank was hanging in the air, practically inviting the Japanese to attack it. The high command surmised they would do just that and took steps to effect a linkup between the divisions and thus close the gap.

In the meantime I had gotten my mortars dug in and thought I was through for the day. I should have known better. Just before the light started to fade I was ordered to take a recon patrol into the gap. I was, to say the least, not happy. Traipsing about No man's land with evening coming on and an enemy counterattack in the works was just about the last thing I wanted to do. I couldn't say which possibility scared me more in the circumstances, running into the Japanese or into my fellow Marines: each was just as likely as the other to shoot or toss a grenade at me, no questions asked. I felt sick to my stomach just thinking about it.

But once again, orders were orders. I needed two men to go with me and asked for volunteers. Don Maines and another man in my section, Eugene Stevens, said they'd go. ("I must have been nuts!" Don said when I interviewed him about this episode.) We headed out in single file; I led the way, setting a brisk pace. Speed was more important than stealth, a risk worth taking—I reckoned we had no more than fifty minutes of daylight left to us, and I was anxious to complete the mission and return to our lines before nightfall.

The gap was deserted and silent. The 4th Marines weren't there. Neither were the Japanese. The emptiness was weird and unnerving. Close by were two full Marine divisions, one to the north and one to the south, and God knows how many thousands of Japanese to the east. But here, in this gap between the lines—nobody.

After thirty minutes of poking around I decided to call it quits. We had probed about two hundred yards into the gap, and that, I figured, was far enough. We went back the way we came, moving very quickly in the fast-fading light, loping along like a trio of wolves, our thumping boots and labored breathing the only sounds in that empty place. We were passing by an air-raid shelter, on our right, when a Japanese soldier bolted from the entrance. I saw him coming out of the corner of my eye, and he was almost on top of me before I could react. But I did react, without thinking, at once turning to face my assailant and stepping away from him. I tripped on the undergrowth and fell backward, but as I was going down I shot him once with my carbine. In the next instant Don Maines, who was right behind me, pumped two or three shots into him. I jumped up to find my carbine clogged with sand—I had jammed the muzzle into the ground when I fell. Maines and Stevens emptied their clips into the shelter's entrance, and then we got the hell out of there.

The Japanese soldier did not have a rifle. He might have had a grenade, but we didn't hang around to check. I don't think he meant to attack us. Probably he didn't see us when he emerged from the shelter and never knew what hit him. He had chosen the wrong moment to make a run for it. Bad luck for him.

We finally reached our lines, and Don and I fell into a foxhole together. We were exhausted, but the shells exploding all around us made sleep impossible. Also, we knew that nightfall would bring Japanese counterattacks. A little while later we spotted two shadowy figures moving toward us from the direction of the air-raid shelter. We assumed they were Japanese and shot them a few yards from our hole. They lay groaning and crying out and sometimes screaming, and there wasn't a damn thing anyone could or would do about it.

The next morning several men went out to inspect the bodies and discovered they were women. They must have come to us seeking refuge from the fighting and we had killed them instead. We all felt bad about that but didn't dwell on it. All I could think was that it could easily have been me lying out there, shot dead by my own men when I was returning from my recent foray into No man's land. Mistakes like that happened all the time. In fact, just such a mistake had happened that same night farther down the line. A green second lieutenant from A Company had gotten out of his foxhole and was walking toward his company commander's hole when one of his own men shot him through the head, mistaking him for one of the many Japanese infiltrators who were just then coming out of the swamp to attack our line.

★   ★   ★

Some time before the Japanese attacked, a captain attached to the division staff, Carl Hoffman, hopped into John Murdock's foxhole to escape a particularly intense interval of shellfire in B Company's sector. John and Hoffman were friends, and John greeted him warmly: "C'mon in, Carl, sit down. How'd you like a drink?"

Hoffman said, "Jesus, John, I'd love a drink!" It was his lucky night. John always went into the field with two canteens, one full of water and the other, his "medicinal canteen," filled with booze. He got the booze from the chaplain aboard ship, Fr. Joe Keehan, a fellow Irishman who could appreciate John's needs and was in a position to satisfy them.

"So we had a drink, me and Hoffman. We shot the shit, talked about things, about what was going to happen."

After the war, Hoffman wrote two USMC historical monographs on the campaign in the Marianas: *Saipan: The Beginning of the End* and *The Seizure of Tinian*. These accounts are considered definitive, but, not surprisingly, neither mentions the night the author spent with John Murdock sipping from John's "medicinal" canteen.

Later that night, gunfire erupted along the line in front of John's hole. First light revealed the bodies of many women and children strewn about the area, more civilians killed while trying to pass through our lines. "It was so sad," said John. "I felt sorry for them, even though they were Japs. I thought, *Oh, Jesus—oh, shit. That's just terrible.* But we had no choice, you know? Anyone who moved might get shot. I'll never forget it. But you go on."

★   ★   ★

That night the Japanese counterattacked at several points along our line. They came across the lake and the swamp, mostly in small groups. At the outset of the fighting, Don Maines scurried off to another hole containing one of my 60-mm mortars. The mortar's crew had lost its gunner, and Don, who had lost his own mortar and crew on the beach, took command of the weapon. Don and his new charges spent the rest of the night blooping out rounds at the Japanese. "It was a stupid damn thing they did," he recalled.

They banzai'd across the gosh-danged swamp, and we just shot 'em up. The swamp was marshy, water up to their ankles or knees. They were charging across in a sort of a line and they were yelling and screaming—they were just a little nutty. I was operating the mortar; we dug the base plate in and fired it that way. We were right out in the open. They fired as they came at us. We were firing from flat ground. We fired into the water and it was very effective: high arc, with a point detonation. We weren't cocky about our situation. Any time you're in combat it's a fearful experience! But it was like shooting ducks, really. I've got the gun sighted in and leveled and the second gunner was dropping the shells in. None of the Japanese who were charging across the swamp reached the shore. They got slaughtered right in the swamp.

Groups of Japanese continued to attack across the lake and the swamp as dawn approached, and were killed to a man. Then, at first light, eight or nine Japanese soldiers appeared in the swamp on the north side of Lake Susupe about a hundred yards in front of holes occupied by my old unit, 2d Platoon. They came walking out of the rushes and tall grass, and although all carried rifles, one of them was waving a little white flag and making other pacifistic gestures to indicate that he and his companions wanted to surrender. Lieutenant Sullivan told his men to hold their fire and stood and motioned for the enemy soldiers to come forward. He spoke to them in Japanese, assuring them that no one would shoot at them.

Dick Stein and Bill Crumpacker shared a foxhole near Sullivan's hole. They also shared a sense of foreboding about Sullivan. "Boy," Dick said to Bill. "I surely wouldn't be doin' that if I were him."

The enemy soldiers approached our line slowly, holding their rifles down, the Marines watching them intently. Then they stopped and conversed with each other. The Marines stared at them, weapons at the ready. No one spoke. A hush had fallen over the battlefield. The Japanese advanced a few more yards then stopped again and talked. They were now about forty yards from 2d Platoon's line. Suddenly they scattered and dropped down out of sight in the rushes behind low humps of mud.

Sullivan pointed to three or four Marines and said, "You guys come with me," then strode out into the swamp. But the Marines he had selected to accompany him hung back.

Bill looked at Dick. "Uh-oh," he said. "This is going to be interesting."

Other Marines reacted with less restraint. All up and down the line they began shouting at Sullivan:

"Get down, Lieutenant; you're gonna get shot."

"Lieutenant, don't go out there!"

"Watch out, they're faking!"

Sullivan was a big man, a former college football player, and a gung-ho Marine, a warrior who thrived on war. Before Pearl Harbor and enlisting in the Marines he had served with the British Eighth Army in North Africa as a volunteer ambulance driver. He carried a Tommy gun, one of the few officers to arm himself with that weapon, because he liked combat. He wasn't satisfied with merely directing his men in battle; he wanted take part in the fighting, getting in among the enemy at close quarters, blasting them with automatic fire. He was fearless and hard and aggressive, and he had absolute confidence in himself and his abilities. Now he walked toward the rushes where the enemy soldiers lay hidden, holding his Tommy gun with the barrel pointed up and the stock resting in the crook of his arm, jabbering at the Japanese soldiers in their own tongue.

Suddenly a shot rang out and Sullivan dropped, a bullet between his eyes.

"Ah, fer chrissakes!" said Bill, and opened fire on the rushes, quickly squeezing off eight rounds from his M1. In that same instant every other Marine on the line, the entire company, began shooting, blasting the rushes with everything they had—machine guns, BARs, rifles, and mortars. A little while later the company advanced into the swamp and met with no fire from the rushes. In killing Lieutenant Sullivan the Japanese soldiers managed to get themselves killed, which had probably been their intent from the beginning.

When I heard about Sullivan's death, I remembered talking about him with a couple of 1st Battalion officers just before the invasion. We spoke of his bravery and toughness and his fierce delight in battle, and we all reached the same conclusion: sooner or later he would become a hero—even if he were killed in the attempt. Well, he did become a hero, and he was killed. Maybe, just maybe, that had been *his* intent from the beginning.

★　　★　　★

Just after Sullivan was killed the 8th Marines went on the offensive. While some units mopped up the rear, others moved into the swamp toward the high ground beyond and also to our right—into the No man's land I had briefly explored late the previous day. My mortar section fired in support of the units attacking into the swamp. The instant after the first rounds popped out of their tubes I felt a stinging sensation in the upper back of my left arm. Our corpsman came over to me and I told him, "I guess I'm hit." The corpsman looked at the wound. Blood trickled from a little hole in my arm—nothing serious, a shrapnel wound. The corpsman said, "Ah, probably no reason to go back," and proceeded to dress the wound.

At first I didn't know where the shrapnel came from. Enemy guns and mortars were firing continuously, but nothing was hitting close by. Then, while the corpsman patched my wound, somebody said, "Hey, you got that from one of your own mortar shells." I thought, *Oh, geez, I guess it could be.* One of the gunners admitted, sheepishly, "Yeah, it was us." His first round had hit a tree branch just overhead, exploding and spraying metal to the ground. My guys were embarrassed by their mistake. I wasn't angry, though—it was just another friendly fire incident. Happened all the time; no use getting upset about it. I didn't receive a Purple Heart for the wound, because I never reported it, but I still carry the shrapnel, a sliver of metal about a quarter of an inch long, in my arm.

Around this time John Murdock also became a casualty, hit while leading B Company on a sweep west of the landing strip, down toward Charan-Kanoa. He recalled:

Opposition was very light on the other side of the strip, and when we got down to the end of it we stopped and a Sherman tank came up to help us. The tank had a phone in the back, and I was on the phone and I'm trying to tell the guy inside where I wanted him to shoot: at the big smokestack in the sugar cane factory. I figured a Jap was up there spotting for his artillery, which was very accurate. Then all of a sudden: BOOM! Shells started falling around the tank and I just knew that the spotter in the smokestack was telling his guns to fire at us. So I ordered the tank commander, "Get that smokestack!" Then I put the phone back and I'm running back to safety, to a hole, and that's when I got hit by shrapnel in the left leg and right elbow.

He felt as though he had been hit in the arm by a baseball bat, a blow so painful that it masked the pain he would otherwise have felt in his leg. Not knowing that he had been hit in the leg, he ran over to a big rock and sat down beside it.

So I'm just sitting there, and the corpsman comes over and starts bandaging my arm, and I looked down—and my pants are all wet. And I said, "Holy shit, I pissed my pants." And the corpsman says, "That's not piss, that's blood." That's when I found out I had been hit in the leg. So I dropped my pants and my drawers and now the corpsman's bandaging up my leg, and the Japs start to shell us again. So I jumped and ran to a hole nearby, which wasn't easy, you know, because my pants and drawers were down around my ankles.

John's exec, Jim Westerman, appeared on the scene, and John told Westerman to take over: "Here, Westy, congratulations: you just made company commander! I'm getting out of here!"

So I headed for the beach, looking for the evacuation team. I wasn't bleeding all that badly, but I was a mess. I could walk, sure, and I walked. I was looking for one particular doctor, Sol Cosol, a dentist. Earlier I had seen him on the beach there, and now I found him and said, "Solomon, my friend: a ticket, please!" Because you couldn't get evacuated without a ticket—they had to put a ticket on you. He looked me over. My right hand wasn't any good, I couldn't use it, and Solomon ticketed me. A little while later I was evacuated in a small boat, and I said to the Navy kid who was driving it, "Hey, find me APA 51, will you?" And he said, "Sure."

We found the ship. And by then I was lying down and the guys on deck called down to me: "We'll pick you up in a boom on a stretcher." And I came up in the basket, and I'm all dirty and bloody. And I see our chaplain, Father Joe Keehan, who I'd become very friendly with; so when they took me out of the basket and put my stretcher on the deck I closed my eyes and pretended I was dead. Father Joe came over and started giving me Last Rites of the Church in Latin. But I can't keep a straight face, so I open my eyes and smile at him. And he goes, "You son of a bitch." He goes right from speaking Latin to calling me an SOB. Then he took me down to the infirmary and they patched me up a bit. Then he took me to his stateroom and put me in his bed. I must have slept all day and all night. I didn't hear a thing. I wasn't feeling any pain. My right hand and arm were numb.

When I came to, I didn't know where I was at first. Then I took a shower, changed the bandages, got cleaned up. That was the end of my war there. My second day on Saipan. My right arm was no good, really. My hand, even today, it's no good. I don't have any feeling in the right side of my hand—the nerve was cut. It was a million-dollar wound, really. Because my thumb and two fingers are good, still good. The next to the last finger and the little finger were dead; they're still dead.

★   ★   ★

The rest of the day passed with little forward movement by either division. Positions were consolidated, lines straightened, beachheads made more secure. Around noon the 2/8 and elements of the 1/29 linked up with 4th Division units at the Charan-Kanoa pier, in the process clearing Afetna and the area east of Lake Susupe. That night my mortar section stayed in the same holes we had occupied since nightfall of the first day and tried to get some rest before the Japanese launched their expected counterattack.

Starting at 0400 on the division's left, the 6th Marines were assaulted by a strong force spearheaded by upward of forty tanks—the largest concentration of enemy armor in the Pacific War. By daybreak the attack had been repulsed and most of the tanks destroyed. Shortly thereafter the entire division resumed the offensive. The 8th Marines' immediate objective was the first line of hills on the approaches of Mt. Tapotchau, east of the swamp and about fifteen hundred yards inland. We advanced across the swamp, encountering no resistance but coming across a lot of dead Japanese. The riflemen in the skirmish lines ahead of my mortar section kicked the bodies and shot them if they moved, and sometimes even if they didn't move.

We emerged from the swamp and moved across flat, open sugarcane fields that were just like the fields around Camp Tarawa on Hawaii. Still no resistance, although shells continued to fall among us. Evidently the Japanese had pulled back into the hills, a sensible move. We liked the look of the land, found it reassuring: there were telephone poles, roads, farmhouses with yards, all very familiar, very normal. The kids from the Midwest said it reminded them of home.

Finally we reached the top of the ridge and dug in. During the night a small enemy force attacked our left and was thrown back after a sharp fight. A mortar round exploded near a foxhole to my left, and its occupant screamed that his arm had been blown off. He screamed for several minutes and then went silent and I assumed he was dead. There was nothing I could do for him. Next morning his buddies found him alive and in fairly good shape considering the severity of his wound, which had clotted and stopped bleeding on its own.

We woke that morning to find that the vast fleet that had been anchored offshore had mostly vanished, leaving only a few ships behind. What a shock that was! The new kids wondered whether the Navy had abandoned us, but the veterans of Guadalcanal quickly set them straight. We had seen this before and we knew what it meant: a big sea battle was in the offing.

★   ★   ★

We were right. A few days later we learned that a great battle had indeed been fought in the waters west of Saipan, resulting in a decisive victory for the U.S. Navy. With their defeat in the Battle of the Philippine Sea the Japanese lost all hope of relieving their forces on Saipan. Now it was up to us—the Marines and the Army—to win the land battle.

The ridge we had seized formed what was designated the O-1 phase line. Now that it was firmly in our hands, preparations could begin for the main offensive, the drive north up the length of the island. The 2d Division's regiments were aligned as follows: 2d Marines on the west coast, facing north; 6th Marines in the center, facing east; 8th Marines on the right, also facing east. The 6th and 8th Marines, in order to get into position for the offensive, had to wheel around to the north, pivoting on the 2d Marines. The 2/8 and 1/29 (still attached to the 8th Marines) were on the outside of the wheel, to 1st Battalion's right, and thus had the farthest to go. The 1st Battalion Marines spent a few days on the O-1 ridge waiting for those units to come up alongside them. From our vantage point we could clearly see the Marine units on our right moving about, shooting and getting shot at by the mostly invisible Japanese. Then they reached our line, and we climbed out of our holes and joined them in the wheeling movement to the north, toward Mt. Tapotchau.

Our brief spell on the ridge had been fairly uneventful, with combat limited to short, sharp skirmishes between our patrols and enemy rearguard elements. The Marines returned from these encounters little impressed by the fighting but mightily concerned about the rugged terrain through which we would soon be advancing. The real action took place above us when Japanese fighters, zooming in from the sea through withering antiaircraft fire, attacked our ships. Some of these planes were hit, exploding in midair or diving into the ground and vanishing in a quick, bright flash; the survivors flew low over our line, sometimes loosing a burst at us in passing. During the night the Japanese on the ground, as usual, crept close to our positions and tried to lure us out of our holes by crying out, "Hey, Joe, I'm hit; help me," and "Corpsman, corpsman!" The veterans weren't about to fall for this old trick and stayed in their holes, but there were a lot of green kids in the line, and at least once that I know of a new corpsman crawled out to help what he thought was a stricken Marine, only to get killed for his effort.

The 2d Division's wheel to the north put it in contact with the 4th Division on its right. The two Marine divisions thus established a more or less continuous line across the island, with the 4th Division's right anchored on Magicienne Bay. But the 4th Division's advance soon carried it north of the bay and into the Kagman Peninsula, which extends east above the bay. The 4th Division began pivoting to its right into the peninsula, and on 23 June the bulk of the Army's 27th Division was inserted into the center of the line, southeast of

Mt. Tapotchau, to fill the gap that had opened as a result of the 4th Division's turning move.

Meanwhile the 8th Marines advanced in columns along narrow trails on a line of march that took us across and up the west face of Mt. Tapotchau through a devil's garden of brush-choked ravines and hillsides, steep, jagged limestone ridges, and sheer cliffs plunging into deep gorges. The 1st Battalion found a ravine on the south face leading to the mountaintop and followed it the whole way up. Japanese rearguard units intermittently contested our advance through that wilderness, staying hidden in the dense foliage and in caves until our forward elements were almost on top of them and then announcing their presence with the sudden furious racket of machine-gun and rifle fire and banging grenades. At which point the column would halt as corpsmen sprang forward to assist the wounded while the forward elements returned fire even as they started to work around the enemy position to take it from the flank or rear. If a flanking movement was not possible in the constricted terrain, we simply bashed our way through. We didn't have tanks—they couldn't operate in that terrain—but we did have mortars, and these became the only means at hand to provide close-in support fires for attacking the rearguard positions.

My mortar section was always about two hundred yards behind our lead elements. An outbreak of small-arms fire in front of us was the signal to stop and set up our weapons. We started firing as soon as we received target coordinates. Once the enemy position was taken, we disassembled the mortars, packed up our ammunition and gear, and moved on with the rest of the column.

Casualties overall were relatively light, with the point men, as usual, getting the worst of it. But not always. Somewhere between the O-3 and O-4 phase lines, while we were taking a break, a random Japanese mortar shell dropped in on our column, bursting among three senior NCOs who were seated on the ground about seventy yards from me. The sergeants went limp and collapsed in a heap and were still. Immediately a corpsman was kneeling beside them, looking for their wounds, trying to help. But there were no wounds to be found, and they were beyond help, killed instantly by the concussion. The corpsman covered their faces and tagged them for the burial-registration people. There was nothing more to be done.

I went over and looked at them for a moment, then we got the order to move out and I turned and walked away. I regretted the loss of three experienced NCOs, but otherwise I was unmoved by their deaths. I felt no sadness or shock or horror. No anger, either. The Japanese killed us and we killed them—it was all part of the job, of the business we were in. Anger had nothing to do with it.

Meanwhile, off to our right on the other side of the mountain, the 27th Division had run into a meat grinder. The Army was attacking on a plateau bordered on its left by a sheer cliff that formed the east face of the mountain and on its right by a series of hills connected by a ridge. The latter was soon dubbed "Purple Heart Ridge" and the plateau became known as "Death Valley," epithets indicative of the hard fighting there.

The Marines from units on 1st Battalion's right, having finally reached the top of the mountain, could stand on the edge of that sheer cliff and watch as the Army units some eight hundred feet below them tried again and again to advance, only to be halted and thrown back each time. The Marines could see groups of soldiers in their ODs moving through the brush and mortars shells exploding among them, cutting them down. Others were felled by machine-gun and rifle fire. The sounds of battle, a constant rattle of small arms and explosions, floated up to the watchers on the summit, and they knew that the GIs were catching hell down there. But there was nothing they could do to help. The Marines were eight hundred feet above them, too high to render assistance.

The Army's failure to advance infuriated the Marine commander of the Saipan operation, Lt. Gen. Holland Smith, who acted quickly to rectify the situation. On 24 June, just one day after sending the 27th Division into Death Valley, he relieved the division's commander, Maj. Gen. Ralph Smith. This move stirred up a hornet's nest of accusation and recrimination as senior Army and Marine generals rushed to defend or condemn the actions of the respective Smiths. The controversy raged on until well after the war was over, with many harsh words exchanged and bad feelings engendered. Representatives for the Army asserted that Holland Smith had acted unjustly and precipitously in firing Ralph Smith—that the latter had handled his division ably in what were very difficult circumstances and that, given just a little more time, he would have prevailed over the enemy. Marine Corps advocates contended that the 27th Division's problems in Death Valley were largely due to errors made by Ralph Smith in its deployment and use and that Holland Smith had acted correctly to remove the Army general before those problems worsened and brought the whole offensive to a halt.

At the time, for the vast majority of Marines, soldiers, and sailors involved in the battle for Saipan, this dispute between generals was as remote as the wrangling of the Olympian gods had been to the Greek and Trojan warriors fighting on Ilium's plain. We knew little about it and cared even less. The generals had their war to fight and we had ours.

On 25 June, elements of the 1/29 on our right captured the summit of Mt. Tapotchau. My unit drove a short distance below and beyond the summit, halting at dusk. We resumed movement at 0800 and kept going until nightfall, digging in on the high ground above Tanapag Plain. Thus situated, we could see all the way to Tanapag town and harbor, which were burning and wreathed with smoke. Between the town and our positions stretched an expanse of open, rolling hills falling gently away to the sea.

My mortar section remained on the high ground for a short time, firing in support of our advancing units. That lofty perch proved ideal for the job. It provided a wide, clear view of the action below, allowing us to easily pinpoint enemy positions and mortar them with devastating accuracy.

Presently we decamped and moved down through the hills behind our frontline units. During this movement Don Maines and his fellow mortar crewmen—John Paypatch and Jim Petty—stumbled on a Japanese supply dump. "We found tins of crabmeat and big bottles of sake, all kinds of stuff," Don recalled.

So we confiscated an oxcart with an ox tied to it and drove it back to the supply dump and loaded all this stuff into it and drove the oxcart back to our unit. And the ground was littered the whole way with these damned Japanese artillery shells and we tried to avoid them but the ox wouldn't let us. We found out that once you get an ox started, he'll go straight ahead, and that's it! So we're rolling over live ordnance. And this Navy photographer comes up and says, "Hey, fellas, lemme take a picture." And he took pictures of us standing in front of the oxcart grinning and holding those big bottles of sake.

When we got back to our unit we broke out the sake—and we had a ball! We all got half-crocked! We weren't worried about getting attacked. We were on a push. So everything was in front of us—way, way in front of us. We spent the night in that position eating the crabmeat and drinking the sake, and we got drunk.

Where was I when Don and his buddies had their little party? Possibly asleep in my hole; possibly back at company HQ. In any event, I didn't find out about their shenanigans until after the war when Don told me the whole story at a reunion. I laughed as he recounted it, especially when he described their terrible condition the next day. Bleary-eyed and tormented by splitting headaches and gut-wrenching nausea, burdened by the weight of their mortar tubes and base plates, the desperately hung-over mortarmen trudged along through the heat of the day thinking that death might be preferable to the way they felt. They were dragging, but I don't remember noticing anything different about them. The truth is, everyone was dragging, myself included. We all looked like hell: weary and wasted, shuffling along like zombies, slack-jawed and blank, with thousand-yard stares that saw everything and comprehended nothing.

★   ★   ★

By 1 July the 8th Marines had driven north of Mt. Tapotchau into rolling country east of Garapan, assaulting and capturing four small but strongly defended hills dubbed the "four pimples." My mortar section and other 1st Battalion units passed an uneventful night on high ground in a stand of trees and rose early the next morning to resume the advance. Around 0800 the rifle platoons formed a skirmish line and moved out. My section and the company's Weapons Platoon stayed in the trees and readied ourselves to move out in another thirty minutes or so, after the lead elements had cleared the area ahead of us. It was a quiet morning; the Japanese had evidently withdrawn from the immediate area. I was resting on one knee next to a tree, holding my carbine upright with the butt plate to the ground, when suddenly WHAM! WHAM! WHAM! Three big shells exploded over our position.

The shells came not from Japanese artillery but from a battery of Army 155s located deep in our rear. Either the battery's fire-control directors had miscalculated or, unaware of how far and fast the 2d Division had advanced, they deliberately targeted an area they thought was controlled by the Japanese. We didn't know what had hit us. Most of us did not hear the shells coming. No one shouted a warning, no one ducked for cover. One of the shells burst in the tree above me, deflecting the force of the blast and most of the shrapnel outward instead of straight down. That's what saved my life. A single piece of metal pierced my elbow. The wound was larger than a bullet hole, about an inch in diameter, and it hurt like hell, but it didn't look serious: it hardly bled and the bone didn't seem damaged.

Still, the wound needed treatment. A few minutes later several hospital jeeps converged on the scene, and I walked over to one of them. On the way, just fifty yards from my tree, I passed a large crater containing the remains of several men from Weapons Platoon who had been playing blackjack when a shell hit their position. They had been blown literally to bits. Several of these men had been my friends since Samoa. I had served in their unit before being commissioned. I could identify only one of them, and only by the glasses he wore.

A few yards further on, a dead Marine lay in a hole beneath a coral outcropping where I had spent the previous night. He too had been killed by the Army's misdirected salvo.

The same shell that killed the blackjack players wounded Dick Stein, then a member of Weapons Platoon. He doesn't remember the explosion or anything else about that day. "One moment I'm standing around with the guys in the Weapons Platoon, and the next thing I know I'm waking up in a tent there in a field hospital and it's around midnight. I woke up and said, 'What the heck am I doin' here?'"

Bill Crumpacker, also in the area but unharmed, watched as Dick was placed aboard a jeep that would take him to the regimental hospital in the former Japanese radio station/communications center outside Charan-Kanoa. Unconscious and limp, bleeding from his wounds, Dick looked close to death, and Bill figured his good buddy had finally run out of luck. He was wrong. Dick Stein never ran out of luck.

I'd got a chunk of meat taken out of my right side, just like you'd take a spoon out of a dish of ice cream. They just put a bandage on it. Nearby [in the hospital] was this Marine screaming to high heaven. They were taking an arm or a leg off and he was cussing and screaming and hollering. I can't remember much else after that. I must have passed out. But after I woke again the next day I said, "Jeez, I'm not gonna stay here; there's nothing wrong with me." Because I felt okay. So I went back up to the front line.

Don Maines was also wounded. The blast knocked him down, and a piece of shrapnel tore through his right side and sliced off part of his scrotum, severing his right testicle. One of our corpsmen gave him a shot of morphine; a few minutes later he got a second shot from another corpsman who didn't know that Don had already been injected. He was then placed on a stretcher in the back of a jeep for transport to the field hospital. On the way there, a sniper threw a few shots at the jeep and the driver stomped on the gas pedal. They sped around a sharp turn and hit a rough patch that bounced Don and his stretcher clear out of the jeep and into the road. Bleeding profusely but giddy with morphine and feeling no pain, he sat in the road laughing, completely oblivious to the severity of his injuries.

After receiving emergency treatment on Saipan, Don was put aboard a hospital ship that took him to a hospital on Guadalcanal. He made a full recovery and returned to the 2d Division in time to take part in the 1945 invasion of Okinawa.

As for me: I too was put on a stretcher and taken by jeep to the hospital outside Charan-Kanoa. On a stretcher next to me lay Pfc. John O. McCarley, one of my squad leaders on Guadalcanal. One of his legs was gone. All he had left of it was a stump, bloody and bandaged.

In all, the shells from the 155s killed or wounded more than fifty Marines. One of those wounded was Capt. Jim Westerman, who had taken over B Company after John Murdock was wounded. Like John, he would spend the rest of the war recuperating. George Stein replaced him as B Company commander.

I spent two nights and most of three days in the regimental field hospital. In the meantime, on 4 July, the 2d Marine Division went into reserve, its place taken on the front line by the 27th Division. The 8th Marines bivouacked in the vicinity of Tanapag harbor.

Late on 7 July, my third day in the field hospital, doctors and corpsmen went through the wards telling all the walking wounded to return at once to our units. They told us that the Japanese had launched a big banzai attack, that our forces had gotten creamed, that the fighting was still going on, and that every man who was able to walk was needed at the front.

CHAPTER NINE

Banzai

THE JAPANESE COUNTERATTACK WAS NOT UNEXPECTED. Everyone from General Smith on down to the lowliest private knew it was coming. And yet, it caught everyone by surprise.

The blow fell on the west side of the island, just north of Tanapag town. The Army's 27th Division was operating in that sector, having relieved the 2d Marine Division, which had pulled back to refit for the invasion of Tinian. When the attack came, most of the 2d Division, including its three infantry regiments, had moved well south of the combat zone. Only the 3d Battalion of the 10th Marines—the division's artillery regiment—was forward-deployed.

Some five thousand Japanese took part in the attack, a disparate force comprising frontline units, noncombatant troops, civilian construction workers, and the walking wounded. They were variously armed: some with the usual complement of weapons and some with grenades only, and others carrying bamboo shafts with bayonets lashed to the tips. They were essentially leaderless, their top commanders having committed hara-kiri after issuing orders for the attack. And they had no objective other than to head south and keep going for as long as they could, for as far as they could, killing as many Americans as they could until they themselves were killed.

The attack began on the night of 6 July in typical Japanese fashion, with patrols probing our perimeter for weak spots. They soon found one: a three-hundred-yard expanse of largely unoccupied ground separating the 1st and 2d battalions of the Army's 105th Regiment. First contact was signaled by smatterings of gunfire and grenade explosions all along the line. Hard on their

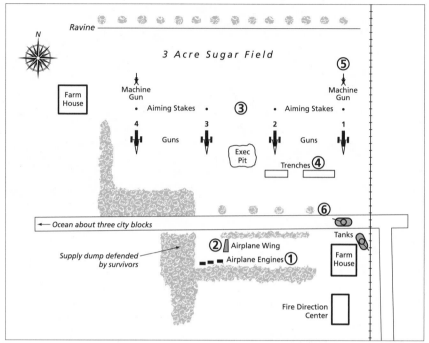

Position During Banzai Attack on Saipan.

Notes:

1. Three airplane engines in crates.
2. Airplane wing.
3. Aiming stakes (one behind each gun).
4. Two trenches, each filled with 55-gallon drums of aviation fuel.
5. Machine gun operated by Holzer and Hoffman.
6. Line of pine trees behind trench.

heels came the main body of the enemy force, conducting what would become the largest banzai attack of the war.

They advanced in three columns. The smallest pushed down the beach at the water's edge. Another drove along the base of the cliff that bounded the Tanapag Plain on the east. The largest force came right down the middle, advancing along a narrow-gauge railroad that ran parallel to the sea on a low embankment about three-quarters of a mile inland.

The enemy host slammed into the two Army battalions and poured through the gap separating them. Positioned some six hundred yards to the rear of the Army units, just to the left (west) of the railway embankment, were the four 105-mm guns of Hotel (H) Battery, 3/10 Marines. Rodney Sandburg, a twenty-year-old private, first class in the battery's instrument section, was on duty in what was known as the "exec pit" when the shooting started. Sandy is my principal source for what happened to the men of H Battery in the desperate hours that followed.

His account, it should be noted, is at odds in certain key respects with official histories of the battle and with books and articles based on those histories. For instance, the official histories and their progeny place H Battery south of Tanapag and state that the Japanese attack began around 0400 on the morning of 7 July. Sandy contends that H Battery was set up north of Tanapag and that the attack started shortly after nightfall on 6 July. He is very firm about this, as are his buddies. I believe they're right, and I also believe that future research on the subject will substantiate their claims.* The account that follows is based mostly on personal interviews I conducted with Sandy in 2004–6 and on an unpublished account Sandy wrote and made available to me. I also interviewed Don Holzer, a machine-gunner in the battery; he passed away in 2005. I trust Sandy's memory. In the course of refuting the official version, he declared—emphatically: "There isn't much I have forgotten about that day, as I live it every day of my life."

On the morning of 5 July, H Battery had moved from positions in southern Saipan to a rest area in the vicinity of Tanapag harbor. All hands thought they would do no more fighting on Saipan and would stay in the rest area for several days, until the island was secured. Next afternoon, however, they received orders to relocate to positions closer to the front, where they would provide support fires for the 27th Division. Army commanders had specifically requested H Battery, because it was more accurate than their own batteries—which, as I had recently learned through personal experience, could be dangerously unreliable.

The battery's destination was a wooded grove on the high ground just north of Tanapag town—Sandy estimates its distance from the ocean to be about "two or three city blocks." They arrived there in late afternoon and set up their four guns among a group of large trees, facing north, in a line about one hundred feet long. Gun 1 was placed on the battery's right next to the railway embankment, which was about two or three feet high and formed the eastern perimeter of the battery's position. Guns 2, 3, and 4 were spread out, in

---

* A mural depicting the battle hangs in the Pentagon. Any discussion of the mural at H Battery reunions always ends with everyone agreeing that it woefully misrepresents what really happened.

that order, to its left. The exec pit—a shallow rectangular excavation bordered by fifty-gallon drums and covered over with a tarpaulin—was dug, as always, between Guns 2 and 3, just beside the trails of 2. The men in the exec pit received targeting information from the 3d Battalion Fire Direction Center [FDC], which also housed the battalion HQ.

Just north of the battery there was a sugarcane field about three acres square backed by a stand of pine trees. A ravine cut across the battery's front at the back (north edge) of the field just in front of the pine trees, but the Marines were unaware of this terrain feature, because the waist-high cane concealed it from their view.

West of Gun 4 a dry ravine filled with underbrush and trees ran more or less parallel (north–south) to the ocean. West of that ravine and a little north of the battery position, at the edge of the cane field, stood a small white farmhouse, which could not be seen from the battery because of the dense undergrowth growing out of the ravine.

Some 100–150 feet to the battery's rear, an east–west road crossed the railway embankment and descended on a gentle incline to the north–south beach road, forming a T intersection where the two roads met. Between the battery and the road, no more than fifteen feet behind Guns 1 and 2, were two twenty-five-foot trenches filled with two rows of 55-gallon drums of aviation fuel in stacks of three.

The area between the road and the battery position behind Guns 3 and 4 was choked with foliage, blocking the road from view and preventing access to it as well.

Behind Gun 1, some fifty to seventy-five feet south of the road and about half that distance west of the railroad tracks, stood another farmhouse. The 3d Battalion FDC tent and the Headquarters and Services (H&S) section were set up behind the house. Batteries I and G were echeloned back and to the right of the FDC; that is, southeast of the railroad tracks and H Battery.

West of the farmhouse in a stand of large trees there was a storage dump containing crated engines for Japanese aircraft. Various other aircraft parts, including wings, were scattered around the site. South of the dump was a small clearing that was bordered on the west by a line of trees and a ravine, and on the east by trees, heavy underbrush, and the railroad tracks.

By the time the Marines of H Battery had set up their guns it was too late in the day to dig them in. Empty 55-gallon drums placed in front of each gun provided some protection. These were to be filled with sand on the morrow.

The gun crews did take the normal precautionary measure of preparing three or four "ready-to-fire" shells for each gun. Each shell consisted of two parts: explosive projectile and powder casing. The casing could hold up to seven bags (each with enough powder to fill a coffee mug). This was the maximum charge, or "charge 7," and it was used only for very-long-range fire missions. For ease of storage and transport, however, the shells came fully assembled with charge 7 in either a three-shell container (known as a "cloverleaf") or a two-shell container. Prior to most fire missions, the shells had to be disassembled for removal of the extraneous bags, then reassembled with the desired charge, which was determined with calculations that took into account the distance to the target, wind direction and velocity, and related factors. If airbursts were desired, the fuzes on the projectiles were set (or "cut," in artilleryman's jargon) to explode at a predetermined distance. Usually this was unnecessary: most fire missions entailed shells exploding on contact with the ground. Battery H's ready-to-fire shells contained two powder bags, considered sufficient for most contingencies.

The Japanese had withdrawn to the north end of the island, beyond the cane field. The Marine artillerymen did not expect any trouble from that direction, or from any other direction, for that matter. Apart from the dangers posed by snipers and infiltrators they felt reasonably secure in their new position. Two battalions of the Army's 105th Infantry Regiment held the front line in their sector, and the presence of these units plus the battery's distance from the line seemed a pretty firm guarantee against having to repel a large-scale attack. To reach the battery a Japanese force would first have to punch through the dug-in Army battalions and then traverse six hundred yards of presumably fire-swept ground. The Marines did not consider that likely. They did not think the Japanese had the wherewithal to attack them in force. "We all felt that the rest of the battle for Saipan was just going to be a matter of cleaning up the few Japanese still on the island," Sandy recalled.

This conviction that the Japanese were all but beaten induced someone in authority to send the battery's trucks back to Tanapag town to fetch the men's packs and the rear-echelon personnel. Many of the latter were already with the battery, having accompanied it in the original move to the new position. These included cooks, clerks, the quartermaster section, truckers—men who normally did not go with the battery to its firing positions and who knew little about operating the guns. The rationale in bringing them was to give all hands a taste of what it was like to be up front, but in relatively safe circumstances.

"We had no inkling of what was to come," Sandy said. "None whatsoever."

At dusk, Sandy went into the exec pit for the night's first shift as battery recorder. Joining him were 1st Lt. Arnold C. Hofstetter, the battery's executive commander; P.Sgt. Richard Mathews; and radioman/telephone operator Pfc. Thomas Moretti. Sandy arranged for Pfc. Gene "Swede" Larson to relieve him at midnight. In the meantime, Swede would dig the foxhole the two men were to share.

Around dusk, Hofstetter ordered Lt. Harold Lane to "survey" the guns, the process by which the guns were arranged so that all four were exactly parallel with each other. Lane and several men from the instrument section went out in front of Gun 1, which was always the first gun in every battery to be surveyed. Almost immediately they began drawing sniper fire. They managed to survey Gun 1, but when Lane reported that the sniper fire was getting worse by the minute Hofstetter decided that the other guns could be surveyed from Gun 1 and ordered the team back to the battery position.

Lane and his men hastened back to the battery. On the way, they set up aiming stakes but did not turn on the battery-operated red and green lights affixed to each stake. These lights served as visual aids for the gunners when firing at night, but since enemy snipers could use them for the same purpose, Hofstetter thought it best to keep them switched off. It was just as well. The gunners did not have time before nightfall to fire into a base point and in any case had no FO (forward observer) in position to correct their fire. The FO would not arrive until morning. There were to be no fire missions that night.

With darkness descending on their position and Japanese sniper fire steadily increasing in volume and intensity, Hofstetter detailed Gun 2's section chief, Sgt. Ralph L. Conner (nicknamed "Pop" because he was older than just about everyone in the battery), to set up two .50-caliber machine guns in front of their position, one on each flank. He also ordered Sgt. Robert Delahunt, who commanded the battery's machine-gun section, to set up two .30-caliber machine guns south of the road in the battery's rear, to guard the storage dump.

The machine gun out front on the right (near the railroad tracks) was a big .50-caliber weapon manned by Pvt. Don Holzer and Pvt. Harold Hoffman. They had set up on a knoll overlooking the ravine that cut across the rear of the cane field. The cane in front of them stood four or five feet high, and their field of fire was patchy: forty to fifty yards in some places, a mere ten yards in others. There were several small bridges across the ravine, but all had been blown out. Holzer and Hoffman were out in the open, but mounds of dirt and cut cane stalks and debris around their position afforded some protection. They were all alone, with no riflemen to provide close support. Nor could they communicate with the battery; everyone had been too busy preparing the main position and setting up the 105s before nightfall to lay the phone line to the exec pit.

After dark, the Japanese began massing in the ravine. Holzer and Hoffman could hear them talking, hollering, making a lot of noise, and all the while shooting up white parachute flares that floated through the air for twenty seconds or so, bathing the area in light. The two Marines couldn't see the Japanese, but they figured the Japanese could see them clearly in the light of the flares.

This went on for hours: flares popping overhead, one after the other, drifting down on parachutes. "All that time the noise kept getting louder and louder," Don remembered. "There wasn't any shooting. Just the noise: the Japanese yelling."

At length it seemed to Holzer and Hoffman that the noise reached a sort of crescendo, indicating that the Japanese were about to attack, and they opened fire. "There were no visible targets. We just depressed the muzzle and fired into the noise, fired into the darkness in the ravine. We knew we were hitting them—we could hear them screaming. We thought we were about to be overrun. It was clear to us what the problem was: they could see us but we couldn't see them. But they still were not firing at us at this point."

According to Sandy, "It was about nine o'clock at night, nine-thirty, when all hell broke loose out in front of our battery, and one of the machine guns started firing."

The other machine gun joined in a few seconds later. The men in the exec pit couldn't tell which gun fired first, the weapon on the right (manned by Holzer and Hoffman) or the one on the left. They were not about to pull the tarp aside to look outside. Had they done so the light from the lantern they kept inside would have revealed their position. Hofstetter demanded to know what was going on and ordered Thomas Moretti, the telephone operator, to get the machine-gunners on the line. Moretti tried, but of course he couldn't raise them. No one in the exec pit knew that there were no phone lines connecting them to the machine-gunners.

"I can't get a hold of them," Moretti told Hofstetter. "I'll see if I can get the communications chief to send somebody to check the wire."

Hofstetter said, "No, we're not gonna do that. I think the machine-gunners are firing at each other. They might fire on the section chief if he goes out there." He added, "It wouldn't be the first time Marines fired on their own. It's easy to do when you're put in position after dark."

The machine guns kept firing. Hofstetter fumed. "Those machine-gunners are gonna be court-martialed when daylight comes," he muttered to no one in particular. He then ordered the 105 crews to report in and told them that the usual practice of relieving the crews at midnight was suspended: every man now at his post was to stay there through the night. "No one will relieve anybody else; those people who are not on duty will stay off duty." And he said to the others in the exec pit: "We'll deal with the machine-gunners in the morning."

"So we sat in the pit under the tarp listening to Hofstetter gripe about the machine-gunners supposedly firing at one another," said Sandy. "We didn't step out of the pit—no way we'd open the tarp and break blackout conditions. We could hear the machine guns but we didn't see the flares. As far as we knew, all the rest of the guys were down in their holes."

Meanwhile, Don Holzer and Harold Hoffman were blasting away at their so-far invisible foes, firing down into the darkness, into the tall cane; traversing the barrel from side to side and back again, firing short bursts and long bursts and intermediate bursts; firing and reloading and firing again. The big gun roaring and bucking on its tripod, spewing long, ragged jets of fire from the muzzle, throwing hot shell casings to one side. The air thick with the smoke and smell of their firing and illuminated by the strange white light of the flares. The Japanese screaming and howling, working themselves into a frenzy.

At length, with dawn's first light graying the sky, the Japanese stopped sending up flares. Holzer and Hoffman kept firing into the cane. And then—

All of a sudden we heard a rustling sound behind us. We turned around and three Japanese, big guys, were standing about ten or fifteen feet from our position. They didn't have rifles but they did have grenades and they started tossing them at us. I grabbed the tripod and tipped the gun over so they couldn't use it. Then I grabbed my carbine and dove into the heavy grass and pulled the trigger. But the carbine was jammed. When I hit the ground I must have hit the clip and pushed it on into the chamber and damaged it.

They jumped us then. Two of them jumped us; the third one, I have no idea where he went. I threw down my carbine and pulled out my KA-BAR. The guy who attacked me, he didn't have a weapon; he came at me and grabbed me. I went for his gut. I got him several times, at least three thrusts. I can still see the expression on his face. He knew he was gone. He knew he was licked. Surprised, like. He didn't say a word. He didn't gasp or shout. He was quiet. And then he went down.

This encounter probably marks the beginning of the Japanese assault on H Battery. By then the Japanese had surrounded the guns, as Rod Sandburg quickly discovered:

> It was just starting to get light when Swede Larson came in the exec pit and relieved me. I took my carbine and started out of the exec pit. There was a guy in a foxhole right outside the door, and he said, "Sandy, be quiet; there's Japs on the road." I looked out on the road, and there's a Jap tank about thirty-five or forty feet from us. There were Japanese infantrymen walking in front of it, five abreast, a whole platoon of them. There were more behind it. I was standing in full sight of them, but it was still just dark enough where they couldn't recognize me as a Marine. They could see somebody standing there, but they couldn't see whether I was a Marine or one of them.

The Japanese tank and its infantry screen approached from the ocean side, heading east on the road toward the railway embankment, spearheading the force assaulting from Marpi Point down the beach road. A couple dozen yards behind the tank marched another large group of Japanese soldiers. Some fifty yards to their rear, on the other side of the brush and trees fringing that part of the road, Sandy could hear a second tank approaching. The infantrymen in both groups "were oblivious to our location and were marching slow and in step, just like they were on a parade ground."

Sandy ducked backed into the exec pit and told Hofstetter about the tank. Just then, Gun 1's telephone operator called, asking for permission to turn the gun toward the tank. "Do it," said Hofstetter. Sandy stepped out of the tent and watched as the crew manhandled their gun into position, pushing and pulling its trails until it pointed at the tank. Then the gunner yanked the lanyard and the gun roared, scoring a hit dead center in the hull of the tank as it started to crawl up onto the railway embankment.

The tank abruptly halted. For what "seemed an eternity" nothing happened. Then an internal explosion rocked the vehicle, spinning the turret around so the main gun was pointing backward; that is, down the road toward the sea. The Japanese infantry in front of and behind the tank scattered, most of them south in the direction of the storage dump.

In the next instant Sandy heard somebody shout, "Look out there in front!"

And I looked out there toward the cane field and, *holy crap,* here comes a line of Japanese at us. They were shoulder to shoulder and the line extended all the way across the field. It looked like the Japanese had been crawling in the cane and all of a sudden they just stood up. I know now that they came out of the woods behind the field and went down through the ravine at the back end of the field. When they came walking up out of the ravine it looked like they were just popping up out of the ground in the cane field.

Hofstetter ordered the guns to fire at will. Moretti transmitted the order to the gun crews, and they responded within seconds, using their ready-to-fire shells. They cut the fuzes to create airbursts at minimum range, thereby putting themselves at risk of being struck by their own shrapnel. But they had no choice, given the enemy's proximity. Thus, a mere four-tenths of a second after the gunners pulled their lanyards, the shells exploded above the onrushing Japanese, felling many of the enemy with fragments that also sprayed the guns and their crews.

Despite the carnage in their ranks the Japanese kept coming. It seemed to Sandy that the airbursts "didn't even slow them down." Sandy stood his carbine against a nearby tree and went to Gun 2 to help as a loader.

Don Holzer and Harold Hoffman were still out in front of the battery when the guns commenced firing. They were hotfooting back to the battery, heading in the approximate direction of Gun 1. The shells from their own guns were exploding above and behind them, but neither man was hit and Don didn't notice the flying shrapnel; his only thought was to get back to the battery position. The Japanese swarmed everywhere around them. The two Marines made their way along the railroad embankment, pausing briefly to catch their breath beside a blown-out bridge spanning a narrow ravine. Suddenly several Japanese came around the corner of the bridge. Don stood face-to-face with one of the enemy soldiers: "We were maybe three feet from each other!" Forgetting that his carbine was jammed, he raised his weapon at the man and pulled the trigger. "It went *click.*" Another misfire.

Then I grabbed it by the barrel and started clubbing him over the head. He didn't have a helmet on. He went down. Then I looked over at Harold, about ten or fifteen yards from me. He'd also been fighting hand to hand with a Jap and had killed his man. We signaled each other that we were going to go through this little ravine that the bridge crossed over and get back to the battery area, where the guns were.

There were lots of Japanese around us, hundreds. We ran right through them. They were just standing around, milling about. We ran as fast as we could. I think we surprised them. I don't think they noticed us until we were past them. Basically, we ran through the Japanese army. I got very close to where the guns were, and there was a big root from a dead tree, and I dove over it, and at that point I was hit. I was hit while I was diving. I recall reaching up in the air to grab my arm where I'd been hit. It was more of a shock than it was painful.

Meanwhile, the gun crews were working at a furious pace. They had quickly expended their meager stocks of ready-to-fire shells and were now firing charge 7 shells straight from the cloverleafs. There was no time to reduce the charges or to cut the fuzes to create airbursts. Sandy recalled that they "couldn't get the shells out of the cloverleafs fast enough."

I was removing the shells from the cloverleafs and handing them to the loader to place into the breech of the gun. As fast as we got a round out of the box it was put right into the gun and the gunner pulled the lanyard. The gunners had the tubes angled down pretty low, firing at the ground. I'm not sure how far in front of us the shells traveled before they hit the ground—not far at all, really. The shells would hit the ground and then they'd ricochet up in the air and explode.

They threw everything they had at the Japanese: HE, antitank, even smoke shells. Burning phosphorus from the smoke shells hit several Japanese in their buttocks, and they threw down their weapons and ran about "jumping in the air holding their ass with their hands."

"We all laughed at that," said Sandy. But not for long.

One wave would pop up out of the ravine and come at us and we'd fire and they'd all go down and by then another wave would pop up and be coming at us. It was just like in a shooting gallery. Some of them didn't have rifles; they came at us carrying sticks with bayonets and knives tied to them. They weren't running; they were walking, sort of hurrying along, hundreds and hundreds of them. They weren't yelling; they weren't shouting, "Banzai." Or if they were, I didn't hear them. Because when those big guns go off you don't hear anything else.

The Marines were also taking heavy casualties. "Dropping like flies," is how Sandy put it, cut down by shrapnel blowing back from their own exploding shells or shot down by the Japanese. The valor of these men cannot be overstated. They were completely exposed, with no cover whatsoever, and yet they stayed with their guns, doing their jobs with cool, workman-like detachment until they were either too badly hurt to continue or they were dead.

Japanese forces were also attacking from the rear. Resisting them were all battery personnel not directly involved in firing the guns, including the battery clerks, cooks, and drivers—men who normally did not go anywhere near a battlefield. They were lightly armed—for the most part with carbines—and ammunition was scarce. They too put up a gallant fight. The second tank that Sandy heard, but did not see, had driven through them but was knocked out between the railroad tracks and the farmhouse where the FDC tent was located, probably by headquarters personnel.

Sandy knew that the Japanese were behind them, but he was much too busy to worry about them. Cpl. Leonard Froncek was then commanding Gun 2, standing in for Pop Conner, who had stayed with the .50-caliber machine gun up front on the left after helping to set it up. Suddenly Froncek was hit in the foot or the ankle. He dropped to the ground beside the gun's wheel, crying, "Sandy, I'm hit! I need help!"

Sandy knelt beside Froncek and attempted to remove his boot so he could treat the wound. But there was a knot in the bootlace and he couldn't untie it. Swede Larson appeared and offered to help. Froncek cried, "Cut it off; just cut it off!" Sandy pulled out his KA-BAR and began sawing through the boot's leather top.

Just then the Japanese onslaught struck H Battery and broke on the position like a mighty wave, flowing over the Marine foxholes and around the guns. Suddenly the Japanese were everywhere—in front of the battery, behind it, on both flanks—and more were coming at the Marines from the cane field, wave after successive wave rising out of the ravine, emerging from the very ground itself like the spawn of the dragon's teeth.

With the battery's position collapsing, Hofstetter gave the only order he could in the circumstances: "Every man for himself!" he bellowed. "Get the hell out of here! Every man for himself! Every man for himself!" (Sandy distinctly remembers Hofstetter shouting this command "at least three times.")

Swede Larson took off, but Sandy continued cutting away at Froncek's boot. Froncek told Sandy to leave him and make a run for it. Sandy refused, saying he would help Froncek escape too.

"No, don't stay around to help," said Froncek. "Didn't you hear the lieu-tenant? He said, 'Every man for himself.' So get the hell of here! That's an order!"

Sandy went to the tree where he had left his carbine. But the carbine was gone. Every artilleryman was issued a carbine and three clips of ammunition, with fifteen rounds in each clip. They didn't carry additional ammo because, presumably, it would not be needed—artillerymen were supposed to fight with their big guns, not carbines. Sandy figured someone who had run out of ammunition had seen his carbine with its clip and made off with it. So he returned to Froncek, telling him: "My carbine's gone. I can't go anywhere. Guess I might as well stay."

Froncek gestured at a tree trunk where another carbine stood. "Take that one," he said.

Sandy had twice been given a direct order by a noncom. He had disobeyed the first order; he could not disobey the second. He grabbed the carbine and took off running toward the road behind the battery, leaving Froncek to his fate.**

Sandy came to the road but stopped before crossing it when a burst of machine-gun fire kicked up dirt in front of him. He took cover behind a tree and checked his carbine. The clip was empty, but he had two loose rounds in his pocket. He inserted one in the carbine's chamber, the other in its clip. He peered around the tree to his left, in the direction of the railway embankment, and found himself looking at the tank that Gun 1 had knocked out earlier. The tank sat immobilized in the road just before the gradient, its main gun pointing uselessly to its rear. In the back of the turret (which was now facing Sandy), there was a ball-mounted machine gun, and this weapon was spraying the road as the Marines fled across it. How the man operating the gun could have survived a direct hit to his tank at point-blank range by a 105-mm shell was a mystery Sandy would ponder at a future date. At the time his mind was entirely focused on the problem of getting across that road without getting shot.

** Years later, at a reunion of the veterans of H Battery, Sandy was astonished—and delighted—to find Leonard Froncek among the attendees. It turned out that shortly after Sandy had left him by the wheel of Gun 2, Froncek had pulled himself to his feet and hobbled back across the road, eventually making his way to a group that was holding out near the house behind Gun 1. In the confusion of the battle, the Japanese, who were swarming all about the area, simply failed to see or notice him. He was evacuated while Sandy was elsewhere; as a result, Sandy assumed that Froncek had been killed. After the war, Froncek, who had served in the Army before enlisting in the Marines, reenlisted in the Army and made a career of it, finally retiring as a colonel. The two men became fast friends and attended several reunions together.

He thought he saw a way. The machine-gunner would sweep the road from right to left and then stop firing and swing his gun back to the right and start firing again. Sandy determined to make a break for it while the machine-gunner worked over the left side of the road. Just then, one of the men in his battery, Eric Johnson, came running up beside him.

"C'mon, Sandy, let's go!" he said, and started across the road.

"Wait, Eric, wait!" cried Sandy.

"The hell with you," Johnson said. "I'm not waiting here!" With that he ran out into the road and was promptly cut down by the machine gun.

Sandy waited until the machine-gunner started another right-to-left sweep of the road and then darted across. On the other side of the road he found a group of Marines lined up to run through a clump of bushes on a path leading to the seashore. Beyond the bushes, the path went down and across some twenty feet of open ground before reaching another patch of bushes. Japanese machine guns set up in a clearing south of the path covered the open area, but the Marines were willing to brave their fire because the path offered the only avenue of escape from the swarming forces of the enemy. They crossed the open area one at a time, each man choosing his moment and dashing to the other side, hoping to reach it before the enemy machine guns got him. Sandy installed himself at the end of the line to await his turn.

He was just about to run when a familiar voice spoke up behind him: "Sandburg, is that you?"

Sandy turned to see Hofstetter standing under the trees. Lying near him on the ground was Capt. Harold E. Nelson, the battery's nominal commander. (Hofstetter had authority over him in all combat situations, because he had more time-in-service than the captain—a statistic that could be more influential than rank in establishing one's place in the Marine Corps hierarchy.) Nelson had been shot through both hips, probably while participating in the defense of the battery's rear area, but had somehow managed to get this far before collapsing.

Hofstetter asked Sandy whether he thought this area—which encompassed the aircraft parts storage dump—could be turned into a fort where they could gather the wounded and protect them from the Japanese. He felt the position was defendable provided it was properly barricaded.

It was typical of Hofstetter to *ask* Sandy for his help. He would not order Sandy or anyone else to stay when doing so probably meant that they would be killed. He was an Old Salt, hard-nosed and crusty, about thirty-nine years old, a veteran of Nicaragua with the permanent rank of sergeant-major, the highest rank an enlisted man could achieve in the Marine Corps. He became a lieutenant in the field, but the rank was temporary by his own choice—he didn't want to give up his status as a sergeant-major. "Most of the guys didn't like him," said Sandy. "He was a tough old boy. But he was fair, and that's what I liked about him. He fought for the guys when they were right. He did more fighting for the guys than they realized. I would be in the exec pit and I'd hear him arguing with the majors, our battalion commanders. There aren't too many lieutenants who are going to argue with a major. He knew his business. He sure as hell did. And I decided that I wanted to stay there with him."

★   ★   ★

After Don Holzer was shot while diving over the tree root, he lay where he fell for a few minutes. Finally a corpsman got to him.

I was shot in the left shoulder, from behind, right through ball joint. The entry wound was lower than my shoulder, but the bullet went up through the ball joint and came out there. The corpsman gave me a pill and I had foam all over my mouth from it—and then he was hit. He was kneeling beside me, and he just fell over, dead.

Harold Hoffman was hit at the same time. He was just a few feet from me. I saw him get hit, but just for a split second. He went down. I had no idea how badly he was hit but I assumed that he was done for. I was right. I was later told he died from loss of blood, not from being shot.

I knew I had to move back. There was too much open space where I was at and that bothered me. There was a gravel road about twenty yards from where I was hit, and heavy woods behind that. I wanted to get into those woods. So I took off my gear and tossed anything I could get rid of—I wanted to be free of the weight when I made a run for it. I looked to the left and there was a Jap tank up there on the road, and I looked to the right and a Jap tank was down there on the road too.

The tanks were facing each other and there was about eighty yards between them—one was forty yards to my left, the other forty yards to my right. There was no infantry. I took my chance and got up and ran across the road right between them. I don't think they fired at me, but I don't know.

The road wasn't that wide; I probably took four or five steps and threw myself in the ditch on the other side. Then I crawled back to where I could see some big boxes, the ones filled with airplane parts. It was daylight by this time and I could see bodies all over the place. I found other wounded men there, but the only ones I really knew were Pat Linder and Ray Forbus.

Don had found his way to the aircraft parts storage dump. There, under Hofstetter's direction, Sandy and several others hurriedly stacked aircraft engine crates along the dump's south perimeter to defend against the attack that all felt was imminent from that direction. There were four crates, each about five feet high and five feet square—Sandy believes they contained bomber engines. Sandy's group included Sergeant Mathews, J. B. Mills, Swede Larson, Everett Hinton, a private named Sayer, and Ken Miller. Several dozen Marines had sought refuge in the dump, and Sandy estimates that more than forty of them were wounded. Several were near death and would in fact die in the minutes and hours that followed. Some, although not mortally wounded, had barely made it to the dump and were incapable of further movement. Many were still capable of fighting but had either lost their carbines or had little or no ammunition.

On completing their barricade Sandy and the others hunkered down behind it and readied themselves as best they could to defend their position. From his vantage point Sandy could see Guns 1, 2, and 3. The powder bags for 1 and 2 were burning, and the fire had spread to the fuel drums in the trench behind the guns, setting the contents on fire. The burning barrels were intermittently exploding, sending their covers sailing through the air.

Sandy realized that they needed more ammo. He asked everyone to hold their fire until a Japanese soldier got close enough so that when he fell Sandy could recover the man's rifle and ammunition.

The first enemy soldier that came their way approached on the path leading up from the beach. He wore a Marine jacket, and with his dark complexion, he looked to Sandy like an American Indian who belonged to their unit. "Say, I think I know that guy," he said to his buddies. The Japanese soldier came closer and stood with his boots planted right next to Sandy's head, oblivious to the presence of the Marines. It was then that Sandy saw that the man was wearing the distinctive Japanese boots with a separate box for the big toe. "Oh, God, it's a Jap!" Sandy exclaimed. The Japanese soldier heard Sandy and looked down at him and started to say something—and then turned and ran back down the path. Sandy raised his carbine and one of the other Marines did the same, and both fired at the fleeing man.

I'd never killed a man before, so I closed my eyes when I squeezed the trigger and I fired into his back when he was down at the bottom of the clearing. I don't know if I hit him; there was no way of knowing. Though we both fired two shots at him, he didn't go down. Course, we were using carbines, and that's like being hit with a .22. It didn't make any difference because I think his own machine gun put him down. A Jap machine gun down there opened up then—I could hear it—and he went down pretty quick after that; he could have taken another few steps after we both put the rounds into his back. But the Jap machine-gunners saw him down there in the clearing and they fired and I think they're the ones that killed him. He got killed by his own guys.

The Japanese machine gun was positioned southwest of the dump in a clearing on the other side of a line of bushes. It guarded a field headquarters the Japanese had established after overrunning the battery's guns. The line of bushes concealed the Marines in the dump from the enemy HQ, and the Japanese would remain unaware of their presence throughout the battle.

Now with one round left in his carbine, Sandy asked the men around him whether they had any to spare. They didn't. He would have to make his last round count. Just then, another enemy soldier obligingly approached their position, running toward them from the north on a driveway that connected the road behind the battery to the storage dump.

Sandy raised his weapon at the man. "He came right into my sights and I squeezed off my last round. He took one more step and down he went. I believe Hinton fired at him too. I crawled to him with my KA-BAR in hand in case he wasn't dead. I relieved him of his rifle and all his clips—and his wristwatch too."

Even in these dire circumstances Sandy couldn't resist taking a good souvenir when he saw one. Typical Marine.

Sandy scrambled back to the stronghold with his booty. The rifle was a bolt-action Arisaka with a full clip. Sandy opened the bolt and was surprised to find that the chamber was empty. Full clip, empty chamber. *Why*, Sandy wondered, *would he go into battle with an empty chamber?*

Every time they captured a Japanese rifle they found the same thing: chamber empty. The Marines could not make sense of this, being unaware of how little ammunition the Japanese forces on Saipan had left.

They fought all morning using Japanese rifles and ammo. More men were hit, and more were killed. J. B. Mills, lying beside Sandy, took a bullet between the eyes and died instantly. Sandy and other Marines nearby pushed Mills into the foliage. They did this with all of their dead, because the bodies bloated quickly in the heat.

Japanese dead lay all around them too. Every now and again another Japanese soldier approached them on the driveway.

> They were coming at us intermittently. They had gotten scattered when we fired the 105s at them, and they didn't know we were there. They knew their headquarters was there, on the other side of this wall of engines we had built. So they were just kind of stumbling on us. They would come down that driveway one at a time and we'd shoot them the moment they came in there. One of them that we shot, he lay out there on the east side of the driveway, feet facing south, his rear end toward us—he lay for a long time hollering, in English, "Wah-ter! Wah-ter! Wah-ter!" Our guys that were wounded that still had rifles and ammunition, they got all upset; they got tired of hearing him, and so they'd pump another round into him. Finally he quit hollering. But it seemed like it took hours and hours before he did.

The Marines in any case had no water to give him, nor did they have any rations. These were to have been brought up that morning by the rear-echelon personnel.

The Japanese may not have known about the Marines in the storage dump, but that didn't make the Marines' situation any less perilous. The air was thick with flying metal: bullets and shells and shell fragments. Lying next to Sandy on his stomach was P. Sgt. Richard Mathews; a piece of shrapnel came sailing in and "hit him in his butt." The metal passed through the soft flesh and struck the stock of Sandy's Japanese rifle between his arm and face, gouging a sizable chunk out of the stock.

Don Holzer lay near Sandy, unable to fire a rifle because of the damage to his shoulder. "There were maybe nine or ten wounded men right near me," Don said, "and we were all pretty well shot up. Ray Forbus had his left shoulder blown out, and the only thing left was his skin connecting his arm to his shoulder; he wanted Pat Linder, also wounded, to cut his arm off, but Pat wouldn't do it."

> The Japanese were all around us. We saw one in a tree and he was shooting at us. Pat Linder was hit again at that point. He swore like everything. He was hit five times before someone took the sniper out. But he survived!

It had rained and there was a tarp there and there was water in it. We were all very thirsty. I had a plastic waterproof cigarette case, and I took out the cigarettes and threw them away and we used it as a drinking cup. I passed the cigarette case around and everyone drank from it. I took a drink and then vomited all over. The rest of the day I was falling in and out of consciousness. I don't remember much.

I would say I was hit at daybreak or thereabouts, and that we were rescued sometime late in the day. Someone put me on a stretcher and I was taken to a truck. But not before I heard someone say, "You might as well leave Holzer, he's dead anyhow." Bob Edwards was sitting on the gate of a truck and they had him move over so they could put my stretcher on the deck. I wasn't in pain, just in shock. The next thing I knew I was in a hospital or an aid station and they were cutting my clothes off.

★　★　★

Soon after Sandy's rifle stock was hit the fighting slackened, at least in their immediate vicinity. The human tsunami had passed over them. The all-out attack they expected never materialized. The Marines in the dump could not know it, but by then the enemy offensive was running out of steam. The valiant defense mounted by H Battery before it was overrun surely deserves a lion's share of credit for slowing the Japanese, who lost many men and much of their momentum in the attack. The destruction of H Battery was a "victory" from which the Japanese would not recover.

But the battle was far from over.

Around 1300 the Marines in the storage dump heard the throaty roar of tank engines on the coast road below them. Sandy said to Hofstetter that they sounded like American tanks. Hofstetter agreed but had doubts that Americans were operating them. "The scuttlebutt is, the Japanese have got gotten some of our tanks," he said.

They talked about this for a minute or two. In the meantime, the tanks drove back and forth on the road, and this finally persuaded Hofstetter and Sandy that the tanks were crewed by Americans. Sandy said that he was willing to go down to the road to get help for the men in the dump.

Hofstetter considered Sandy's offer. "Would you do that?" he asked.

"Sure," said Sandy.

"You don't have to go, you know."

"No, I'll go; it'll be okay."

Hofstetter looked at the Japanese rifle Sandy held. "Well, you sure as hell aren't going to take that, because if you do run into Americans, they're going to think you're a Jap and shoot you."

Hofstetter found a carbine for Sandy and ordered everyone who had carbine ammunition to give it to him. They produced enough to fill one clip. Just as Sandy was about to leave, Hofstetter told him: "When you get down there to those tanks, the first thing you do is, you take your helmet off so they can see you've got blond hair and know you're an American."

"Okay," Sandy said, and with that he began crawling along the south side of the road leading down to the ocean. He somehow avoided running into any Japanese. At the junction where the inland road met the coast road he came upon three Army Sherman tanks heading north; a fourth tank had stalled in a small shell hole in the sand on the seaward side of the road and sat there abandoned with its hatches sprung open.

Sandy hurried over to one of the tanks and pounded on its hull with the butt of his carbine. No response. He stepped back, raised his carbine, and fired a round at the tank's hull.

A second or two passed and then the turret rotated toward Sandy and leveled its 75-mm gun at him. Sandy lowered his carbine. His face was just a few feet from the cannon's muzzle, and he was staring up the big black bore of the gun tube when it occurred to him that now would be a very good time to take off his helmet and flash his blond hair at the men inside that tank, who were doubtless watching him through periscopes. Sandy removed his helmet and silently prayed that the men inside were indeed Americans. Another second passed and then the main turret hatch began opening, slowly and cautiously raised by a hand that was followed by an arm that was finally followed by a head with, thankfully, an American face on it. The tank commander glared down at Sandy.

"What the hell do you think you're doing?" he demanded.

Sandy quickly explained the situation, telling the tank commander that he was with an artillery unit that had been overrun, that the survivors were holding out in a supply dump a little way inland, that many were wounded. "Could you come help us out?"

The tank commander thought about this for a moment and then said, "Wait just a minute," and dropped down into the turret. He reemerged a few seconds later and said, "Sorry, can't help you—we've got a fire mission." Then, with Sandy standing in the intersection watching, the three tanks shifted into gear and moved off to the north.

Sandy crawled back to the dump and reported to Hofstetter, telling him that the tanks had driven off—they were too busy fighting to help the wounded Marines; too busy, even, to send a message for help. Hofstetter observed that the tanks were just then returning from their fire mission. "Do you think you can make it back down there?" Sandy said he could, and Hofstetter told him: "If they won't come, ask them if they'll send a message to the rear and tell them we need help. Tell them to send a message to the Marines, not the Army."

Sandy started on his second trip from their beleaguered position with Hofstetter admonishing him to be careful: "I don't want to lose you."

Sandy felt confident that he could again make it safely to the beach road. He hadn't run into the Japanese on his first trip to and from the road and was reasonably certain that he would not encounter any on this trip. He was across the road from the farmhouse that stood to the west of Gun 4 when he spotted several Japanese kneeling in a ditch on the other side of the road. They didn't have rifles but they had plenty of grenades, which they proceeded to fling at him.

Sandy dove to the ground, scrambling to pick up the grenades and hurl them back at the Japanese: "As fast as they threw the grenades at me I would throw them back." Some of the grenades burst in midair, others exploded among the Japanese. After one explosion his enemies screamed, evidently wounded by the blast. Realizing the danger to themselves from their own fragmentation grenades, they started throwing concussion grenades at Sandy.

The third concussion grenade they threw hit him in the helmet, bounced off, and landed on the ground in front of him. He was reaching for it when it exploded.

Then a strange thing occurred. I felt like I was floating in the air but I could see myself, my body, lying face-down on the ground. Across the road I saw two Japs helping a third going into the farmhouse. A fourth Jap lay motionless on the north side of the road. And off in the distance there was a big bright light. It was like I was in a tunnel, and it looked like the light was coming closer and closer to me; then it would back off, and then it would come again, and then back off again. I don't know how long this went on. It seemed like a long time. But it was the most serene and peaceful time in my entire life.

Eventually the pulsating bright light receded and vanished, and Sandy suddenly found himself back on the ground crawling down to the beach road.

The tanks had moved on, but he did come upon a wounded soldier leaning against the tank that had stalled in the shell hole. He asked the soldier if he was with the tanks. The soldier said that he wasn't and asked Sandy for a drink of water.

Sandy didn't have a canteen, but he saw two five-gallon cans of water strapped to the back of the tank turret. When he proposed to get one of the cans, the wounded soldier warned him to be careful—there was a sniper sitting in a palm tree just south of them between the road and the shoreline. Sandy hurriedly climbed up onto the tank's engine deck, grabbed one of the cans, and jumped back down. He filled the soldier's helmet with water. When the soldier had finished drinking from it Sandy asked him when the tanks would return. The soldier said he didn't know. Sandy decided to take matters into his own hands. He climbed into the tank through the driver's hatch and tried to start the engine. He couldn't get it going, though, and was pulling himself back up through the driver's hatch when the sniper opened fire on the tank.

Sandy dropped back down into the tank and stayed there for a few minutes listening to bullets pinging off the tank's hull and turret. When at length the sniper quit firing, Sandy exited the tank through the machine-gunner's hatch and slithered down the tank's front glacis where the sniper couldn't see him.

The tanks that Sandy encountered on his first trip to the beach road were now returning from their mission. Sandy flagged them down and spoke with the same tank commander about getting help for the survivors of H Battery. This time the tank commander was willing to send a message. Sandy had to wait several minutes for a reply, and all that time the sniper in the palm down the beach was shooting at them and rounds were whipping by them or pinging off the tank. Finally, the tank commander poked his head out of the turret and said, "Message sent," adding that help was on the way.

Sandy made his way back to the storage dump. A few minutes after he arrived, the defenders heard a burst of gunfire to the south and the sound of a tank approaching from the same direction. The tank hove into view, another Sherman, but it was a Marine tank, and a platoon of Marines walked behind it. Sandy and the unwounded men quickly pushed aside the crates to make an opening in their barricade, and the tank and the infantry came on through.

"What a beautiful sight that was," Sandy recalled.

The tank commander climbed down from his turret and conferred briefly with Hofstetter, informing him that he'd wiped out a machine gun on his way there. After a few minutes of discussion he said to Hofstetter: "Okay, I guess you guys will be all right," then climbed back into his tank. The tank and the infantry platoon moved off across the battery position to the north.

Not long after the appearance of the Marine tank Hofstetter asked Sandy if he thought he could make it back to regimental headquarters to request ambulances for the wounded. Sandy told him that he would sure try. Walking east on the road behind H Battery's position, he came to the railroad tracks and encountered a jeep on the road that ran along the east side of the embankment.

The jeep was from H Battery, and in the front passenger seat sat Lieutenant Fletcher from the battery's instrument section. Two H Battery Marines sat in the back seat. One was Cpl. Ralph Mills, older brother of J. B. Mills, who had been shot between the eyes while lying next to Sandy in the storage dump. Ralph had been in charge of one of the guns and had taken off across the road when Hofstetter had shouted, "Every man for himself." He had made it back to the rear and had now returned to find his brother.

The jeep stopped, and Fletcher got out and asked Sandy where he was headed. Sandy told him he was going to 10th Marines headquarters to see whether he could get some ambulances and trucks brought to the dump to collect the wounded. Fletcher said that Sandy could have his jeep and told the other men to get out. Sandy approached Fletcher and said quietly, "I'm not going to tell Ralph, but his brother got killed up there. You're going to have to tell him." The lieutenant said he would. Sandy got into the jeep, and the driver turned around and started back to regimental headquarters with Sandy feeling "safe for the first time that day."

The 10th Marines HQ was located on a hillside just above Tanapag town, in a driveway leading up to what was left of a basement garage and the ruins of the house that stood over it. Reporting directly to Col. Raphael Griffin, commander of the 10th Marines, Sandy told him what H Battery had been through, explained the present situation of the men in the storage dump, and requested immediate transportation for the wounded. The colonel issued orders for all units under his command to dispatch every available vehicle to the regimental HQ. "I want those vehicles moving by the time you acknowledge this message," he told his unit commanders over the phone. "If I don't see any trucks or ambulances here real quick, heads are going to roll."

A few minutes later Sandy saw all manner of vehicles—trucks, ambulances, jeeps—streaming up from the south on every negotiable road, track, and trail. But they could not come quickly enough for Colonel Griffin. After the first several vehicles had arrived, congregating at the foot of the driveway, Griffin exchanged his jeep for Sandy's and led that group to the storage dump. A few minutes later, a second convoy departed with a headquarters officer leading the way in his jeep. Sandy left shortly thereafter in Griffin's jeep.

He arrived at the dump to find the wounded being placed aboard the trucks that had preceded him. Typically, Sandy pitched in to help, despite being in tremendous pain himself. He watched as the badly wounded Ray Forbus was placed on a stretcher. Ray cried out and Sandy saw that his arm lay on the ground but was still attached to his shoulder by a string of flesh. "I hollered at them and they stopped and I ran over and picked his arm up and I put it across his chest and held it there while they walked him over and put him on the truck. And off to the hospital they went."

After the vehicles left with the wounded, Ralph Mills came to Sandy asking to see his brother's body. Of course, Sandy had seen J. B. fall before him with a bullet between his eyes and had helped to push his body into the bushes where it still lay, and where, Sandy knew, it was now hideously bloated, foul smelling, and crawling with flies. Sandy and Everett Hinton took Ralph aside and gently explained that seeing his brother's body was not a good idea.

"Ralph, you don't wanna see him," Sandy told him. "Think of him the way he was when he was alive, not what you're gonna see."

Ralph nodded grimly and said, "Well, I want to get his personal effects."

Hinton said that he would collect J. B.'s things and went off to get them. He soon returned with J. B.'s wallet, ring, and other items, and handed them over to Ralph. Waiting until Ralph was out of earshot, Hinton told Sandy, "Jeez, I had to cut his damn finger off to get his ring."

Sandy said, "Well, you got it—that's the important thing."

A while later the battery's trucks returned from delivering the wounded to the hospitals and aid stations, driving up the road behind the guns. Sandy joined a group comprising men from the entire regiment to help hitch the guns to the trucks. H Battery's dead lay all around them, but orders were given to leave them where they lay for collection the next day. While the Marines were hooking up the guns, three Japanese holed up in the farmhouse north of Gun 4—the same men Sandy had fought the grenade-tossing duel with a few hours earlier—poked their rifles out the windows and started shooting. They were too far away to hit anyone, but that mattered little to the Marines in Sandy's group. Most of them had not been with the battery when it was overrun, and the presence of those Japanese combined with the sight of their dead comrades enraged them. Thirsting for revenge, they started toward the house, only to be recalled by their officers, who told them that the infantry would deal with the problem.

One man kept going, however, a lieutenant named James Brandt.

Brandt was an expert shot with a pistol, and he went into battle carrying two fancy pearl-handled six-shooters, worn gunslinger-style in two holsters on an intricately tooled leather belt. During the voyage to Saipan he had entertained one and all with demonstrations of his marksmanship, shooting half-dollar coins thrown up in the air and earning the nickname "Two-Gun Brandt." Now, with the rest of the Marines hanging back as ordered, Brandt drew his pistols, shouted, "I'll get those bastards," and charged the house.

Sandy recalled, "We all hollered at him, 'No, no! Don't go out there! You're gonna get yourself killed!' But he kept right on going with his pistols out, just like a gunfighter in a Western movie, just like John Wayne—and they shot him dead. He lay where he fell until the next morning."

After Brandt was shot, one of the truck drivers ran over to his lifeless form to make sure he was dead. While the Japanese potted at him he stripped away the lieutenant's pistols as well as his holsters and gun belt and returned unscathed with his prizes. For some inexplicable reason no one acted to relieve him of these personal effects for shipment to Brandt's next of kin, and he disappeared into the crowd with them. To this day his identity remains unknown, although many names have been advanced at the battery and regimental reunions, where the episode continues to be a topic of discussion among the dwindling number of veterans who witnessed it.

Many of the bodies were unrecognizable, and Sandy and the others had to reach into the bloody remains for the dog tags that would identify them. Discovering which one of their friends each charred and mangled corpse had been inflicted wounds on the survivors of H Battery that would never fully heal. What Sandy described as a "horrible traumatic experience" would haunt every one of them, in some form or another, for the rest of their days.***

★   ★   ★

There are various estimates of the number of Americans and Japanese killed in the attack. As near as I can determine from what I saw and have since read, the Japanese lost upward of 4,000 men. Some 500 Americans were killed, most of them from the two Army battalions that were overrun (and nearly wiped out). Approximately the same number were wounded.

H Battery suffered 152 casualties in the attack: 75 killed and 76 wounded. It is estimated that some 600 Japanese were killed on the open ground directly

---

*** Although Sandy didn't fully realize it at the time, he had also suffered tremendous physical trauma. Shortly after the final battle on Saipan he began to have blackout spells and related episodes that seemed to indicate that he had sustained significant neurological damage. Initially the diagnosis was "combat fatigue," but further examination revealed that he had suffered a broken neck from the grenade explosion that had caused his "out-of-body experience." He eventually made a full recovery.

in front of the battery's guns. Another 2,500 dead were subsequently found in the cane field and in the ravine at the back of the field.

The numbers on the Japanese side of the ledger are, of course, inexact. The attacking force was thrown together willy-nilly, at the last minute, and records identifying the participating units and individuals are accordingly imprecise, when they exist at all, making any tally of those killed problematic. The condition of the bodies, many of which were blown to pieces or simply blown into oblivion, leaving scarcely more than molecular traces of their corporeal existence as evidence that they had once walked the earth as men, also hindered an accurate count of the dead.

And the killing was by no means over.

★   ★   ★

The same morning that Sandy and his buddies were engaged in the heart-rending task of identifying their dead, I arrived on the scene with my company to mop up the battlefield.

I had left the division field hospital with my right arm in a sling, carrying my carbine in my left hand. No transportation was provided to those of us who had been ordered to return to our units. We were simply told to get out of the hospital and find our units as best we could.

And so out we went, guided only by a general sense of where our units might be. There were no shore patrolmen or MPs to monitor and enforce our progress, to prevent the fainthearted from going off in some other direction. None were needed. We had our orders and we obeyed them.

I got rid of my sling shortly after leaving the hospital. Wearing it might lessen the pain and speed the healing process, but I couldn't be bothered by such concerns now that I was returning to the battle zone. I needed both arms for the fighting to come, and I could use my right arm without the sling. It was stiff and it hurt, but it was functional.

I found C Company camped a short distance from the hospital. I also found that I was effectively in command of the company. In my absence the former commander, Maj. Harry Phillips, had been appointed 3d Battalion's operations officer. He had been replaced by Capt. Melvin Seltzer, and I had been moved up to executive command. But Seltzer had been called away from the company the previous day and had not yet returned, and we had been ordered to move out ASAP for the front. Since we couldn't wait for Seltzer to show up, it fell to me to command C Company in the forthcoming action.

This was an unexpected development. For a moment I didn't know quite what to do. Everything was happening so fast. I'd been wounded, sent to the rear, sent back to the front. Now I was in command of a company headed back into battle. I realized, *This is it, I'm the main guy.* It was all a bit confusing and I felt somewhat disoriented.

But the moment quickly passed and I regained my bearings. I had C Company form up, and we moved out in column of march on the coast road. We arrived at the edge of the battle zone a little over an hour later in the vicinity of a place known as Harakiri Gulch. We came on positions occupied by soldiers who sat or stood without moving or talking and stared at nothing with dazed, unfocused eyes, their faces devoid of expression. In front of their position and extending as far as the eye could see to the north and east were the bodies of their attackers.

We took a break and I approached one of the soldiers and struck up a conversation with him. He was an older man, late twenties or early thirties. We chatted casually about the recent fighting and his experiences, and he explained in a quiet sort of way that he didn't "belong" on Saipan: "I didn't ask to be here, you know—I was drafted." He paused, and when I didn't reply he went on, "You guys, you Marines, you're a lot younger than we are. You probably take more chances than we do. When you're younger, you'll take more chances than an older man does."

He said the soldiers in the Army units were demoralized. Many, perhaps most of them, were draftees like himself. Most were older than the Marines. Many were married and had left families and real jobs back in the States. "We didn't volunteer, like you guys," he said. "We didn't ask to be here."

We passed on through their positions and deployed in skirmish lines extending from the water's edge to the railroad tracks, with the 6th Marines advancing along the shore and the 8th Marines on their right. (The 2d Marines were attached to the 4th Division to take part in the final drive on Marpi Point.) Thus arrayed we picked our way slowly through the battle zone, our weapons at the ready. All around us the dead were thick on the ground in numbers that defied comprehension. Bodies and pieces of bodies everywhere. Artillery had pounded the area and chopped up the bodies, turning the battlefield into an immense open-air abattoir strewn with torsos and limbs and heads and chunks of unidentifiable flesh burned black by fire. I could re-create the flow and ferocity of the battle, the patterns of fight and flight, by the numbers and positioning of the dead. There would be places, pockets of resistance, where bodies were piled on top of bodies, dead Japanese entangled with dead Americans, frozen in attitudes of hand-to-hand combat, clutching and plunging bayonets into each other, locked in their death struggles. Our machine-gun positions were tableaus of butchery, with the bodies of the Japanese heaped in front of the positions and the bodies of American soldiers slumped over their guns.

For men who didn't want to be there, these U.S. Army soldiers had put up a hell of a fight.

Not all the Japanese were dead, of course. As usual, some were shamming. We knew that this would be the case and were very quick on our triggers if we saw any movement. If one of those bodies so much as twitched, we poured fire into it. Even if we didn't see movement, if a body or group of bodies looked suspicious, we shot it through and through. Bushes big enough to provide concealment were preemptively blasted into wood chips and leaf bits.

Now and then as we advanced across the battlefield a "dead body" rose suddenly to throw a grenade or shoot at us. Some Japanese jumped to their feet and tried to run away. We shot them all, just shot them right down. No prisoners were taken. We moved forward at a steady pace, hardly breaking stride, rarely halting. We just kept walking through that killing ground, looking around, scrutinizing the bodies, firing at the Japanese, at the living and the dead.

In a few places we encountered something close to real resistance. No problem. We took cover wherever we could find it—behind a log, a palm tree, whatever. Then we methodically moved in on the enemy position and killed the defenders. For most of us, combat veterans all, it was routine. The Japanese weren't using mortars or machine guns, and many didn't have rifles. Others ran around in front of us like scared rabbits. But they wouldn't surrender. They never surrendered. Which is why we didn't take any prisoners, didn't even try.

We'd sometimes approach a hole where several Japanese sat in apathetic silence, clearly in shock and utterly bereft of hope. They did not look much different from the American soldiers we had recently encountered. But where our soldiers were benumbed and confounded by what they had been through and the fact that they had survived their ordeal, the Japanese were fully aware that their own deaths were upon them. They didn't shoot or throw grenades at us. We could walk right up to them if we wanted and they wouldn't do anything until the last moment, when one of them would explode a grenade. I had never seen anything like this: they wouldn't fight, they wouldn't surrender, but they would explode a grenade and kill themselves and any Marines who ventured too close to their position. So we killed them.

My friends in B Company, operating more or less alongside C Company, had similar encounters with the Japanese. Bill Crumpacker was sickened by the slaughter and would not do any shooting that day. He recalled, "I went over to the railway and I looked down the tracks and I could see all these Japanese guys just sittin' there with their legs folded. Our guys shot them where they sat. Not me, though. I thought to myself, *I don't want to have anything to do with this.* But I could understand why everyone else was shooting. They were upset over all the American soldiers who had gotten killed. They were just getting some payback."

Harold Park, now a corporal and a fire-team leader, arrived in the battle zone to find a wide drainage ditch clogged with dead Japanese.

The ground was covered with bodies. There were stacks of bodies in some places. You couldn't believe the stench. We got into the ditch and we were going around checking to see if they're dead. A lot of them were playing possum. I checked over this one guy two or three times before somebody realized he was alive. And this other guy shot him. But I thought he was dead. He sure looked like he was dead. After that the guys passed the word, any bodies laying around, make sure they're dead, whether they look dead or not. We had to make sure they were dead. Either shoot them or bayonet them. I told my guys, "If they got a head on their bodies, shoot 'em again. You never know."

They took a meal break about halfway through the area, but no one could eat because of the sickening and pervasive reek of corpses rotting in the heat. After a little while of just sitting around, B Company moved out, turning to the left to go down to the shore. Harold stood on the beach acting as a spotter for one of his men, who was firing his rifle at a number of Japanese who had fled out to the reef a short distance offshore and were now clustered on the coral awaiting their fate. He heard movement behind him and turned toward the sound just in time to fend off an attack by a charging Japanese soldier armed with a samurai sword that he slashed at Harold's head.

He had been hiding in a hole under a tree, and when I turned he had just crawled out of the hole. He was coming right out at me with his sword held high. He was so close that I thought that if I stuck my rifle up he would just knock it away with his sword because of the way he was swinging it. I started to back up to where I could get a shot at him, and when I did I tripped and fell on the ground on my back; as I fell I could feel the damn air of that damn sword as it went by my face. When I hit the ground I put eight rounds through him, from my M1. It all happened so fast that nobody could do anything to help me.

Dick Stein witnessed the incident and might have helped Park—if he hadn't had his eyes to the ground, searching for souvenirs. "That was my weakness," he allowed.

Every time I'd see something that looked good, I'd take it. My pack was full of stuff—I had lots of little Buddha figurines and those little pipes they smoked. Park was about ten or fifteen feet off to my right. Then, all of a sudden, this Jap jumped up with a sword. He didn't have hardly any clothes on him at all. It looked like all he had on him was a jockstrap. He slashed at Park two or three times. Park kept backing up, backing up, then he tripped or stumbled and fell backward. He fell back and landed on his ass, but he shot the Jap while he was falling. Boy, I'll tell you, it was a lucky shot, because he was backing up and he didn't even aim; I think he just kind of pulled his rifle up and shot the guy. I thought for sure he had been slashed.

"After I got him," said Harold, "I was sort of in shock. But not too bad. I'd had other close calls, although none like this one. I just kicked some sand over his face so I wouldn't have to look at him. The other guys didn't congratulate me. There was so many other things going on, they were all doing different things. Some of 'em were checking out these ditches and stuff, for stragglers; and some of 'em were taking a position farther up the hill. They didn't take time to go around and pat anybody on the back."

Harold retrieved the sword of the man who almost killed him and brought it back to the States. It is now in his son's possession, mounted on the wall of his home outside Chicago.

★ ★ ★

It took us all day to move through our assigned area, and in that time C Company must have killed about 150 Japanese. A few of us received minor wounds, but nobody was killed. We were exhausted, though, and our nerves were frayed. You get very tense walking among so many bodies knowing that some are not dead, knowing that some will suddenly spring up and try to kill you. As well, the killing had been wanton and largely unopposed, and for reasons we could neither understand nor articulate, that did not sit well with us.

We finished our sweep late in the day and broke for chow, eating our field rations as millions of flies engorged on the flesh of the dead buzzed around us. Bulldozers had already been brought up to the battlefield and were digging long trenches that would serve as mass graves for the Japanese. My men and most of the other Marines involved in the mopping up would spend the better part of the next few days dragging Japanese bodies to the edge of those excavations and piling them up for the bulldozers, which would then push them in and cover them over as if they were so much carrion to be disposed of. At the same time our own people were retrieving the bodies of fallen Americans for proper burials in individually marked graves.

Next morning, while my men hauled corpses off the battlefield, I went back to the battalion aid station to have my wounded arm rebandaged. I was alone, and I cut cross-country through brushy terrain because that was the shortest and quickest route to the aid station. I should have followed the main road south because it was safer, but that would have taken longer and required more effort, and anyway, I didn't feel that safety was an issue. I had reached a point in my career as a combat Marine where I had lost the capacity to be afraid in all but the most extreme circumstances; that is, when the Japanese were actually shooting at me. This was not bravery, nor was it an instance of taking a calculated risk. It didn't occur to me that I was being brave, because I couldn't imagine that there was any risk involved in what I was doing. My sense of danger had been dulled by too much exposure to it.

I should have been afraid—or more cautious, at least. The area was crawling with Japanese. I mean that literally. They were crawling around in the brush, individuals and small groups, survivors of a massacre that had claimed most of their army, still able to fight and kill Americans even if they were themselves slain in the attempt. It is likely that many of these survivors wanted to die and were ashamed to be alive after the death of their comrades. Probably most thought that they *should* have died. But there were a few who could not decide what to do, who were neither ready to die nor committed to living. I know such men existed: I ran into three of them.

Actually, I very nearly stumbled over them. They were hunkered down in the brush a few feet to my left, and they must have seen me coming well before I reached their hiding place, strolling cluelessly along like some green recruit. They could easily have killed me, but instead they kept still, no doubt hoping that I would pass by without noticing them. But the brush was not dense enough to fully conceal them, and that proved to be their undoing. When

for no particular reason I glanced down in their direction and saw a leg in
the foliage I thought at first that I had happened upon a dead Marine killed
in the previous day's sweep of the area. But then I looked again—and the leg
moved! Peering into the brush, I found myself just about face-to-face with
three Japanese soldiers.

For the briefest of moments nobody moved; we all just stared at each other.
They were very young, moon-faced boys, their eyes wide with fright. Suddenly
they began squirming and scrambling about like puppies in a whelping box,
trying to get away, and like puppies, they were making little grunting and
squealing noises. It was a slapstick performance, a flurry of fumbling and
bumbling and entanglement, a virtual comedy of errors—but I wasn't laughing.
My heart practically leapt into my throat, and I stood bolt upright and pointed
my carbine at them. I cut loose just as one of them began thumping a grenade
against his helmet. I killed him before he could arm the grenade and then I
killed his companions, emptying my clip into all three.

And just like that, it was over. From start to finish the whole encounter
had not lasted more than a few seconds. I hurried on to the aid station, cursing
myself for a fool. I was plenty scared, but more than that I was angry with
myself. I wasn't eager to tell the people at the aid station about the incident
and tried to sound nonchalant when I did: "Say, if any of you guys want some
souvenirs, I know where you can find them." I then explained that I had killed
three Japanese on my way to the aid station and told them where they could
find the bodies. Immediately one of the Marines rushed out of the tent. He
returned a few minutes later, after a corpsman had cleaned and dressed my
wound. "Yep, he killed 'em, just like he said," the Marine declared.

I returned to C Company by way of a safer, more traveled route. I told my
officers what had happened, and I was straight up with them, admitting my
stupidity and carelessness. They all ribbed me unmercifully and had a good
laugh at my expense, and I laughed right along with them. Even so, I had a
strange, unpleasant feeling about killing those Japanese boys. I could see their
smooth, round faces and their eyes wide with the terror I had put into them. I
told myself that it was my job to kill Japanese, but that didn't change the way
I felt. I knew I hadn't done anything wrong, but I couldn't shake the feeling
that what I had done was unnecessary. Maybe, I thought, I should have just
let them go.

To this day I can still see those faces, still see the terror in their eyes. And I
ask myself: did I really have to kill them?

That same night some forty Japanese who had been skulking in the brush
conducted a mini-banzai attack on the battalion aid station and the 81-mm
mortar platoon dug in beside it. All of the attackers were killed.

CHAPTER TEN

The Last Campaign

A LITTLE OVER THREE MILES SOUTH OF SAIPAN SAT TINIAN, just twelve miles long and six miles across at its widest point, defended by nine thousand Japanese soldiers and naval personnel. On the morning of "Jig-day," 24 July, most of them occupied positions around Tinian town on the southwest coast, expecting us to assault the spacious beaches in that area. We feinted in that direction with a task force that included the bulk of the 2d Marine Division and instead landed the 4th Marine Division on two small beaches on the northwest coast. The feint succeeded, fixing the Japanese in place in the south and allowing the 4th Division to go ashore virtually unopposed.

The 1/8 landed in late afternoon, the only 2d Division unit involved in the J-day operations. The regiment quickly established a reserve position behind the beachhead's perimeter, digging in and stringing barbed wire in anticipation of an enemy counterattack. All movement around the perimeter ceased at dusk as Marines disappeared into their foxholes and readied themselves for the coming battle: locking and loading weapons, preparing grenades, checking ammo clips, stubbing out cigarettes.

The hours passed with gunfire intermittently flaring in the darkness, tense Marines shooting at phantoms—everyone on edge, green replacements and veterans alike, maybe the veterans especially. This was, for me and many other 2d Division Marines, the fourth combat operation in just eighteen months. The previous three—Guadalcanal, Tarawa, and Saipan—had all been difficult, each in its own way, taking an enormous physical and emotional toll on the survivors. Most of us had been wounded at least once; all of us had been sick. On

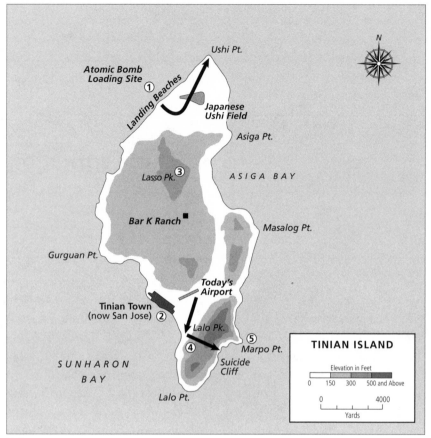

Tinian.

Notes:

1. 1st Bn. 8th made assault landing here on 24 July and advanced rapidly over Japanese airfield to Ushi Point. Marines repulsed furious counterattack on artillery positions first night ashore.
2. The Japanese expected the Americans to land at Tinian Town where a feint was made against heavy enemy artillery fire.
3. Location of enemy reserve forces.
4. 1st Bn. 8th took this ridge and held it against a final strong counterattack during the night.
5. Enemy military personal and civilians committed suicide, jumping off Marpo Point.

Saipan the division suffered sixty-three hundred casualties, including thirteen hundred KIA; and the official total of five thousand wounded was certainly low, since many wounds went unreported because they were treated in the field. Just about everyone who saw combat had unreported injuries. Clipped by bullets, nicked by shrapnel, concussed by shellfire, dinged by grenade fragments—it was all in a day's work. The Air Force could have dropped bushels of Purple Hearts on our frontline units, and every Marine who grabbed one would have deserved it.

There was something else. We felt used up and worn out, tired of spirit. We were becoming increasingly fatalistic: we felt that our bill was coming due, that our luck was running out. The kids—the replacements—were scared, sure, but they didn't know what they were scared of. The veterans, on the other hand, knew what was out there. We had seen it before, and it had seen us. It knew all about us. It had a list and we were on it. It would be stalking the battlefield looking for us, looking to take us away as it had already taken so many of our buddies, looking to draw a line through our names.

That first night ashore, waiting for the Japanese to attack, I thought my name might be near the top of the list. I know that many other old hands felt the same.

The Japanese counterattacked at three points along our perimeter. The first attack struck the 1/24, in front of the 1/8's positions, at 0230. The battle started with a sudden tremendous roar as the frontline Marines opened fire all at once on their attackers. Within seconds star shells fired by our warships burst overhead, clearly illuminating several hundred Japanese navy troops led by officers wearing white gloves. At 0230 a second enemy force assaulted our center. Beaten back, the Japanese reorganized and attacked again, this time breaking through with a small group that reached positions occupied by a company of 75-mm pack howitzers. At 0400 my unit, C Company, was dispatched to help the artillerymen. By then a third Japanese force, supported by a few tanks, had attacked our right flank.

With battles raging across our front and in our rear, C Company moved in column toward the beleaguered battery. We were all scared as hell, knowing that we were violating a basic tenet of Pacific War combat: you don't move around at night when the Japanese are nearby, especially during a battle. With the way unmarked and no paths to follow, we headed in the battery's general direction and hoped for the best, an uncertain journey across unfamiliar ground. Our vision was confounded by swift and radical alterations between light and dark, the photo-flash brilliance of the flares contrasting with the pitch blackness of the night, leaving us blind and groping toward our destination. All around us the racket and commotion of battle rose and fell, and our every step was taken with the stomach-churning fear that we might be walking into an enemy ambush or, worse, a position held by trigger-happy 4th Division

Marines. Our brethren were blasting away at the Japanese with a formidable assortment of weapons—rifles, machine guns, 81-mm and 60-mm mortars, 75-mm howitzers, and, most terrifying, 37-mm antitank guns firing canister rounds. A slaughter was taking place, and we were rightly afraid that we would be among its victims.

But luck was with us. We made it to the battery position without incident and formed a skirmish line in front of the guns. Dawn revealed a landscape pocked with shell holes, covered with corpses. Later it was determined that more than twenty-seven hundred Japanese had been killed in the fighting.

Many of the attackers were still alive; we could see them, or rather the round tops of their helmets, in the shell holes. About a hundred yards of open ground lay before us, and when we received the order to advance, we emerged from our foxholes with the sickening feeling that it was our turn to suffer heavy losses. The Japanese had attacked with reckless fury during the night, and we expected they would perform the same way on defense. But when we formed up and started forward the Japanese threw a few unaimed shots our way and that was all. No one was hit.

What a pleasant surprise. But also baffling. *What were they up to now?*

We crossed the open ground, braced for the worst. Here and there an enemy soldier poked his head up over the rim of his hole and was instantly obliterated by a fusillade of rifle and BAR fire.

As we approached each shell hole its occupants would bang grenades on their helmets, hold the grenades to their chests, and blow themselves to pieces. They could have thrown the grenades at us but chose to kill themselves instead. It was a replay of the mopping-up operation on Saipan but on a bigger scale. We didn't have to scurry around doing the fire-and-movement routine. We didn't have to dive for cover—not once. We just kept moving, standing up straight and walking at a steady pace, and when we got close to a shell hole: *Blam!* It was the damnedest thing. We commented on it as we advanced. *Blam!* "There goes another one." *Blam! Blam!* "Two more!"

It was all very strange, even to the veterans. The new kids were flabbergasted. But no one was complaining. If only the Japanese were always so obliging.

Accompanied by tanks, we continued past this killing ground and advanced rapidly against light opposition north and east along the coast. Advancing on our right were the regiment's 2d and 3d battalions, which had landed early that morning and had now joined us in the offensive to clear the island's northern tip. Ahead and moving steadily before us a rolling barrage from our heavy artillery on Saipan thundered continually, kicking up massive black divots of earth and smoke shot through with fire. In the shallow water on our left, turreted amtracs puttered slowly along the shoreline occasionally firing their machine guns and 75-mm howitzers. Late that morning we ran into a pocket of resistance near the water, circled around it, came in at its flank, and wiped it out. Then we moved on for a short distance and halted for the night.

Next day, 26 July, we overran the two Ushi Point airfields, advancing on debris-strewn runways past the charred skeletons of Japanese aircraft and hangars gutted by bombs and artillery fire, stepping over and around engines and wings and tail sections, charred rubber wheels, and broken Plexiglas canopies. Seabees following immediately in our wake swiftly cleared away the mess. Just two days later U.S. Army P-47 Thunderbolts were taking off from the airfields, providing us with close air support; within weeks squadrons of B-29 Superfortress bombers would be using the airfields as bases for attacks on the Japanese home islands.

We reached the east coast around noon. In the meantime, the 4th Division on our right had seized Mt. Maga and Mt. Lasso in the center of the island. The entire 2d Division was now ashore and had linked up with the 4th Division to form a continuous line across the island.

On 27 July, while the two divisions attacked south, the 8th Marines went into reserve. We were supposed to mop up the north of the island in what was now the corps rear, but there wasn't much mopping up to do. Most of the Japanese in this sector had been killed or had withdrawn to the south. With little work to do, we sat around and rested and watched as dive-bombers from Saipan worked over enemy positions in the path of the two-division offensive. The aircraft used napalm bombs, something new to us. We watched in amazement as the bombs fell earthward, tumbling end over end, and exploded on a ridge that instantly erupted in flames and oily smoke along its entire length. About ten seconds later a gust of hot air from the ridge blew over us. Next day 1st Battalion elements moved up on the ridge and poked around the scorched landscape. Most of the undergrowth had been burned away. The ground was black and reeked of gasoline, and the foxholes were filled with corpses of Japanese soldiers blackened and shriveled by the incinerating fires.

On the twenty-eighth the island was hit by a typhoon that lasted two days. Our foxholes filled with water, forcing us to sit and sleep above ground in heavy blowing rain. After the storm passed, the sun came out and steam rose up from the mucky red soil like primordial mists on a prehistoric landscape. On the thirtieth the 8th Marines went back into action in the center of the line near the island's southern tip. Enemy resistance was steadily increasing:

with their backs to the sea and no escape possible, the Japanese fought with characteristic tenacity.

Bill Crumpacker was hit late in the day while B Company advanced through a cane field toward the island's southernmost plateau. Japanese artillery shelled the field, and Bill along with several others took cover behind a stone water cistern in the backyard of a farmhouse. With shells exploding just thirty yards from the cistern Bill's platoon leader, Lt. Robert Munkirs, hollered, "We gotta get up on the plateaus and dug in by night." Bill and his companions grabbed their rifles and took off running toward the plateau's escarpment. They had gone but a few yards when a shell burst in their midst.

Shrapnel hit Bill in the head, neck, and arm. His helmet went flying, and he dropped to the ground. "It was like someone hit me in the head with a sledgehammer," Bill recalled. "But it didn't knock me out. I felt dizzy, woozy— like being on a merry-go-round." Nearby his helmet lay upside down with "probably two inches of blood in the bottom and holes in the steel pot and the liner that you could have dropped an egg through."

Corpsman Robert Wolland knelt beside him and wiped the blood from his face. "Is that you, Crummy?" he asked.

"Yeah, yeah," Crumpacker replied. Then: "You better back off, Bob. They're gonna be dropping another one here in a few seconds."

"Oh, those cross-eyed little bastards can't hit the same spot twice," said Wolland, and proceeded to cut off Bill's pack with his KA-BAR. Bill propped himself up on his left elbow and looked at his right arm. About three inches of bone had been blown out of his right humerus, and it seemed to Bill that his forearm was coming out of his shoulder.

"And I thought, *Boy, when I get to the aid station all the doctor's gonna need to take off what's left of my arm is a Boy Scout knife.*"

Wolland was applying compresses to his wounds, trying to stanch the bleeding, when Dick Stein sauntered over and squatted down next to him. He looked at Bill, and he looked at Bill's wounds, and he saw that his friend was in a very bad way, all pale and gray and covered with blood. Dick didn't think he was going to make it. He tried to cheer Bill up, giving solace to what he thought was a dying man, saying, "Crumpacker, you'll do anything to get out of combat!"

"He just gave me a sick look," Dick told me.

Bill was carried to the aid station, a tent set up some distance to the rear. Medical personnel laid him out on a table, and the doctors looked him over and did what they could for him; then he was taken outside and lowered into a recently dug trench with fresh dirt piled on either side. Bill lay on his back and a corpsmen bent over him, examined his dog tags, and said to another corpsman, "Go get a priest; this guy's a Catholic." A few minutes later a priest appeared and gave Bill absolution. When he finished he asked Bill whether there was anything else he could do for him. Bill asked for a cigarette. The priest lit a cigarette and placed it between his lips and held it there while Bill puffed on it—by then he was so weak from loss of blood he couldn't use even his good left hand to hold the cigarette. After a few puffs the priest discarded the cigarette, saying, "I've gotta go; I've got some other work. I'll see you later on." Bill said, "Yeah," and the priest left, leaving Bill in what looked to him like the grave in which he would soon be buried.

Bill didn't die, of course, but the war was over for him. As of this writing he's alive and well and living in California, one of the dwindling cohort of Marine veterans from the Second World War.

Morning, 31 July. We advanced toward the plateau at the southern tip of the island, attacking through a burned sugarcane field taking fire from all directions by Japanese hidden in the wrack of broken stalks. Three Japanese tanks appeared at the edge of the escarpment and fired down at us with their turret guns. But they used armor-piercing rounds ineffective against infantry rather than high-explosive shells. "Everyone started running through the cane field to get away from the tank fire," recalled Harold Park. "I saw this one guy, he was running, and his legs were going up and down like pistons, and this armor-piercing shell went right between his legs and traveled a way beyond before it hit the ground. There was no explosion like you'd get with HE, and nobody was hurt."

From my usual position at the back of our company's column I saw corpsmen hustling to the rear carrying a stretcher with Captain Seltzer on it. Shortly thereafter 1st Lt. Al Tidwell, an old-breed former top sergeant on Larry Hays' staff, appeared by my side. "Seltzer got his legs blown off," he said. "The CO says wants you to take over the company."*

I immediately went up to the front of the column to direct our platoon leaders. We struggled on through the cane field, engaging and killing Japanese

---

* A few months after returning to the States, I learned that Captain Seltzer had been evacuated to Guadalcanal and had his leg amputated. He became so depressed that he took his own life. I heard he had been a professional dancer before the war and couldn't bear to live with only one leg.

machine-gun crews and riflemen. Before us loomed the sheer cliff walls of the plateau, seemingly unscalable. We reached the base of the massif around noon and at first couldn't find a way up. Then elements from A Company on our left discovered a steep winding road with hairpin curves leading to the top. We pushed up the road, fighting every step of the way, taking heavy fire from the plateau, from bunkers in the caves and fissures in the cliff wall, from the dense vegetation on both sides of the road. With dusk approaching, Larry Hays frequently radioed his company commanders, urging us to move faster. "You've got to get your company to the top," he said. "You've got to get up there and dug in before nightfall. The Japs are gonna banzai tonight, and if we aren't in position we're gonna get murdered." Hays was taking a lot of heat from the regimental commander, Col. Clarence R. Wallace, who was in turn getting pressure from division HQ.

Finally reaching the top, we fanned out to the right along the edge of the cliff. Darkness overtook us as we hastily strung wire and dug in as best we could in the hard coral. My radioman and I dug a foxhole fifty feet to the right of the road, the last foxhole on C Company's right; the rest of the company was deployed to my left. George Stein, B Company's commander, shared the adjacent foxhole to my right with his radioman. The rest of B Company deployed to their right.

The Japanese attacked after nightfall, charging our line with customary courage and disregard for casualties. Also customary: our response, the roar of many weapons firing all at once, an earsplitting din. As always in night battles, the situation quickly became confused, the fighting desperate. Tracers streaking every which way, explosions, flares bursting overhead, shouting and cries for help, shadowy figures running this way and that. Bushes around my foxhole limited my view of the battlefield; I couldn't see my men, much less issue orders that might guide their efforts, so I hunkered down beside my radioman and waited for the Japanese to come. George Stein's radioman was wounded in the melee. Down the line to my left, in my company's area, the volume of fire intensified, and I heard our 37-mm antitank guns in that sector banging away at the enemy, firing canister rounds without letup.

With the battle on our left still raging, firing broke out in the rear, on the road below us. A large group of Japanese had penetrated our line, pouring through a gap to our right between the 1st Battalion and elements of the 4th Marine Division, overrunning several vehicles parked on the road and setting them on fire. My radioman received an urgent radio request from his buddies, who were laying telephone wire along the road for our battalion's

81-mm mortars. I heard him reply, "I'll meet you down on the road below our position, if I don't get my head shot off." Then he scrambled out of our hole and disappeared into the night, armed only with a .45 automatic.

We found his body on the road the next morning.

Harold Park was involved in the fighting on the road. He belonged to a detachment providing security for the battalion CP, positioned near the top of the road just below the rim of the plateau. "Around midnight," he recalle:

> A bunch of Japanese came walking up the road and went right up to the CP. Our guys had a password, "Little Lulu Loves Lollipops." On account of the "Ls," which the Japanese had trouble pronouncing. There was a jeep on the road. Its engine was running, and some people were approaching it and I heard one of our guys challenge them. Then a grenade exploded and the engine stopped and the guys in the jeep jumped out. There must have been about a dozen Japanese down there and they were behind a big clump of bushes. We started shooting at them but we couldn't see them in the bushes. We could hear them, though, arming their grenades against rocks or by knocking them against their helmets or whatever. They were throwing a lot of grenades, and we were throwing a lot of grenades and shooting at them too. I got hit down in the lower part of my leg just above my ankle. I went looking for a corpsman, and also to see if I could talk anybody out of their grenades, because we'd used ours up. I found a corpsman and he put a bandage on my leg and I went back to my position.
>
> The next morning we got out of our holes and went down on the road to check things out. That's when we realized how many Japanese were there. They were all lying in a group down there in the bushes. They all had real clean clothes on, and they had these chrome-plated bayonets with hand guards. I wanted to get one of those but I didn't.

The strongest attack came just before daybreak. About five hundred Japanese rushed, howling, at our line, again directing their main effort at our left. We slaughtered them with support fire from our 81-mm mortars and direct fire from our antitank guns. In the process, however, they nearly wiped out one of our 37-mm gun crews, killing or wounding eight of the ten men. Typically, the two unhurt gunners continued to service their weapon, firing without letup until dawn, when the Japanese finally withdrew. By then, scores of Japanese dead lay heaped in front of the gun position, bloody testimony to the lethality of canister shot but also, and most especially, to the bravery of the

Marine gunners, living and dead, who stayed at their post and held it against the ferocious enemy assault.

Shortly after sunup Japanese artillery began shelling us. Airbursts exploded above our positions, and there was no escaping the shrapnel that rained down on us. I pushed myself flat to the ground at the bottom of my hole and hugged the earth until the shelling stopped. In the meantime, Sherman tanks moved up the road, killing the remnant of the enemy force that had broken through our line during the night. Then we climbed out of our holes, formed a line behind the tanks, and started across the plateau. The brush was thick, and it was easy to get separated from the men beside you, and all of a sudden I found myself alone. One of my platoon leaders was a little way behind me, and as I looked over my shoulder at him several rifles cracked and then a machine gun cut loose. I could tell by the sound that it was a Japanese machine gun, but I couldn't determine its position. I threw myself to the ground, more frightened than I had been at any other time in the war. *I've come this far,* I thought, *and now I'm going to get killed by a machine gun.* I felt sort of like a coward for thinking that, but I couldn't help myself.

All in all, it was a harrowing experience, worse than anything I had gone through on Guadalcanal, on Saipan, even on Tarawa.

★   ★   ★

We swept across the plateau, driving the Japanese before us. As we approached the cliff overlooking the shoreline I heard a powerful explosion and then saw the body of a Japanese soldier soaring above the treetops, arms and legs flapping like a rag doll. Evidently he had committed suicide by detonating a large explosive charge.

The terrain in this area was flat but rugged, seamed by jagged coral crevasses, some of them fifteen feet deep and the same or more wide. It was ideally suited for defense, and if the Japanese had chosen to contest our advance, they could have made things very difficult for us. But the Japanese had no more fight in them. They were ready to die, if not yet to call it quits. For the most part they went over and down the Marpo Point cliff wall and went into the many caves that pocked that steep surface and waited for us to come and kill them.

My company dug in along the edge of the cliff and set up our machine guns and mortars to fire down at the Japanese. There were hundreds of Japanese soldiers below us on the rocks along the cliff wall, armed but not using their weapons. A Navy motor launch appeared offshore, and an officer in the bow stood, put a bullhorn to his mouth, and began speaking in Japanese to the enemy soldiers, giving them a deadline for surrendering. But of course they would not surrender, and when the deadline expired, we opened fire.

Many Japanese were killed by our fire, but many also jumped from the ledges, dashing themselves on the rocks below. In front of my unit and to its right Japanese civilians as well as soldiers jumped from a place that we immediately dubbed "Suicide Cliff."

"The cliff had a little bit of a curve to it," Dick Stein recalled, "and they'd jump and about halfway down they'd hit the side of the cliff and their heads would pop off. I saw that happen two or three times. Sometimes they'd take children with them. I remember this one Jap officer, he scooped up a couple of these kids and bailed over the side with them. And this one little girl hung on to him for several seconds and she just looked up at me. And I'm looking over the side of the cliff. This is happening about ten feet below me."

Plenty of Japanese didn't jump. That night several dozen scaled the cliff and attacked one of the battalion's strongpoints. All were killed at close range in a brief but noisy firefight. Next day we sent patrols down among the caves accompanied by interpreters with bullhorns. This time a number of civilians did surrender. But a goodly number of soldiers remained in the caves. So we killed them.

It was a tough, nasty fight. My old unit, 2d Platoon, B Company, was in the thick of it. Dick Stein remembers coming to the edge of the cliff and leaning over to look down. A few feet below him two Japanese soldiers stood on a ledge in front of a cave entrance. Dick shot one in the shoulder, and he tumbled off the side. Then Pfc. George Wasicek, regarded by everyone who knew him as the world's most fearless Marine, jumped off the edge and landed on a ledge in front of the cave entrance and shot the other Japanese soldier. Dick lay down at the edge of the cliff and watched as Wasicek went to work on the cave's occupants. A grenade thrown from the cave hit Wasicek's helmet, bounced off, and exploded in midair, leaving Wasicek unhurt. Then a Japanese soldier came barreling out of the cave straight at Wasicek, like a blitzing linebacker. Wasicek casually sidestepped the enemy soldier, who ran off the cliff, arms flailing cartoonishly as he fell to the rocks far below. Then Wasicek went into the cave. A flurry of rifle shots. When he emerged just a few seconds later, seven Japanese soldiers inside the cave lay dead.

Dick Stein described Wasicek as "the bravest guy I ever saw."

He wasn't afraid of anything. He probably killed more Japs than a whole company put together. On Saipan and Tinian, he'd jump right in where the fighting was hottest. He was like that on Tarawa too. He'd be out in the open, firing his rifle, and I'd think, you're not gonna last long. But that son of a gun, he did. He didn't know what fear was. I met his wife one day and I told her, boy, if anyone ought to get that Medal of Honor, George should. He was kind of a funny guy, you know—quiet, kept to himself, not too sociable. I had a lot of respect for him. We all did.

I tried to interview George for this book, to get him talking about his exploits, but I didn't have much success. George told me a few things but didn't go into detail. A taciturn man, he didn't want to talk about himself. He passed away in 2005, shortly after our meeting, a good man and a great Marine.

Tinian was declared secure on 1 August. First Battalion pulled back about a mile from the coast and set up camp. The end of the fighting was very abrupt: suddenly we didn't have anything to do. There was no enemy activity in our immediate area. No danger, no shooting. I just sat back and tried to enjoy the situation. This wasn't as easy as you might think. I was exhausted and filled with a lingering dread, a sense that I had used up all my lives. I had become conditioned to wondering whether I was going to survive another day, and then all of a sudden all the causes for concern had vanished, as though I'd been given a reprieve from a death sentence. I could hardly believe it. A strange feeling.

I didn't have long to dwell on it. A few days later I received orders to return to the States.

Thirty-two months after leaving San Diego, I was going home.

Epilogue

THREE WEEKS LATER AT PEARL HARBOR, where I had been marking time in the transit center, I boarded a giant Martin Mars flying boat for the final leg of the journey to the States. After a long, long flight the plane came in low right over the Golden Gate Bridge. Everyone aboard, servicemen from every branch returning home, watched in utter silence as the bridge passed beneath us.

We landed at Alameda near Treasure Island, and I stepped out on American soil for the first time in more than two and a half years. A woman Marine driving a jeep waited for me on the dock. I stared at her for a moment before getting in. Amazing. Women in the Marine Corps.

I reported to the Marine facility and was granted a thirty-two-day furlough, one for every month overseas. Later that day I visited a barbershop. While I was sitting in the chair, one of the patrons began bitching about the terrible state of things in the country. I listened to him for a while and then I exploded. "You don't know what terrible is," I told him. He shut up after that.

I left for Spokane the next day.

The war wasn't over. No one had any idea how long it would last, but most Americans thought that it would go on for another three years at least. "Golden Gate in '48" was the catchphrase of the day for servicemen in the Pacific theater. We believed the Japanese would fight ever more tenaciously in the island battles to come and that eventually we would invade Japan and fight our way up and down the home islands. I was fairly sure that I would be sent back into combat sooner or later.

I was serving on the staff of Basic School in Quantico, Virginia, when the atomic bombs were dropped on Hiroshima and Nagasaki. Still the war went on. Then, on 15 August, after a night of devastating bombing raids on eight Japanese cities, the Japanese announced their intention to surrender. For Americans and most of the rest of the world the announcement signaled the end of World War II, even though the formal surrender didn't take place until 2 September.

A few weeks later our classes were terminated and orders were cut by the thousands to release men from active duty. I was asked whether I wanted to stay on and take a regular commission in the Marine Corps. I was tempted. I had started as a private and made captain at age twenty-four—no small achievement—and there was the potential for further advancement in the postwar Corps. At first I said yes and signed the requisite papers. But after sleeping on it I changed my mind. Next day I withdrew my papers.

Shortly thereafter I was released from active duty. I bought a 1940 Chrysler convertible, and in October I drove cross-country to Spokane, a five-day journey. I had never seen the country up close like this, and it was a very moving experience. I didn't stay in motels; mostly I just pulled off the road and slept in the car. Somewhere in the Midwest I pulled off the road near a farmhouse, and the family who lived there invited me in. I stayed overnight.

In a tavern in Des Moines I met a Marine Corps major, in uniform but without any campaign ribbons. I asked him where he had served, what campaigns he had participated in. "None," he said. "I was at Wake Island. I've been a prisoner of war—I just got released."

He told me he had been second in command of the Marine garrison on Wake, serving under Maj. James P. S. Devereux. He spent much of the war working as a slave in coal mines in Japan. I asked how he had been treated. He said, "A little better than the enlisted men, but not much better." We talked for several hours. He was very interested in my campaign ribbons and asked what each was for. I told him about my experiences. He'd been back only a few days. He was thin and very subdued, almost meek. All the vinegar had been taken out of him.

I don't recall his name. In 2007 I contacted Gregory J. W. Urwin of Temple University to help me identify this man. Dr. Urwin is a professor of history, associate director of Temple's Center for the Study of Force and Diplomacy, and the author of *Facing Fearful Odds: The Siege of Wake Island* (Bison Books, 2002). He very graciously offered his assistance and researched the subject. In an exchange of e-mails he told me that Major Devereux's executive officer on Wake (and the commander of the Wake Island Detachment, 1st Defense Battalion, 5-Inch Group) was Maj. George H. Potter Jr. "If any Marine officer would identify himself as Devereux's second-in-command," Greg wrote, "it would be Potter." Although, he added, "some authors refer to Maj. Paul A. Putnam, the commander of VMF-211, as Devereux's second-in-command on Wake. Putnam, however, always insisted that he was sent to Wake with a separate command and that he was directly under the orders of Admiral Halsey. That did not stop him from cooperating with Devereux during the siege—especially after all his planes were gone."

Potter, an Annapolis grad, hailed from Montana and was appointed to the Naval Academy from that state. Which raises the question: why would he have been in Iowa when I drove through? On the other hand, Putnam, although born in Milan, Michigan, moved with his family to Iowa while he was a boy and completed one year at Iowa State College before enlisting in the Marine Corps in 1923 (he was appointed a second lieutenant "from Iowa" on 5 March 1926).

Greg's conclusion: Putnam must have been the officer with whom I conversed.

Maybe, maybe not. I don't recall aviator wings on the major's uniform. And Putnam was then forty-two years old; it seemed to me that the major was closer to thirty. Thus I think it more likely that I was speaking with Potter. But I don't suppose I'll ever know for sure.

★   ★   ★

I spent that night at the University of Iowa at Ames, where I met and partied with two boy-crazy college coeds. One was homely; the other was a knockout. Naturally I was interested in the latter, but the homely one advised me: "She's just a tease. You go out with me, you'll have a lot more fun."

I didn't heed her words and went out with the pretty one—and found out that the homely one was right.

I arrived in Spokane a few days later. I stayed with my parents for the next two months, sleeping in my childhood bedroom. In January I reenrolled at Washington State and was soon immersed in my engineering studies, trying to make up for all the time I had been away, trying to remember what I learned before the war. The classrooms were filled with former servicemen like me, and we all had to work very hard to get back in the academic and peacetime grooves, to get on with our lives.

It was a tough transition. But we made it.

★   ★   ★

In 1954, ten years after my last hostile encounter with the Japanese, I met a Japanese-American structural engineer named Justin Matsuda at North American Aviation, where we were both employed. I told him about the diary I had taken off the body of a dead Japanese soldier on Guadalcanal, and he translated it for me. Later he counseled me to return the diary to the soldier's family in Japan.

At Justin's invitation, I spoke at the East Los Angeles Buddhist Church about my experiences on Guadalcanal. My wife, Vera, and my three young daughters accompanied me. It was difficult for me, because I had to be careful how I referred to my former enemies. The audience members were elderly and most had been born in Japan, and I could not understand why they were interested in hearing about my experiences.

They explained that they were from the northern part of Japan and were not familiar with what had happened to their men who had fought on Guadalcanal. The soldiers on Guadalcanal were mostly from the Tokyo area and other large population centers to the south.

I used a map and Justin translated. After my presentation the church's Buddhist priest presided over a memorial service that began with the sounding of a large gong. Each of us was given a smoking incense stick and a single rose, and we lined up, with me first in line and my family behind me, followed by the entire congregation. Silently and solemnly we filed past the stage, placing our roses on it.

After the ceremony we joined the Buddhist priest in his parsonage for a sukiyaki dinner with beer. The priest was new to America and spoke no English. With Justin translating, he told me about his experiences as an army officer in China, where he had on one occasion played dead when Chinese soldiers overran his unit. He also discussed Japan's expansionist policies, which he believed to have been justified.

The priest also recommended that I return the personal effects I had taken from the dead Japanese soldier—a lock of hair, a first-aid kit, a photograph of a group of soldiers, and a "thousand-stitch belt." A few weeks later, Justin's wife mentioned that she had a cousin playing baseball on the Japanese team in a world championship playoff in the United States. The team had lost its first game and was returning to Japan. She had told her cousin about the personal effects, and the entire team seized on the opportunity to take them back to Japan, a face-saving gesture to compensate for the early loss in the playoffs. Their plane had a stopover in Honolulu, and the cousin was the first passenger to disembark, carrying the dead soldier's personal belongings wrapped in a small white box draped from his neck. Word of his coming and of his precious cargo had preceded him, and several Buddhist priests were on hand to welcome him and his companions.

News of the event flashed across the Pacific to Japan. By the time the plane landed in Tokyo a large crowd that included many Buddhist priests had gathered outside the airport, standing in heavy rain to await its arrival. The Japanese media picked up on the story, and soon newspapers throughout Japan published articles concerning the return of the lost soldier's effects to his family. My name figured prominently in those articles, of course, and for a brief time I became fairly well known among the Japanese.

Interestingly, the return of the group photograph led to a reunion of that unit. The soldiers in the photograph had served in China with the soldier but not on Guadalcanal. The papers showed a picture of them at their reunion looking happily at that photograph.

The diary and lock of hair were presented to the soldier's wife. She was moved and very thankful to get his diary and to read how he felt about her. She was particularly relieved to learn that he had directed her to remarry if he died, which was contrary to Japanese custom—a widow was supposed to continue serving the deceased husband's family. She had indeed remarried but had remained troubled by her decision to do so. The words in the diary finally freed her from her sense of guilt.

Years later, Akio Tani, once a Japanese artillery commander on Guadalcanal and by then a good friend (see below), delved into Japanese army archives to find out more about the slain man. From his records we learned that he was 1st Sgt. Masamitsu Manabe of the 228th Infantry Regiment, holder of the Order of the Golden Kite (5th class), killed in action on 13 January 1943 on what was known to the Japanese as Sakai Ridge. In 1955 I received a formal thank-you letter, exquisitely crafted in Japanese calligraphy, from the soldier's eldest brother, Mitsuo Manabe. Tani translated the letter from Mitsuo (who died in 1977 at age seventy-three) as follows:

> It is at the end of 1955, it is very cold but I think you are very glad and working well. I have not seen you but I am writing you. My brother died over ten years ago and I have been wanting to know how he died and what he left. I am always thinking of my brother and looking at his picture. I believe he did his best, although our country was defeated. I am very sad because I can't see even his bones.

Years have passed since then and Japan has been preparing a peaceful country. Everyone has been inclined to forget the men who devoted their lives for their country. I think it is a sad thing, especially for me, who lost a brother. I am very obliged to you for informing me about his last time and I'm very happy to get the following things: a seal, a pocket memo diary, a picture of the soldiers, a business card, food, his picture, handicraft (the thousand stitch belt added to by many people).

As you know, they were fighting each other but you were very kind. I don't have more words to thank you. I suppose he is at peace in heaven. Thank you very much again. I am the luckiest person because there are few who can obtain the personal things left. I will keep them forever. I am praying for your safety and soundness far away from Japan.

Sincerely yours,
Mitsuo Manabe
December 27, 1955

★   ★   ★

In 1980, after retiring as an engineer at Lockheed, I decided that it was high time to return to the Pacific. It had long been my dream to revisit the Pacific battle sites where I served as a young rifle company lieutenant in the 2d Division, at times wondering whether I would live to see another dawn. My motivation for doing so was heightened during a trip my wife and I took to New Zealand in April 1982. The high point of that trip was a tour of the site of Camp Paikakariki north of Wellington. There we met two New Zealanders, Ian and Enid Milne, the official "greeters" for visiting Marines. Ian told me about a Guadalcanal reunion planned for August of that same year coinciding with the fortieth anniversary of the Marines' initial landing on the island. I decided right then and there that I was going to attend.

I subsequently took two trips to the Pacific, the first lasting six weeks, from August through September, and the second in November 1983 to coincide with the fortieth anniversary of the Tarawa operation, lasting four weeks.

For my first trip in 1982 I decided to travel on my own, without a set schedule (apart from the reunion ceremonies on Guadalcanal), so that I could visit sites that were meaningful to me. Ultimately I visited thirteen islands that had been either occupied or attacked by the Japanese. My first stop was Tarawa.

My plane landed at the international airport on Bonriki, eighteen miles east of Betio. From Bonriki I took a ferry to Betio, my anticipation building as we neared the island. The ferry arrived, and as I waited for the ramp to drop, I thought back to my previous attempt to "visit" the island. Then the ramp went down and I walked ashore, setting foot on Betio for the first time.

Betio had changed greatly since the war, of course. Nature had long ago repaired the blasted landscape of November 1943 with lush vegetation and tall palm trees. The long pier was gone, and little remained of the beached freighter *Niminoa*. Absent these landmarks it was at first difficult to track the course of the battle. But I soon found that evidence of the battle was not lacking. In fact it was everywhere and abundant. You would have had to be blind to miss it, and even then you would probably have stumbled over it.

A little while after landing I returned to the reef where so many of our LCVPs had run aground on that fateful second day of the Tarawa operation. The tide was out, exposing the sandy bottom of the lagoon, and I was able to walk to the reef without getting my shoes wet. It was strewn with debris from the war, mostly small, unidentifiable fragments that time and tide had battered but failed to wash away. I stood where I thought my LCVP had been so abruptly halted by the reef and then walked about one hundred yards toward the shore, stopping at the approximate location where I had intercepted a Japanese bullet. I stood there for a minute or so, remembering the names and faces of the brave young men under my command who had died alongside me in the lagoon and on Betio itself. Then I walked on in to the shore.

I returned to Betio in November of the following year to take part in the ceremonies commemorating the fortieth anniversary of Operation Galvanic. I was the leader of a tour group that included five 2d Marine Division veterans, three of them from my platoon: Bill Crumpacker, Dick Stein, and John Durst. As the representative of the commandant of the Marine Corps, the secretary of the navy and, indirectly, President Ronald Reagan, I was given the honor of reading their statements to the attendees. I also presided over the Marine portion of the ceremony, held in a large *maneaba,* a thatched-roofed, open-sided meetinghouse a short distance inland from the location of the long pier. It was an intensely emotional experience for all involved, but especially for my former comrades-in-arms and me.

Later during this trip my Marine friends and I—Crumpacker, Stein, Durst, Roy Thaxton, and Joe Souza—took a ferry in from the reef to what had been Red Beach 2. We laughed and talked excitedly the whole way, and when we stepped off the ferry onto the concrete ramp that now covered Red 2, Dick Stein raised an open can of beer and proclaimed, "This time I'm landing with a beer instead of my rifle, and that's the way I like it!"*

We subsequently explored the island from end to end. We found the landing beaches strewn with relics of the war and the Japanese concrete bunkers in a good state of preservation; the rusted hulks of about twenty amtracs littered the area. The best-preserved amtrac lay half-buried in sand behind what had been Red Beach 1. Although covered with graffiti it was otherwise in excellent condition and positioned in a way that made it look as if it might spring back into action at any moment. When it was unearthed in 1974 during the installation of a sewer line, the amtrac contained the remains of three Marines. Two were identified and buried with full military honors eight years later.

Somewhere near this amtrac Pfc. Anthony O'Boyle had been killed, the top of his head shot off as he peered over the seawall. Here John Murdock had briefly held Anthony in his arms before laying him aside in the sand near the waterline. We reflected sadly and reverently on Anthony's fate, shared in one form or another by so many of our buddies.

From this same spot we could see the turret of a Sherman tank protruding from the water at low tide just west of Red Beach 2. I looked several hundred yards east toward the location where the long pier had jutted out from the shore. Somewhere in this vicinity I had been gut-shot by a machine-gun bullet. Nearby on the left flank of Red Beach 3 stood the mount for a Japanese multipurpose gun, one of the last of many such weapons that had killed or wounded so many of the 8th Marines as they waded to the beach. Just behind the gun mount is the "Memorial Garden" that served as an interim American burial site—a place where I might have easily ended up but for the grace of God and the efforts of two brave men in my platoon.

★　★　★

---

* In peace, as in war, Dick Stein was the man that life simply could not kill, although it was not for want of trying. A motorcycle police officer for the Los Angeles Police Department, he survived numerous crashes and injuries from violent encounters with armed criminals—"about nine of them were hand-to-hand combat." He also walked away from several plane crashes (he learned to fly on the GI Bill). "When I retired from the police department," he recalled, "the city gave me a commendation on being there for twenty-five years, and I had the record for being injured on duty thirty-three times! That was thirty-three trips to the hospital. And then I had a couple of airplane crashes; I lost the engines on takeoff. I done a number on my neck and back; I broke 'em."

In 1982, after a very emotional two days on Tarawa, I flew to Guadalcanal, where I stayed for a week, using the city of Honiara at Point Cruz as my base of operations.

I had joined an organized tour sponsored by the Guadalcanal Campaign Veterans that included about thirty American veterans, but I arrived several days before they did, flying into the international airport located at the site of what used be Henderson Field. On the taxi ride from the airport to Honiara I noticed that a pier that once projected into Ironbottom Sound near Red Beach was gone except for a few pilings. Resting in the shallows were several wrecked landing craft and amtracs. Remnants of aircraft and trucks were scattered in the fields beside the road.

We crossed the Lunga River heading west, passing a golf course on our right built on the site of another airstrip designated Fighter 1. Then we crossed the Matanikau River on a single-lane Bailey bridge, itself a relic of the war, located near the site of the floating bridge we used during the war. Just west of the bridge (to my left) I recognized the low ridge now called Vavaea Ridge, running parallel to the beach almost to the northwestern tip of the island. I led several reconnaissance patrols there in early November 1942, and memories of those forays came flooding back. A large, modern Catholic church, Holy Cross Cathedral, was built on the ridge in the late 1970s a short distance from the river, in the area where one of my patrols killed three snipers in a large tree over the command post of the U.S. Army's 182d regiment.

I soon realized that my hotel was close to the location where I had shot a sniper. Next day I hiked into that area. Just after starting out I was drenched by a brief but heavy downpour, triggering more memories. I stood on the east bank of the Matanikau beside the bridge and gazed upstream at a perfectly lovely tropical setting. The river was pristine, but in my mind's eye, I could see Japanese bodies floating in it.

After visiting the Catholic church at the top of the ridge where my platoon had been deployed, I resumed my trek. Looking down toward Point Cruz, I spotted the hotel where I was staying and realized that I was near the location of the Japanese sniper who had harassed us while we held this position for several hours.

Several Japanese were staying at my hotel, and I later asked one of them whether there were any Japanese war veterans among them. He said, "Yes, by coincidence there is one in a room close to yours." He took me to the man's room, and there I met Akio Tani.

We talked for hours, each with his own tape recorder running. We had a difficult time conversing, but Tani could read English well. The most important information he imparted was that he had commanded the battery of 105-mm guns collectively known as "Pistol Pete."

Next day, at Tani's suggestion, the two of us drove west on the coast road toward Cape Esperance, following the route taken by retreating Japanese forces in the final weeks of the campaign. Our destination was the Vilu Cultural Village and War Museum near Doma Cove, but we made several stops along the way at places meaningful to Tani. The first of these was the site near Kokumbona village where his guns had been positioned for nearly two months. Nearby stood a memorial to his unit that Tani had established with the help of islanders. As we walked around the site, Tani pointed to a ridge a few hundred yards inland where his observation point (OP) had been. He told me that the command post of Lt. Gen. Harukichi Hyakutake, who took command of Japanese forces on Guadalcanal in mid-August 1942, was situated on the White River just behind and below Tani's OP.

Tani had visited the site of his OP a day or two before we met and had also been there on his two previous trips to the island. On each occasion he had worn his old uniform—a tattered shirt and trousers—and climbed down into the pit to get the feel of the place and to reflect on his experiences. From that vantage point he had peered through his telescope, spotting for his guns and other artillery batteries, directing bombardments against our ground forces and ships. I observed that his efforts had frequently sent me scrambling for cover, and we both laughed.

While Tani showed me around, several children from the village approached us and greeted Tani by name, and he promised to bring them candy on his next visit.

One of the old Pistol Pete guns is at the Vilu museum, which we visited later that day. The others were removed from Guadalcanal, and their current locations are unknown. Tani thought one was in Australia and another in the United States. As we viewed the gun at the museum, he spoke of it as if it were an old friend. He had previously offered the museum's owner, Fred Kona, a considerable sum to purchase the gun for return to Japan, but Kona refused the offer. He considered the gun a national treasure and wasn't interested in the money.

★   ★   ★

The ninth of August marked the fortieth anniversary of the naval battle of Savo Island, a disaster for the Allies that resulted in the loss of the U.S. cruisers *Quincy*, *Vincennes*, and *Astoria* and the Australian cruiser *Canberra*. The latter's namesake, the recently commissioned frigate HMAS *Canberra*, hosted a wreath-laying ceremony held over the spot in Sealark Channel where the old cruiser had gone down. Participating in the event were some thirty American veterans of the Guadalcanal campaign (me included) and a large group of dignitaries and guests. Most notable among those attending were Joe Foss, Marine air ace and Medal of Honor recipient; Martin Clemens, an Australian army officer who became a coast watcher and leader of native scouts during the war; Sir Jacob Vouza, a much-decorated Solomon Islander who served under Clemens; and about seven veteran coast watchers from the Solomons campaign. Tani also attended: he came at my urging and with some reluctance, concerned lest his presence give offense to his former enemies (it didn't).

While aboard *Canberra* I surveyed our surroundings and reflected on my wartime experiences on Guadalcanal. Powerful emotions welled up in me as I beheld Guadalcanal rising out of the sea, crowned with clouds, and I recalled a passage from Masamitsu Manabe's diary in which he described it as "a beautiful island that speaks so loudly."

★   ★   ★

My chance meeting with Tani on Guadalcanal blossomed into a warm friendship. In the years that followed we corresponded often, trading information and memories about the Guadalcanal campaign. He also corresponded with several other American veterans who were equally interested in finding out about the campaign from the perspective of a former enemy soldier. In January 1985 I spent ten days with him at his home in Tokyo. He was a gracious host and very humble about his service record. He classified himself as a "quiet patriot" but was critical of Japan's governmental bureaucracy, which he felt had held back the nation's economic development.

During that visit with Tani I met a Japanese army veteran named Ohno, a marketing executive for Cannon Business Equipment, who had been a corporal in Tani's battery on Guadalcanal. I found it interesting that both Tani and Ohno, one an officer and the other an enlisted man, disliked their commanding officer, whom Tani referred to as typical of the "upper crust." He felt that way about many of the ranking officers on Guadalcanal, with the notable exception of Lt. Gen. Harukichi Hyakutake, whom he admired. Most of the others, Tani said, were more interested in getting decorations than in the welfare of their troops. Tani also told me that the younger generations in Japan didn't want to hear the truth about the war and that, sadly, it was too late to get the correct information out because the generation that fought the war was passing away and memories were fading.

Tani's commanding officer, a colonel, drowned in July 1943 when his ship sank on the way to Bougainville. His widow was still alive in 1985. Despite his feelings about the colonel, Tani and Ohno had befriended the man's widow and assisted her in any way they could.

Tani and I discussed the possibility of revisiting Guadalcanal together in August 1992 on the fiftieth anniversary of the campaign, but his health failed in the interim, preventing him from making the trip. He died in 1994.

★   ★   ★

A few days later I headed off into the rough country west of the Matanikau, determined to find the foxhole on Hill 81 where I had spent thirty-four difficult days doing my part to hold the line against the Japanese. An islander who lived in the area accompanied me, and I carried the battlefield map I had used during the campaign, still legible, and I hoped still a reliable guide to the former battleground. On the way, we met and chatted with a police special investigator, Lemuel Luiramo, and when I told him what I was searching for he immediately offered his assistance. It turned out that he knew exactly where the front line had been located and led us straight to it.

Tramping along the ridge on an afternoon as torrid as those I had sweated through almost forty years ago was no easy task—it had been hard enough when I was a young man of twenty-one—but at least I wasn't weak from malaria or twitchy from stress or wasted physically by the rigors of fighting a war in the thoroughly miserable circumstances of that place. Best of all, no one was trying to kill me. I took genuine comfort in knowing that this time the heat was the only threat to my well-being.

At length we came to a shallow depression no more than eighteen inches deep. I looked around to get my bearings; I consulted my map; I looked around again. And then I realized: this was it!

I stood there for a long while, lost in thought. This insignificant declivity had been at least twice as deep when I inhabited it, and yet it never seemed deep enough—especially at night, with enemy artillery and mortar fire crashing around it or the Japanese creeping about just a few yards away, haunting the darkness beyond the wire. I remembered the brief but savage clashes, "alarums and excursions," grenades flying back and forth, shadowy figures darting this way and that, explosions, bright flashes, flares, machine guns chattering, shouting. I remembered the heat, rain, and thirst. I remembered the weariness, illness, and boredom; and I remembered the excitement, the thrill of battle, the camaraderie. Only thirty-four days, just a little over a month: 11 December 1942 to 13 January 1943. But at the time it might as well have been just a little less than eternity. At the time I wanted nothing more than to leave. Now, I felt as if I had come home.

The area was littered with debris from the war. I began to poke around in the dirt, looking for souvenirs—old habits die hard, sometimes never. Four teenagers from a nearby group of thatched huts joined me in my search. We collected bullets, grenade and shell fragments, first-aid pouches, clothing, and all types of personal gear. We even found what I initially thought could be a magazine for a Thompson submachine gun. I eventually took it to a gun shop in Spokane where, very much to my disappointment, I learned that it was for a Reising gun.

Carrying my relics in a plastic bag, I retraced the steps of our final drive. I wanted to find the spot where my friend Marine Gunner Otto Lund had been killed. There was a good deal of construction going on in the area, which made it difficult for me to get oriented, but I finally found the approximate location of his death on a ridge above a new residential development.

I also searched for the location on the opposite side of the ravine to find where Silver Star recipient Joseph Washvillo had been killed. I paused there and recalled how Corporal "Ski" Wilski, a very capable man in combat, lost his normal composure at this location.

I continued retracing my steps and came to the place where I had collected personal effects from the body of Masamitsu Manabe. I recognized the draw with a small stream at the bottom where the enemy had been dug in like gophers. I recalled how we had thrown grenades into the openings, killing many Japanese huddled in the blackness deep inside. Did those caves still contain the remains of those doomed men? I didn't go in to find out. I hadn't entered the caves in 1943, and I wasn't about to enter them now.

★   ★   ★

After Guadalcanal, Saipan. The day after arriving on Saipan I walked along the beach where the 8th Marines had landed. There were several Japanese bunkers in the area, some engulfed in bright flame trees and showing surprisingly little damage from the air and naval bombardment that preceded the invasion. On the reef sat the hulks of two Sherman tanks, forever halted short of their objective, possibly knocked out by gunfire from those bunkers. The tide was out and the water was shallow, and I waded in, heading for the reef, holding my camera above my head and thinking of all the Marines who had bailed out of their shot-up amtracs and waded ashore under heavy fire holding their rifles in that position.

Later I retraced the route of our advance beyond the beach. I especially wanted to find the air-raid shelter where Don Maines had shot a Japanese soldier but was at first stymied in my search by the profusion of tangan-tangan thickets growing where sugarcane once stood. A bush with acacia-like leaves that grows to a height of nearly twenty feet and nearly impenetrable thickness, tangan-tangan was introduced into the area shortly after the war to prevent soil erosion. But it had proliferated and proved impossible to control, spreading rapidly and aggressively over both Saipan and Tinian, transforming the landscape with an ecology-altering onslaught that effectively choked the life out of the sugarcane growing in its path. Most of the land formerly devoted to sugarcane cultivation was now overgrown with tangan-tangan, and the sugarcane industry that was so important to the prewar economy of the two islands was dead.

I persevered, however—and got lucky. Driving up to a shack near where I thought the shelter might be located, I asked the people who lived there whether they knew of any such structure in their vicinity. To which they replied, "Yes, it's in our backyard—how did you know?" Then they took me back to see it. They now did their outdoor cooking there—it was, in effect, their kitchen. As I inspected the shelter I could see in my mind's eye the Japanese soldier emerging from the entrance, running straight at me as I tripped and fell backward, and Don Maines shooting him in almost the same instant, killing him before I hit the ground.

Subsequently I made my way to the northwest end of the island, exploring the area where the biggest banzai attack of the war had begun on the night of 6 July 1944. Here in the aftermath of the battle we had performed the grisly task of collecting the bodies and body parts of many of the four thousand Japanese killed in the fighting, dumping them into long open pits excavated by bulldozers. I thought I would readily find those mass graves, but I was wrong about that. After the war, the land above them was developed for commercial and residential use, obliterating every trace of their existence. Nor had their locations been recorded beforehand. As a result, the mortal remains of count-less Japanese soldiers are irretrievably lost, and though it seemed inconceivable that the dead in all their numbers would not find a way to make their presence known to the living, such was indeed the case. I found this merely troubling, but the Japanese who came to Saipan intent on unearthing the bones of their fallen countrymen and returning them to Japan for proper burial found it nothing short of tragic.

As I wandered about, I observed buses filled with Japanese tourists passing through the area without stopping, and I had to wonder whether the passengers were aware of what had transpired here or even cared. The island is studded with Japanese war memorials, but they seemed of little interest to the people who had the most reason to feel a connection with them. Saipan had become a popular destination for Japanese vacationers, especially newlyweds, and for most the war simply did not matter anymore. I struck up a conversation about the war with one of the honeymooning couples in front of their beachfront hotel, and when I asked them whether they would have committed hara-kiri like their forefathers, they replied, no. They were young, in love with each other and with life, and the war was ancient history to them.

I posed the same question to older Japanese tourists, men around my age and older, and often received equivocal answers that revealed subtly different feelings. I realized from talking with them that many were still influenced to some extent by the Bushido code and that they looked disapprovingly, albeit with understanding, on the soldiers who had surrendered or allowed them-selves to be captured rather than committing hara-kiri.

There are two interesting Japanese monuments at Banzai Cliff on the north tip of the island. Funded by Japanese schoolchildren and erected in 1969, one represents a mother kneeling and facing south, mourning her sons killed in the South Pacific. The other smaller structure represents a kneeling child facing Suicide Cliff on Mt. Marpi, memorializing the many small chil-dren who also died in that spot, carried to the rocks below by their parents. On display at the base of the cliff, incorrectly dubbed the "Last Command Post" (the Japanese HQ at the time of the banzai attack was actually located several thousand yards to the south, near Matansha), are numerous Japanese war relics, including a tank, several artillery pieces, a torpedo, and a fortification that housed a naval gun.

When I visited the two monuments on my second trip to Saipan in 1983, I found that many prayer boards had been placed at both sites. I also noted white birds soaring serenely above the cliff. According to local legend, the birds did not appear in the area until after the mass suicides took place, when the liberated souls of the dead took flight in avian form. Japanese vacationers golf at a picturesque course extending from the misnamed Last Command Post south toward where the banzai attack started. Who could have foretold this?

★   ★   ★

It should be noted that the battle for Saipan did witness the surrender of Japanese in numbers that were unusual for the Pacific War. Many, perhaps most, did so at the inducement of Guy Gabaldon, who was living on Saipan when I visited the island. I looked him up at his home, and the two of us spent several hours reminiscing about our experiences. A veteran of the 2d Marines, Guy was born into a large Mexican-American family in East Los Angeles but left home at age twelve to live with a Japanese-American family, there becoming fluent in what he called "backstreet Japanese." On Saipan he had repeatedly ventured out alone in search of the enemy, not for the purpose of killing them but rather to coax them to lay down their arms willingly, without fighting to the death or committing suicide. Standing by the entrance to caves in which his enemies were ensconced, he would promise them decent treatment if only they would give themselves up.

This tactic had been tried before on countless occasions in countless battles of the Pacific War, and it almost always met with failure. But Guy's ability to speak in the idiom of the common Japanese soldier gained him a hearing instead of a grenade, the customary response to such blandishments; and this plus his considerable powers of persuasion also gained him their trust and finally, in most instances, their peaceable capitulation. Guy claimed to have singlehandedly convinced some fifteen hundred Japanese soldiers and civilians to choose life over death in the course of the Saipan campaign, a truly extraordinary achievement that earned him the Silver Star, later upgraded to the Navy Cross. Eventually the "Pied Piper of Saipan," as he came to be known, got the attention of Hollywood, which immortalized his exploits in the 1960 film *Hell to Eternity*. Subsequently he wrote his memoirs, *Saipan: Suicide Island*, published in 1990.

Guy passed away in August 2006 in Old Town, Florida, and was buried with full military honors at Arlington National Cemetery. As of this writing, efforts are being made to upgrade his Navy Cross to the Medal of Honor, and the case is under review by the Department of Defense.

During our visit Guy told me about meeting a certain Capt. Sakai Oba a year or two earlier when Oba and other Japanese veterans were visiting Saipan. Following the banzai attack and the collapse of Japanese resistance on Saipan, Oba had led a group of survivors up into the hills, where they held out for fifteen months before they were finally persuaded to surrender on 1 January 1945—more than three months after the end of war. Guy had captured one of Oba's men in a cave about halfway up Mt. Topatchau and was told by his prisoner where he might find them. Guy subsequently had tried his hand at capturing Oba, only to be severely wounded in an ambush prepared by his elusive foe.

Oba wrote a book about his experiences with Don Jones, himself a Marine veteran of the Saipan campaign. I met Jones several years later at a 2d Marine Division Association reunion, and he let me read an early draft of the manuscript. First published in Japan in 1984 under the title *Topatchau*, it received a mixed reception in Oba's homeland, especially from veterans of the war, many of whom thought Oba made a mistake by not committing hara-kiri with the others and then compounded the error by writing his book. In 1986 the book was published in the United States by Presidio Press with the title *Oba, the Last Samurai: Saipan 1944–45*.

I met Oba at his home in Gamagori, Japan, in January 1985 after my visit with Akio Tani. I left Tani's house in Tokyo early in the morning to board the bullet train that took me to Nagoya, 250 miles away, where I transferred to another train for Gamagori. My interpreter was Yukiyasu "Yuki" Katow, who had been in the United States a few years earlier, staying in our home for several weeks on a cultural exchange program. We caught a cab, and as I started to describe where Oba lived, the driver said, "No, you don't have to. He's well known here." He took us directly to Oba's home.

The driver and many others had already read about Oba in *Topatchau*, and he told us that Oba was very active in the community. He had been a city councilman and owned rental property.

The street to Oba's home resembled an alley—very narrow, barely allowing cars to pass. The homes were attractive in that area but were on very small parcels of land. We stopped in front of an immaculate home with an appealing garden in front accented with a pool and fountain. Oba and his wife greeted us warmly, and we spent the rest of that afternoon reminiscing with him about Saipan.

I had already read Jones' manuscript about Oba's experiences, so my questions started from that common ground. During a break in the interview his wife served pork, rice, and mussel soup that she had purchased already prepared. Oba said he had returned to Saipan four times but couldn't walk up into the Topatchau mountain region because of his bad heart (he had undergone open heart surgery in 1979).

Oba elaborated as best he could on details of the banzai attack but conceded that his memory of it was fading. After much discussion and poring over maps, Oba and I determined that I had probably passed through his unit on my way to the aid station after mopping up in the wake of the banzai attack. The three young Japanese soldiers I killed may have belonged to his unit. He told me that for six months following the end of organized resistance on Saipan he hid out in a cave just to the west of the Mt. Topatchau's summit. Two months after Japan surrendered he walked out, leading forty-six soldiers down from the hills inland from the town of Garapan. He met the Americans near the old Japanese hospital to surrender his sword.

I asked Oba if his sword had been returned. He replied, no. I asked him if he knew where it was and he replied, yes, and said no more. He was very gracious about it and didn't complain. However, I let him know that I realized how important a samurai sword was to an old samurai.

Our discussion then moved on to the Bushido code. He said he was very much torn at the time over whether to live or die. Was it better to try to survive in the hope that the Japanese navy would come back to retake the island and give him an opportunity to fight further for the emperor? Or should he commit hara-kiri as most of the others had done to avoid capture? He doesn't consider that he surrendered, however, because the war was over when he finally came down to present his group to the Americans.

Our discussion then shifted to events leading up to his tour of duty on Saipan. Before joining the army in 1935, he had been a geography teacher for three years. Then he spent four years, 1935–39, on the Manchurian border until Soviet forces routed the Japanese in the Battle of Khalkin Gol in August 1939.

His unit was sent from Manchuria to Saipan in early 1944, a few months before the Americans landed. En route, a U.S. submarine sank his troopship, killing more than half the men in his unit. He jumped overboard and floated on a wooden plank until he was picked up by a destroyer that took him on to Saipan. At the time the Americans landed, he was in charge of a medical station on the northern end of the island near Matansha.

At the end of our visit, Oba and his wife drove Yuki and me back to the train station. As we boarded the train and waved good-bye to the Obas, they stood together waving farewell to us.

In the fall of 1986 Oba toured the United States to promote his book. In the course of his travels he attended the 2d Marine Division reunion held in Orlando, Florida. Not a few of the Marine veterans were chagrined about his presence, primarily because they didn't believe that he could have outfoxed the Marines as he claimed he did. Such hard feelings after all these years are difficult for me to understand. After all, Oba was merely being a faithful warrior to his cause, just as the Marines were being faithful to theirs.

★ ★ ★

Very few tourists who visit Saipan bother to go to Tinian, but I wanted to retrace my steps through the denouement of my career as a combat Marine. I did so after visiting with Guy Gabaldon, traveling as the only passenger on a single-engine aircraft making the short hop to Tinian with a cargo of groceries. Even from the air I could see that Tinian, too, was overgrown with tangan-tangan thickets. But the southeast quarter of the island was still open and grassy, providing excellent pasturage for the Bar-K cattle ranch, which occupies most of the area.

My plane landed at the old Japanese airfield just north of San Jose, previously known as Tinian town. No rental cars were available at the airport, so I hitched a ride into San Jose with a local resident who took me to the manager of the Bar-K Ranch. The manager signed a pass allowing me access through all the cattle gates on the ranch, and I rented a small pickup truck, ideal for the muddy roads I would encounter. Then I drove to the city hall of San Jose, where a municipal employee was assigned as my guide.

I had a lot of ground to cover before the plane returned later that afternoon to Saipan, and there was much I wanted to see. First I toured the north end of the island, visiting the landing beaches where two Marine divisions came ashore and the airfield a few hundred yards to the west that we captured on the second day of the campaign. The airfield was mostly covered with brush, and I had to stop frequently to remove branches and deadwood blocking my path as I drove alongside the runway. At the northwest corner of the field I found the site, marked by a plaque, where the first atomic bomb was loaded aboard *Enola Gay*.

My guide and I then stopped at a nearby restaurant, where several government officials had gathered for lunch. I tried to strike up a conversation with them, but they reacted coolly when I told them that I was a Marine veteran of the Tinian campaign. They asked whether I had found the Japanese hospital on Mount Lasso, and I replied that I didn't know about it. Appearing relieved, they warmed up to me and we talked for a while about the campaign.

Later, after returning to Saipan, I met with Ted Oxborrow, an American historian and consultant to the local government, and mentioned the strange behavior of the men in the restaurant. Ted showed me an article he had written for the local Marianas newspaper about his search for the hospital. I learned that when the Japanese in the hospital refused to surrender, a bulldozer sealed the entrance, effectively burying them alive. The people of Tinian are superstitious about the place, fearing that any attempt to open it will release the spirits of those interred there. Ted's article didn't say that he had actually found the cave, but he told me that he had. He had kept this to himself, however, because he didn't want to upset the islanders.

After lunch my guide and I drove down to Mt. Lalo at the southern end of Tinian. The mountain stands at the north end of a long cliff with a plateau on top, and we followed the road to the high ground, opening and closing the many cattle gates we encountered on the way. Our destination was Marpo Point on the eastern shoreline, and we had to walk the last half mile, pushing through dense jungle and then crossing a broad swath of coral cut with jagged crevasses. It was more or less the same route taken by the advancing 2d Battalion of the 8th Marines on the last two days of the campaign. Evidence of the war was plentiful; Japanese mess kits, personal gear, and pieces of shrapnel were strewn about. My guide had previously tied fluorescent ribbons to the trees to mark the way, and I asked him whether other Americans had explored this area. "No, only Japanese survivors," he replied.

We returned to the truck to find it surrounded by cattle. My guide shooed them away, and we drove back to the plateau. Next I searched for the steep, winding road that the Marines ascended after spending most of the day urgently looking for a path to the top of the plateau's seemingly unscalable cliff. After some probing back and forth along the edge of the cliff, I finally found it. Somewhere nearby was the location of the foxhole that I occupied during my last major engagement of the war. The foxhole no longer existed, but I could well remember the violence and anxiety attendant to my brief stay in that all-too-shallow declivity. The heaviest fighting had taken place a short distance down the line, but it was bad enough around my foxhole and I cannot remember any time during the war when I had felt more vulnerable and more unsettled by events. My memories of that night haunt me still with the possibility of what might have been—of what, it still seems to me, I escaped by only the narrowest of margins.

★ ★ ★

During the battle for Saipan, a GI asked Bill Crumpacker, "What makes you damn Marines so wise, so cocky?" He answered, "Well, I was in three battles, and every battle I was in, if I had Marines on either side, all I had to worry about was what was in front of me."

> And that was the feeling—that we all protected one another. You wouldn't believe it, the way we operated. Which sounds self-serving, but it really isn't. I talked to a fella who was in the field artillery on Okinawa, Army. And he said, "Boy, I never was so glad that I was in the Army on Okinawa." I said, "Whaddaya mean?" And he said, "Because we used to sit and watch the Marines take an objective. And they just kept goin' at it, up and down, back at it, back at it. You wouldn't believe the way those guys operated." I said, "Yeah, I would."

★ ★ ★

On 22 November 1993, the fiftieth anniversary of the battle for Tarawa, I attended a ceremony in Yonkers, New York, to rededicate Anthony O'Boyle Memorial Park in the name of the fallen private from my platoon. Also attending were Anthony's good friends and foxhole buddies, Bill Crumpacker and Dick Stein; our company commander, John Murdock; and several other Tarawa veterans; as well as a number of high-ranking Marines, including Lt. Gen. John J. Sheehan, then a member of the Joint Chiefs of Staff. It was a cold, gray day with an icy wind blowing in off the Hudson River, quite a contrast to the tropical heat and brilliant sunlight on Betio when Anthony had met his end. Shot in the head while peering over the seawall on Red Beach 2, Anthony had fallen back into John Murdock's arms, still alive but unconscious, his body twitching, his eyes open but empty. John held him for a brief time, spoke to him—and then set him aside on the beach among the bodies of other slain Marines, where he died a few minutes later.

All the solemnities appropriate to the occasion were observed, all the rites performed. The colors were trooped; speeches were given; music was performed; prayers were offered. We sang the national anthem, the "Marine Hymn," and "Amazing Grace." There was a presentation of military testimonials; proclamations were made. John Murdock gave a talk about Anthony, then presented Anthony's brother with the Purple Heart, a fitting gesture from the man who comforted Anthony in the final moments of his life. An honor guard fired a twenty-one-gun salute, taps was played—and we all wept. Our tears were shed in both sorrow and joy. There was cause for both. Anthony's life had been short, his dying hard, his glory everlasting. There was no bitterness, no disillusionment, no anger. His life had mattered; his death also. And we remembered both and knew that both had meaning and purpose. The biographical sketch in the program for the ceremony expressed our feelings well in this regard and serves as a fitting epitaph for every Marine in the Second World War:

If the world had been different, if he had been born at another time, Anthony, with his sunshine smile, could have married, raised a family, had grandchildren, and lived a quiet, typically traditional American life.

But the early 1940s were not normal times. A fascist dictator who threatened to conquer Europe had forged an alliance with the militarists who controlled the Japanese government. In their distorted plan for world domination, an unprepared and unsuspecting United States became a primary target. The American people were shocked into action by the Sunday morning arrival of Japanese bombers over Oahu.

Like hundreds of thousands of other young Americans, Anthony felt compelled to volunteer to serve his country. He simply could not stand aside while America was under attack. . . .

Anthony gave his life on Tarawa for his country, his corps, and for his fellow Marines. He was not a famous hero, mourned by millions, extolled in the press, immortalized in magazine articles or books. He was no one special, just another Marine Private First Class. The American people should thank God eternally for Anthony and his fellow Marines, Soldiers, Seamen, and Airmen who persevered and won a magnificent victory over a wickedly evil enemy.

Semper fi, brother. You are not forgotten.

Index

About the Authors

Dean L. Ladd is a Marine combat veteran of World War II, serving as an officer in the 8th Marines, 2nd Marine Division, in the battles for Guadalcanal, Tarawa, Saipan, and Tinian. After the war he served in the Marine Corps Reserve, participating in numerous active-duty training tours and completing courses in amphibious warfare and management in the Department of Defense. He was promoted to major on September 14, 1951, and to lieutenant colonel on September 15, 1960. In all he served thirty years as a Marine (Reserve) and has since remained active in the 2nd Marine Division Association, Marine Corps League, and other veterans' groups. In the 1980s Ladd returned twice to the Pacific islands on which he fought and also traveled to Japan to meet with Japanese veterans of the island campaigns. Ladd currently resides in Spokane, WA; his wife, Vera, is deceased.

Steven Weingartner is a historian and writer specializing in military history and military affairs. The recipient of the 1998 Carl Sandburg Award for Nonfiction as co-author of *Lala's Story: A Memoir of the Holocaust*, he is currently writing books about chariot warfare and the Russo-Japanese War, and he is a regular contributor to magazines and journals and other publications focusing on military history. He has served as a consultant and on-camera commentator for the History Channel's *Battles B.C.* series and contributed to entries for Sandhurst/Praeger's forthcoming *Philosophers of War* multivolume book series. He lives in La Grange Park, IL, with his wife and two border collies.